D0073377

NICOLAS SLONIMSKY
Writings on Music

VOLUME TWO

NICOLAS SLONIMSKY
Writings on Music

VOLUME TWO
Russian and Soviet Music and Composers

Edited by Electra Slonimsky Yourke

ROUTLEDGE
New York and London

Published in 2004 by
Routledge
29 West 35th Street
New York, NY 10001
www.routledge-ny.com

Published in Great Britain by
Routledge
11 New Fetter Lane
London EC4P 4EE
www.routledge.co.uk

Routledge is an imprint of the Taylor & Francis Group.

Printed in the United States of America on acid-free paper.

10 9 8 7 6 5 4 3 2 1

Library of Congress Cataloging-in-Publication Data

Slonimsky, Nicolas, 1894–1995
    [Selections. 2003]
    Nicolas Slonimsky : writings on music.
      p. cm.
Edited by Electra Slonimsky Yourke.
Includes bibliographical references (p.) and index.
      ISBN 0-415-96866-6 (v. 2 : alk. paper)
      1. Music—History and criticism. I. Yourke, Electra. II. Title.
      ML60.S646 2003
      780—dc21   2003011569

Deus Ex Musica

REVEALING SOME REVOLTING AND BLASPHEMOUS CLAIMS TO DIVINE
REVELATION BY SOME CONTEMPORARY COMPOSERS; WITH AN EX-
ORDIUM, CITING EXAMPLES OF TRUE PIETY IN MUSICAL HISTORY;
ALSO, AN ARDENT APPEAL TO ESTABLISH A COMPETENT BODY OF
CHURCHMEN AND MUSICIANS TO PASS UPON SUCH CLAIMS AND DE-
CIDE WHETHER THE ENEMY OF MAN MAY NOT BE THE AUTHOR OF
THIS PROFANE VANITY; FOR GOD BEING GOOD, AND THE DIVINELY
INSPIRED WORKS MOSTLY BAD, THIS MAY NOT BE SO.

by Nicolas Slonimsky

Exordium

True piety was revealed when the Church ruled that only triple time should be used by God-loving composers; for "it hath its name from the Blessed Trinity which is pure and true perfection."

True piety was again revealed when Boethius ruled: (concerning the holy origin of the octave): octave is good, for 'twas on the eighth day *(octave die)* that Isaac was circumcised after the circumcision of his father, Abraham.

Exposition

One Arnold Bax, musician, when asked how he came to compose his second Symphony, answered blasphemously and unwarrantably that he was guided by Divine Powers while sojourning in the vicinity of Monte Carlo.

Upon the examination of the music written by Arnold Bax, it appears that there is no coherence nor any perceptible plan therein; but God being all-wise and all-powerful, it is impious to propose that He could have fathered a work of human weakness.

One Igor Stravinsky, musician, when asked to reveal his plans concerning a new opera, stated in a letter that not he, but God is the master of his gifts,—that his duty is so to use his gifts as to acquit himself honorably before the Giver.

At another time, he dedicated one of his works to the greater glory of God. Yet it has not been shown that more glory has redounded to God since the writing of the work.

Lamentation

What are we, humble children of the Lord, to do in the light of such declarations? Are we to step aside and witness the glory of God dimmed through attribution to Him of musical works, many of them using intervals other than the octave? Is it not our plain duty to appeal to all brethren, musical and secular, to set up a Body of Judgment invested with the power to destroy such works by fire? In the meantime should not we seize such false prophets and inquire diligently into the origin of their claims? The true Christians of Germany have already crushed the power of Darkness, but as yet lit insufficient fire under the wicked works of open enemies of God, that chew the cud but use not the octave.

Appeal

Then, forth! Let us assemble and set up a body of Judgment and select a presiding member upon the proof that God has truly spoken to him through the fire or any other element! Let us summon Jean Cocteau, who, like Apostle Paul, had been wicked, but repented and proclaimed the glory of God in hog Latin! Let us summon the meek and teach them to listen to the Lord when their creative powers fail!

But let us beware of false Gods that speak through false prophets. Ours alone is the world!

from *Panorama*, December 1933

CONTENTS

Preface ix

A Note from the Editor xiii

PART I. THE ROOTS OF RUSSIAN MUSIC

1. Russian Music 3

2. Russian Folk Music 21

3. Russian Music in Art Songs 25

PART II. SOME MAJOR COMPOSERS

4. Nikolai Rimsky-Korsakov: Muscovy's Musical Merlin 33

5. Alexander Glazunov: Keeper of Russian Tradition 41

6. Reinhold Glière 45

7. Alexander Scriabin 48

8. Nikolai Miaskovsky: The Man of Twenty-three Symphonies 57

9. Alexander Tcherepnin—Septuagenarian 63

10. Igor Stravinsky 73

11. Serge Prokofiev: His Status in Soviet Music 79

12. Dmitri Dmitrievitch Shostakovitch 84

13. Shostakovitch's War Symphony   115

14. Shostakovitch after the Seventh   120

PART III. AFTER THE REVOLUTION

15. Development of Soviet Music   127

16. The Soviet Opera   135

17. Soviet Composers in War and Revolution   138

18. Soviet Music at Quarter-Century Mark   142

19. The Changing Style of Soviet Music   149

20. A New Tune in Soviet Music   176

21. Schoenberg in the Soviet Mirror   183

PART IV. PERSONAL EXPERIENCES

22. Russia Revisited   191

23. Stimulating Talks Reveal Extraordinary Paradoxes   196

24. Moscow: Musical Interlude   199

25. Cultural Explosion in the U.S.S.R.   204

    Index   243

PREFACE

Selecting the articles for this volume has been harder than for the other volumes because of the profusion of writings available. Russian/Soviet music was, of course, one of my father's major subject areas. He was personally a product of the great Russian musical tradition—born in St. Petersburg, his family part of the cultural elite, and he attended the famous Conservatory there. His considerable talents gave him entrée to Russia's musical world as a young man, even as it was shaken and overturned by war, revolution, and exile. The Russians who had the good luck to find exile in Paris constituted a core of musical life there, and he was part of that exalted group.

Although he moved on to identify and promote American modern music in particular, he remained in a unique position to monitor the eventful tale of Soviet music as it unfolded from the late '20s. He was professionally in full throttle, especially qualified to read and interpret politically driven musical policies as they were first handed down, then reversed, conceived anew and re-promulgated, around and around. He maintained direct contact with musical sources as best he could, with due regard for his counterparts' safety. He read Soviet bulletins, journals, and embassy publications, and he subscribed to the *Daily Worker*. He analyzed the effect the zigzagging policies had on individual composers' works, and he reported on their public mea culpas when they found themselves a step behind the latest government dicta.

In due course all these contacts across (or through or around) the Iron Curtain attracted the attention of the FBI. It is not clear when his file, obtained via the Freedom of Information Act, was first set up. The Bureau was, naturally, interested in his activities with supposedly Communist, or subversive, or pro-Soviet, etc. organizations which, if one

credits the agency, proliferated in the Boston area during the 1940s. Most
of the ones my father admittedly associated with—by allowing his name
to be put on a masthead or playing the piano at an event or signing a
telegram to FDR—said they were dedicated to Russian war relief, Soviet-
American friendship, progressive causes, and peace. His *Daily Worker*
subscription is repeatedly noted in the official FBI file, which also contains an offprint of "The Changing Style of Soviet Music" (originally published in the American Musicological Society's *Journal*), which is included
as Chapter 19 herein.

At one point, the agency put a mail cover on him for a month. The
pursuit of "leads" from the items intercepted constitutes one of the fun-
niest reports I have ever read. It hardly need be said that the file reveals
far more about the FBI than it does about Nicolas Slonimsky.

It all ended happily. After all the years, the special agents sought and
received authorization to actually interview him in May 1953. To his
astonishment, they had precise questions about quite a number of Russia-
oriented organizations and publications, as well the dates of his appearances and writings and contacts with various individuals. When they asked
his views on Communism, he loosed a blast against Soviet repression,
brutality, hypocrisy, and the suppression of artists. The encounter is fully
described in his autobiography, *Perfect Pitch*. It is also quite fully and
fairly reported in the FBI file (which my father never saw—I obtained it
after his death). Almost immediately after the interview, his file was
closed.

Given his credentials, my father was often asked to write articles on
Soviet music as it evolved, and especially after the unleashing of each new
political orientation. The writings are all interesting, but obviously there
is a lot of overlap. I have selected the most comprehensive and analytic
articles and regretfully left aside many others that contained material of
value but, overall, are less informative now than they were at the time.
Inevitably there is a certain amount of repetition of the history up to the
date of each article; but the commitment of this collection is to preserve
the articles as they were written, with no editing whatever. Accordingly
such repetition—and even some contradiction—is inevitable.

The articles on individual composers form an admittedly unbalanced
section. The total collection from which to choose was also unbalanced,
ranging from strong, serious writings to more lightweight introductory
biographies for general newspaper readership. The former were given

priority here. Accordingly, a long piece on Tchaikovsky's correspondence
with Mme. von Meck is not included, nor are less comprehensive writings
on composers already represented. Then why three Shostakovich articles? Because they're good. The reader is also directed to Volume I, with
several interesting articles on Russian composers, especially Stravinsky,
originally written for the *Boston Evening Transcript*.

Although most of my father's writings are of an objective, analytic, or
reportorial nature—albeit well spiced with opinion—some few are personal. Clearly the experiences dearest to his heart involved visits back to
his native land. In 1963, the U.S. State Department sent him to several
countries in Eastern Europe and to Russia as a kind of musical ambassador from the U.S. to the musical world of these several countries. He
seems to have carried off his mission in fine form, meeting with the musical establishments and also the anti-establishments that were beginning
to be tolerated in the more relaxed political environment. The lively nar-
rative that concludes this volume captures some of these experiences and
shows what a good ambassador he was, both above and under ground. He
was thrilled to meet so many bright and talented composers, some of
whom he already knew through correspondence, and they seem to have
been equally thrilled to meet this authentic Russo-Western modernist
who could speak with them on their own terms and in their own languages—and show them a thing or two.

To me, this exuberant saga is a perfect counterbalance to the rather
sober, dictionary-like opening chapter, carefully laying out history to date.
After observing from afar the twists and turns through half a century, he
finally plunges back into the transformed musical geography of his youth.
He finds talent in abundance, he observes their hunger for a new and free
artistic life, he feels their urgent desire to find out what has been going on
in the West during their long period of deprivation. This is the human
side of Soviet musical history.

As the years passed and my father was no longer in the lead of
Russian-American musical communication, he continued to take great
pleasure in the re-emergence of Russian (no longer Soviet) musical greatness. Among those who not only survived but prevailed was his own
nephew Sergei Slonimsky. Sergei and his family now live in the apartment
in St. Petersburg that his parents moved into after their marriage early in
the twentieth century, a lineage amazingly unbroken in the cultural history of that great and beautiful city. Sergei's numerous compositions,

including symphonies, operas, ballets, chamber pieces, and songs, are all published and widely performed. His 70th birthday this year was the occasion of major national recognition of his achievements. He and my father were very proud of each other, and it was gratifying to observe their deep, natural, spontaneous communication. It was in the language of music, but it was only possible in the language of family. No more fitting legacy could be imagined for my father than the primacy of his lateral descendant in the musical life of his nation.

Electra Slonimsky Yourke
New York, November 2002

A NOTE FROM THE EDITOR

Every article in these volumes is presented in full without any editing whatever. I have also preserved the orthography and other stylistic elements as they appeared in the original publications or manuscripts. Changes were made only in the rare instances of errors or misprints obvious to me. Accordingly, readers will encounter a wide variety of spellings, especially of Russian names, and the disparate punctuation policies of dozens of different publications. I believe that fidelity to the originals helps highlight the historic nature of these documents, and preservation of the record, warts and all, was of great importance to my father, a lover of language in all its flowerings.

—E.S.Y.

Part I

THE ROOTS OF RUSSIAN MUSIC

1. RUSSIAN MUSIC

Russian music, as a separate, individual and recognizable entity is at least one thousand years old. The first folk melodies originating in European Russia (Asiatic Russia was not incorporated into the national and cultural complex until centuries later) date from the tenth century. The most ancient Russian folk songs are entirely *sui generis*; the Byzantine influence was marked chiefly in Russian religious music, and was clearly an alien importation. Thanks to the intelligent work of Russian folksong collectors, an enormous amount of authentic musical material has been gathered and published in Russia during the last century and a half. It is now possible to reconstruct the principal elements of original Russian folk songs as preserved by tradition through many generations.

P. Sokalsky, in his book *Russian Folk Music in its Melodic and Rhythmic Structure* (Kharkov, 1888), summarizes the essential characteristics of ancient Russian folk songs in these four points: (1) the melodic motion of Russian folk songs is predominantly descending; (2) the range of folk modes may be as narrow as a fourth, but occasionally is as wide as an octave and a fourth; the older the song, the narrower the range; (3) the intervals of the fourth and fifth determine the modulation to the new keys; (4) in ancient Russian folk music, only three tones are used, a whole tone, and a tone and a half, adding up to the interval of the fourth.

The rhythm of Russian folk songs is determined by characteristic grouping of two short notes followed by a long note, as exemplified in the familiar Volga Boatmen's song. As to the metrical arrangement of musical phrases, Russian folk songs have a large incidence of uneven metrical units, such as 5, 7 or 11 to a musical phrase. The great masters of Russian music have made use of such typical time-signatures as 5/4 (Glinka), 7/4 (Borodin) and 11/4 (Rimsky-Korsakov).

The first collection of Russian folk songs was compiled by Vasily Trutovsky, a singer at the court of Catherine the Great, and published in 1782. Much more important was a book of Russian folk songs by the Russianized Czech Ivan Pratch. The first edition appeared in 1790, and a second in 1806. The 150 songs in Pratch's collection were noted down for him by Nicolas Lvov, a musical amateur. The publication of the collection found immediate response. The famous Italian composer Paisiello expressed his admiration and amazement at the beauty of these songs created by simple peasants. When Beethoven wrote his String Quartet, op. 59, dedicated to Rasoumowsky, the Russian ambassador to Vienna, he incorporated in the music Russian themes taken note for note from the Pratch collection.

During the nineteenth century, the task of collecting and classifying Russian folk songs was continued. The most significant publication was that by N. Paltchikov (Moscow, 1888), comprising 125 melodies with texts, collected in the village of Nicolaevka, in the Ufa Government. Paltchikov gives as many as eight versions of each song, thus according general deductions as to the chief characteristics of Russian folk music. Harmonizations of Russian folk songs published by Balakirev (1886), Rimsky-Korsakov (1877), Tchaikovsky (1868), Liadov (1894) and others, further increased the interest in the subject.

A beginning of scientific musical ethnography was made by Eugenia Lineva, who was the first to use the phonograph to record Russian folk songs. She published, in 1905 and 1912, two volumes of transcriptions of Russian folk song under the general title *Peasant Songs of Great Russia as They Are in Folk's Harmonization, Transcribed from Phonograms.* Each song begins with a solo, followed by a chorus, in which the basic melody is freely embellished and ornamented. The number of individual parts in the chorus is usually two or three, but instances of four-part singing were also found by Lineva. This impels her to support the theory that Russian folk music is essentially polyphonic. There is, however, no proof that ancient songs of Russia were anything more than single musical phrases, without secondary parts. The later polyphony of peasant choruses may have been influenced by part singing in the church choirs.

Further advances in musical ethnography have been made after the Revolution. Numerous collections of regional songs have been published under the auspices of the Academy of Sciences, in the folklore series of the Institute of Anthropology, Ethnography and Archeology. Thus, two substantial volumes of songs from the relatively small region of the Pinega River basin were published in 1937. Revolutionary songs of the Tsarist times are included in the collection *Russkaya Narodnaya Pesnia* (Russian Folk Song), published in Moscow in 1936.

The tradition of folk singing is deep-rooted in Russian folklore. The legendary figure of Bayan is recalled in the *Chronicle of Prince Igor*, dated circa 1200:

> Bayan, as he recited the strife of bygone times, set out ten falcons after a flight of swans, and the one that was first overtaken began her song. But in truth, brethren, not ten falcons did Bayan loose on the swans, but his wise fingers did he lay on living strings, and they by themselves sang the glory of the princes.

The string instrument played by Bayan was the ancient *gusli*, a sort of zither, or horizontal harp, with a wooden sound chest, having ten or more strings. The *gusli* is no longer in practical use in Russia. Rimsky-Korsakov includes a part for *gusli* in his opera *Sadko* to evoke the atmosphere of old Russia, but in actual performance it is usually replaced by a harp. Other string instruments of ancient Russia are the *domra* (similar to the guitar, and played with a plectrum), and the *gudok* (a three-stringed instrument with a pear-shaped body, and played with a string bow). The *domras* have been recently revived in Soviet Russia, and are often included in new orchestral composition: F. Szabo has written a sinfonietta for an ensemble of four-stringed *domras* (1936). In the Ukraine, the *domra* is known under the name of *kobza* or *bandura* (from the Polish *pandura*). The popular *balalaika* is in all probability a development of the *domra*. In the eighteenth century, the *balalaika* assumed its familiar triangular shape. It usually has three strings, and is played like a guitar, by plucking, and without a plectrum. An ensemble of *balalaikas*, organized by V. Andreyev early in this century, gave numerous and successful concerts in Russia and abroad.

Among Russian wind instruments, the following are typical: the *rog* (or, in the diminutive, *rozhok*), which is a hunting horn; the *dudka* (a vertical flute), *zhaleika* (a double reed, with two pipes connected at an angle, with a single mouthpiece) and the *svirel* (a panpipe, composed of several reeds of different lengths, bound together). The nomenclature of these instruments varies, however, according to locality and time of history.

Finally, the Russian bagpipe, the *volynka* (so named probably because of its supposed origin in the district of Volynia), should be mentioned. It consists of a goatskin bag and two pipes. The usage of the *volynka* in Russia life is reflected in the locution *zatianut volynku* (to strike up the bagpipe, meaning to begin a tedious tale).

The most remarkable development of Russian primitive instruments was the formation of an orchestra of hunting horns (*rog*), initiated by Simeon Harishkin in 1751. Forty-nine hunting horns of different sizes were manufactured, ranging from three inches to the enormous length of 24 feet, the latter capable of producing the low A under the bass clef staff. Every member of the ensemble could play only one note, and patient rehearsing was required to give a performance of even a simple polyphonic composition. That it was successfully accomplished, is testified by the German resident of St. Petersburg, one Jacob von Stallin, in his interesting memoir, *Nachrichten von der Musik in Russland*, written in 1770, and published, in a Russian translation, in *Musikalnoye Nasledstvo* (Musical Heritage, Moscow, 1935).

Ancient Russian percussion instruments were drums, metal bars and bells. The most interesting instrument is the *buben* (tambourine). A huge *buben*, called *Nabat*, (*bit v nabat*, meaning to beat alarm, is still a living locution in the Russian language) was so large that it had to be carried by a span of four horses, and eight men were required to operate it.

Very early in history, singing and instrumental music in Russia were used for entertainment. The first musicians were the Russian minstrels, *skomorokhi*, who are mentioned, with great deprecation, as early as 1068, in Nestor's chronicle. Nestor complains that the entertainment provided by the *skomorokhi* drew the people away from God, and that churches stood empty, while the populace amused themselves by playing the *gusli*, blowing trumpets and dancing. According to thirteenth-century sources, the *skomorokhi* used panpipes (*svirel*), string instruments (*gudok*), and the tambourine (*buben*). In the fifteenth century, the *skomorokhi* introduced a new type of entertainment, the puppet theater, which ultimately developed into the popular carnival play, *Petrushka*.

The wide popularity of the *skomorokhi* in medieval Russia is vouchsafed by the fact that numerous villages in Central Russia were named *Skomorokhovod*. Simultaneously with the spread of the *skomorokhi*, the opposition of the church and lay authorities to them grew stronger. Tsar Aleksey took drastic measures against the *skomorokhi*. In his decree of

1649, he ordered ruthless persecution of the godless *skomorokhi* with their *domras* and *gusli*, and instructed the police authorities to destroy all musical instruments found in the possession of the *skomorokhi*.

Very little is left of musical compositions sung by the *skomorokhi*. Nicolas Findeisen, in his valuable two-volume edition, *Sketches of Music History in Russia from the Most Ancient Times to the End of the Eighteenth Century* (Moscow, 1928), cites songs and verses, preserved in oral tradition.

Parallel to the development of folk music, the Church played an important role in establishing the foundations of organized musical learning. The pioneers of musical education in Russia were Greek and Bulgarian clerics who introduced Byzantine chant into Kiev after the Christianization of Russia. As early as in the eleventh century, there were texts with musical notation derived from the Byzantine system of neumes, in use in the Kiev churches and monasteries. In the thirteenth century, the Russian system of notation, known as *znamenny* (*znamia*, sign) or *kriuki* (hooks, from the angular shape of the notes), emerged as a native version of the Greek system. In 1551, Ivan the Terrible, who had some knowledge of music, and wrote several religious chants himself, established schools for teaching musical notation for use of church choirs. Later still, the eight modes of the Russian Znamenny Chant were organized according to typical melodic figures, called *popievki* (singing patterns). About 1700, the five-line notation current in Europe, was universally adopted in Russia churches.

The first beginnings of polyphonic choral music in Russia date from the eighteenth century. In 1713, Peter the Great formed a choir of sixty singers, and Russian noblemen organized private choruses of their own. These so-called *capellas* (from the Italian word *cappella*, for chapel, or choir) developed into Russian choirs justly famous for their fine qualities and virtuosity. The *capella* founded by Peter the Great is still flourishing in Leningrad.

The father of Russian religious music in the polyphonic style was Dmitri Bortniansky (1751–1825), who studied in Italy, where he acquired the technique of part-writing. Maxim Berezovsky (1745–77) wrote, during the short span of his life (he committed suicide at the age of 31) numerous sacred works of high quality. Alexei Lvov (1799–1870), the author of the Tsarist National Anthem, also composed sacred music, and wrote a treatise of the structure of Russian religious songs. In modern times, Tchaikovsky and Gretchaninov have contributed to Russian church music, writing in a free contrapuntal style.

In the field of secular music in Russia, the initial impetus was given by the Italian musicians who went to Russia in the eighteenth century, at the invitation of Russian Empresses Ann, Elizabeth and Catherine the Great. Among these Italians were several world-renowned names, Francesco Araja, Vincenzo Manfredini, Giuseppe Sarti, Baldassare Galuppi, Tommaso Traetta, Giovanni Paisiello, Domenico Cimarosa and others. They were largely responsible for the flourishing state of the opera and ballet in St Petersburg during the second half of the eighteenth century. They acted as choir masters, teachers, concert players and composers. The first opera with a Russian text, *Cephalus and Procris*, was written by Francesco Araja, on the libretto by Sumarokov, and produced in St Petersburg in 1755. Its serious defect is inaccurate prosody of Russian verse which resulted from Araja's ignorance of the Russian language.

Under the influence of Italian music, several Russian-born composers wrote operas during the reign of Catherine the Great, among them, Evstigney Fomin (1761–1800) the author of the opera *Amerikantsy* (in the sense of Indians, depicting a romantic story in Mexico), Vassily Pashkevitch, the composer of the opera *Tsarevitch Fevey*, to a libretto by Catherine the Great, and others.

On the threshold of the nineteenth century, Russian music attained a degree of cultural evolution when the establishment of a national style of composition had become feasible. The Russian art song, in the folkloric manner, was cultivated by Alexander Alyabyev (1787–1851), Nicolas Titov (1800–75) and Alexander Varlamov (1801–48). Alexey Verstovsky (1799–1862) wrote an opera on the Russian subject *Askoldova Mogila* (Askold's Tomb, 1835), which, despite its Italianate idiom, reveals traits of Russian nationalism in the treatment of material.

The acknowledged founder of the Russian national school of composition was Michael Glinka (1804–57), who is to Russian music what Pushkin is to Russian literature. Glinka integrated the elements of Russian musical folklore into a language that possesses unmistakable attributes of national music. His first opera, originally named *Ivan Susanin*, was produced in 1836, under the title *A Life for the Tsar*. Taken from Russian history, the subject of the opera is interpreted by Glinka along purely national lines, with the songs and choral passages reflecting the Russian spirit. Glinka's second opera *Ruslan and Ludmila* (1842), after Pushkin's poem, is remarkable for its brilliant colorism. In his symphonic dance *Kamarinskaya*, Glinka gives the first instance of orchestral treatment of Russian dance rhythms. In Glinka's songs and ballads, the vocal line of Russian songs received its perfect expression.

Quite different from Glinka's style of composition is the music of Alexander Dargomyzhsky (1813–69), less brilliant in color, but rich in musical characterization. Dargomyzhsky's opera *Russalka* (The Mermaid), which retains the traditional division into arias, is nonetheless in a distinctly Russian folkloric style. In his posthumous opera, *Kamennyi Gost* (The Stone Guest), Dargomyzhsky appears as an innovator, abandoning the Italian model in favor of operatic realism, with vocal declamation in place of conventional recitative.

Both Glinka and Dargomyzhsky remained little known outside Russia. It was only with the appearance of the great symphonic and operatic works of Tchaikovsky, Rimsky-Korsakov and Mussorgsky that Russia became a powerful factor in the general course of music history. The spirit of nationalism in Russian music was accentuated in the formulation of aims by a group of Russian composers known as the *Mogutchaya Kutchka*. This epithet, which literally means *A Mighty Heap*, was bestowed upon Balakirev, Borodin, Cui, Moussorgsky and Rimsky-Korsakov by the Russian critic Vladimir Stasov (1824–1906). But the individual talents and the measure of contributions to Russian national music by these composers were far from equal. Certainly, César Cui (1835–1918), who was a military engineer by profession, and who wrote several operas in a conventional romantic style, could not be included among the 'Mighty Five' except by accident. Mili Balakirev (1837–1910) played the role of a spiritual head of the group, and did much to inspire his companions with the ideals of Russian national art. But he wrote little, and only his oriental fantasia, *Islamey*, survives the test of time. It is more appropriate therefore, to speak of the Mighty Three of Russian music, Borodin, Rimsky-Korsakov and Mussorgsky. It is interesting to note that not one of them was a professional in the narrow sense of the word. Borodin was a professor of chemistry, Rimsky-Korsakov, a naval officer, and Mussorgsky, a government employee.

Of the three, Nicolas Rimsky-Korsakov (1844–1908) was the most prolific. In his many operas, he recreated the spirit of Russian folklore and history. Russian legends and folk tales are reflected in Rimsky-Korsakov's operas *Snegurotchka* (Snow-Maiden, 1882) and *Sadko* (1894);

and Russian history in *Tsarskaya Nevesta* (Tsar's Bride, 1893). He wrote operas to two fairy tales by Pushkin, *Tsar Saltan* (1899) and *Zolotoy Petushck* (The Golden Cockerel, 1906). Rimsky-Korsakov's religious opera *Skazanye o Nevidimom Grado Kitezhe* (Tale of the Invisible City of Kitezh, 1907) reveals an influence of Wagner's *Parsifal*. In the symphonic field, Rimsky-Korsakov's *Scheherazade* (1881) is epoch-making in its coloristic treatment of the musical material.

Alexander Borodin (1833–87) was the protagonist of an orientalistic music. In his symphonic sketch *In the Steppes of Central Asia* (1886) he introduced elements of Russian orientalism for the first time. The same orientalism is shown in the famous 'Polovtzian Dances' from Borodin's opera *Prince Igor* (1869–87, completed posthumously by Rimsky-Korsakov and Glazunov). In the purely Russian style of composition, Borodin succeeded in creating epical work in his Second Symphony (1870) which, without an explicit program, paints a panorama of Russian *byliny* (epical chronicles).

Modest Mussorgsky (1839–81) was regarded by his contemporaries as an erratic genius whose technical equipment was inadequate for the tasks he undertook. In historical perspective, however, Mussorgsky appears as the greatest of the Mighty Five in the boldness of musical invention and in his profound understanding of the essence of Russian national folklore. Many of his harmonic procedures anticipate developments of modern music. Mussorgsky's greatest work is the opera *Boris Godunov* (1869). It is usually performed in the version of orchestration prepared by Rimsky-Korsakov, in which certain crudities and unconventional harmonic progressions are smoothed out. Recently, however, the original score of Mussorgsky has been restored, and the opera has been performed in the authentic version in Russia and abroad. A reorchestration of *Boris Godunov* was also undertaken in 1941 by Shostakovitch. Mussorgsky's opera *Khovanshchina* (on a historic subject) was completed by Rimsky-Korsakov. In his short opera *Marriage* (after Gogol's play), Mussorgsky applies the modern treatment of operatic dialogue. Mussorgsky's piano suite *Pictures at an Exhibition* is remarkable for the variety of characterization, from light humor to grandiose tonal painting. The suite has become extremely popular in the orchestration by Ravel.

The cause of nationalism in Russian operatic music was ably served by Alexander Serov (1820–71), the author of *Vrazhya Sila* (Enemy Power), which was produced posthumously, and has remained in the

Russian theatrical repertoire. Serov's music, however, lacks the revolutionary originality of Mussorgsky's music or the effectiveness of Rimsky-
Korsakov's operatic panoramas. Similarly lacking in force are the numerous operas of Anton Rubinstein (1829–94), who left a mark in Russian
musical culture as the first great Russian pianist, and founder of the St
Petersburg Conservatory (1862). His opera *Demon* (after Lermontov)
enjoys great popularity, as do his effective piano pieces. Anton's brother
Nicholas Rubinstein (1856–81) was a celebrated pianist of his day. He
founded the Moscow Conservatory (1866).

The unique and solitary figure of Peter Tchaikovsky (1840–93) domi-
nates the symphonic music of the second half of the nineteenth century in
Russia. Tchaikovsky stood aloof from his musical contemporaries, and followed his own line, intensely individual, subjective, and often morbidly
introspective. Although Tchaikovsky's music is unmistakably Russian, he
but rarely resorts to literal quotations of Russian folk songs (as in the finale
of the Fourth Symphony). Tchaikovsky's nationalism lies in the extraordinary power to create a peculiarly Russian mood by means of expressing his
own inner sentiments. In view of Tchaikovsky's pessimistic outlook on life,
his predilection for minor keys in composition, and his choice of titles
(*Chanson Triste, Melancholic Serenade*, etc.) some interpreters of Russian
music conclude that the "Slavic soul" is inexpressibly sad. This conclusion
appears unwarranted. Even in Tchaikovsky's own music, there is much that
reflects joy and merriment. The programmatic designs of Tchaikovsky's
symphonies are invariably dark and somber. The Fourth and the Fifth
Symphonies express the inexorability of fate and the futility of struggle.
The Sixth Symphony, surnamed *Pathétique*, which Tchaikovsky conducted
in St Petersburg a few days before his death of cholera, is pervaded with
the spirit of dejection. There is a characteristic musical quotation from the
service for the dead, occurring in the first movement of the *Pathétique*.
But each of these symphonies contains material that is full of life and
movement. The subject matter of Tchaikovsky's symphonic poems is also
romantically somber (*Romeo and Juliet*, 1869; *Francesca da Rimini*, 1876),
but the music itself possesses great vitality. Tchaikovsky's operas, *Eugene
Onegin* (1878) and *Pique-Dame* (1890), both after Pushkin, are extremely
popular in Russia, as are his ballets, *Swan Lake* (1876), *Sleeping Beauty*
(1889), and *The Nutcracker* (1892).

The course of Russian music during the last decades of the nineteenth century and the early years of the twentieth century was deter-

mined in varying degrees by the influence of Tchaikovsky and that of the
Mighty Five. The followers of Tchaikovsky cultivated the romantic type of
symphonic, operatic and vocal music. The musical nationalists of the
modern school were active in St Petersburg, where the Mighty Five had
flourished before them, while the stronghold of the romantic school was
in Moscow, where Tchaikovsky taught at the Conservatory.

The heir of the Nationalist School of St Petersburg was Alexander
Glazunov (1865–1936), who wrote eight symphonies, violin and piano
concertos, and chamber music, but no operas. As Director of the St
Petersburg Conservatory from 1906 to 1927, Glazunov played an important role in the education of the new generation of Russian composers.
Anatole Liadov (1855–1914), not a prolific composer, distinguished himself principally by short symphonic poems in the Russian folkloric manner (*Baba-Yaga, Kikimora*). Nicolas Tcherepnin (born in 1877) is known
chiefly by his songs in Russian style.

The representative of the 'Moscow School' was Sergey Rachmaninoff
(1873–1943), whose most enduring contribution to Russian music is contained in his piano compositions, which elevated the Russian pianistic style
to new heights. His second Piano.Concerto has become a classic of piano
literature. Rachmaninoff's songs, poetic and lyrical, are in the Tchaikovsky
tradition. Rachmaninoff spent the last 25 years of his life away from Russia,
chiefly in America, and his works of this period are of lesser significance
than his earlier music. Close to Rachmaninoff in the sources of inspiration
was Anton Arensky (1861–1906), who wrote effective piano and chamber
music. Vassily Kalinnikov (1866–1901) is remembered by his First
Symphony, which shows a fine though not original talent.

Sergey Taneyev (1856–1915), Nicolas Medtner (born in 1880),
Alexander Gretchaninov (born in 1864), Ippolitov-Ivanov (1859–1936),
Reinhold Glière (born in 1875), and Sergey Vassilenko (born in 1872) follow the general line of the Moscow School, with some stylistic departures
towards the Nationalistic. Sergey Taneyev was a great master of counterpoint, and author of a monumental treatise on contrapuntal technique.
Little of his creative compositions (a symphony, chamber music, songs)
has achieved popularity. Nicolas Medtner writes almost exclusively for
piano, and his style is a modern adaptation of Chopin and Brahms. After
the Revolution, Medtner left Russia and settled in London. Gretchaninov
is the composer of several operas, which contain elements of the
Nationalist School, particularly in the selection of subject matter from

Russian epical legends. His songs and choral works reflect the spirit of Russian romanticism. Having left Russia in 1925, Gretchaninov eventually settled in America, and continued to compose.

The name of Vladimir Rebikov (1866–1920) merits a place in the history of Russian music. He began as a follower of Tchaikovsky, but later was attracted to modernism. He was the first Russian composer to make use of the whole-tone scale, not as an incidental device, but as a basic thematic structure.

The title of the first true modernist of Russia rightfully belongs to Alexandre Scriabin (1872–1915). His early piano works are strongly influenced by Chopin, while his orchestral music owes much to Wagner. But superseding these influences, Scriabin developed his own, highly individual technique of composition. He enhanced the harmonies of Liszt and Wagner to the point where tonality all but ceases to exist, and dissonances supplant concords. As a new harmonic basis for his music, Scriabin made use of a six-note chord, which he called Mystic Chord. Religion and philosophy occupied an important place in Scriabin's esthetics, and his major works bear indicative titles such as *Divine Poem, Poem of Ecstasy*, and *Poem of Fire*. In the latter work, also known under the name *Prometheus*, Scriabin includes a special part for a *clavier à lumières*, which was supposed to produce colored lights, changing in accordance with the music. Attempts to put this color keyboard into practical use were, however, unsuccessful. Shortly before his death, Scriabin made sketches for a pantheistic work called *Mystery*, in which he intended to unite all arts. Scriabin's music stands outside of Russian national culture, and is the product of a purely musical development of the modern times. Yet his innovations in technique, and his explorations in the field of new sonorities, have affected deeply the development of the new generation of Russian composers.

The modern period of Russian national music is associated with the name of Igor Stravinsky (born in 1882). In his early works, Stravinsky continued the tradition established by Rimsky-Korsakov, with whom Stravinsky studied. Colorism in instrumental treatment and programmatic depiction of Russian fairy tales, characteristic of Rimsky-Korsakov's last period, are the mainstays also of Stravinsky's early compositions. His *Fire-Bird* (1910) is a colorful symphonic panorama of Russian folklore; his *Petrushka* (1911) portrays the scenes of the Russian Carnival. Both scores were written for Diaghilev's Ballet Russe in Paris. With their production, Stravinsky went abroad, and remained in France until 1939, when he settled in America. Paradoxically, Stravinsky became the acknowledged leader of Western modernism, through his works which are intensely Russian. His most revolutionary score was *Le Sacre du Printemps* (1913), which gives a modernistic representation of the rituals of pagan Russia. In this music, Stravinsky breaks away from tradition, and introduces polytonal and polyrhythmic innovations of unprecedented boldness. After 1924, Stravinsky changed his style in the direction of neo-classicism. His works of this period are based on pseudo-classical formulas (*Apollo Musagètes*, 1927; *Oedipus Rex*, to a Latin text, 1928; *Symphony of Psalms*, 1930), or are pasticcios of music by other composers (*Baiser de la Fée*, on Tchaikovsky's themes, 1928).

Diaghilev's Ballets Russes attracted several Russian composers living abroad, who were commissioned to write ballets for his productions. Among them, Sergey Prokofiev (born in 1891) is the most prominent. He returned to Russia in 1933, after an absence of sixteen years, and has since identified himself with the cause of Soviet music. Of the younger men, Vladimir Dukelsky (born in 1903), Nicolas Nabokov (born in 1903) and Igor Markevitch (born in 1912) wrote effective ballets in the neo-classical manner, which have been produced by Diaghilev.

The period of Russian music after 1917, or Soviet music, provides the historian with many contrasts. The political revolution did not signalize developments of extreme leftism in music. True, there were attempts by ultra-modernists to do away with the musical heritage of the past, and to inaugurate a new revolutionary type of music, but such attempts were doomed to failure, when confronted with the necessity of creating a music for the masses. On the other hand, the emphasis on mass appeal and revolutionary subject matter put by the adherents of proletarian music was equally unsuccessful. The compromise was effected in the formula of Socialist Realism, which postulates an art socialist in its content, and national in form. These changing trends in Soviet musical esthetics parallel the changes in the political and social structure of the Soviet Union. The development of Soviet music may be subdivided into three phases (1) the initial period, from 1917 to 1921, marked by the spirit of absolute innovation; (2) the period of conflicting trends from 1921 to 1932, signalized by the rise and fall of proletarian music; (3) the formulation of Socialist Realism in music, and its practical application, from 1932 on.

In the atmosphere of famine and civil war during the early years of the Soviet regime, there was not much room for creative composition.

Yet, concert life continued, and the new audiences of soldiers and workers eagerly patronized the opera, the ballet, and the symphony. The revolutionary ideology had little affected the repertoire although there were attempts to inject a social note into the familiar pieces of the theater. Thus Puccini's *Tosca* was rewritten to become a story of the Paris Commune; Meyerbeer's opera *The Huguenots* was changed to *The Decembrists*. But after a few performances, the old libretti were restored.

The first operas on Soviet subjects were *Za Krasnyi Petrograd* (For Red Petrograd) by Gladkovsky and Prussak, to a libretto depicting the Petrograd campaign of 1919, and *Ice and Steel* by Deshevov, on the subject of the Kronstadt rebellion of 1921. Neither opera obtained any success. More interesting was *Severnyi Veter* (North Wind) by Leo Knipper, an opera on the subject of the civil war and intervention. But it was only with the advent of Ivan Dzerzhinsky, young Soviet composer, born in 1909, that Soviet opera came into its own. Dzerzhinsky selected Sholokhov's famous novel *Tikhyi Don* (The Quiet Don) for the subject of his first opera, which was produced in Leningrad on October 22, 1933, and at once obtained great success with the audiences. His second opera, also after Sholokhov, *Podnataya Tselina* (Soil Uprooted) was staged in Moscow on October 23, 1937, and was equally successful. Other Soviet operatic composers of significance are Oles Tchishko, the author of the opera *Battleship Potemkin*, and Tikhon Khrennikov, who wrote the opera *Brothers* based on an episode from the civil war. The Ukrainian composer Boris Liatoshinsky has composed an opera, *Shchors*, on the life of a Ukrainian civil war hero of that name.

While in creative composition there were few radical departures from the natural course of musical evolution, in the field of performance, and in musical science, many daring innovations were introduced during the early years of the Revolution. In Moscow, a conductorless orchestra named *Pervi Simfonitcheski Ansamble* (First Symphonic Ensemble), or *Persimfans*, was organized in 1922 as a protest against the system of autocratic conductors. It flourished for five years, and presented numerous works of the classical and modern repertoire. In 1922, the Soviet engineer Leon Theremin gave in Moscow a demonstration of the first electronic instrument, the *Thereminovox*, capable of unlimited variation of pitch and tone color. Further progress of electronic instruments resulted in the construction, in 1943, of the electrical piano, the *Emiriton*, built by a grandson of Rimsky-Korsakov.

With the reestablishment of communications with Western Europe, Russian musicians became acquainted with the new music of Germany and France. The Association of Contemporary Music in Leningrad, formed in 1927, was active for several seasons, in presenting works by European modernists. Machine music, exemplified by such compositions as Honegger's symphonic poem *Pacific 231*, was cultivated in Russia by Vladimir Deshevov, who wrote *The Rails*, imitating the noise of a railroad train in motion, and Alexander Mosolov, who composed the industrial ballet *Zavod* (Factory), which included in the orchestration a metal sheet, for realistic effect. Prokofiev wrote a ballet on the theme of the Soviet industrial development, *Le Pas d'Acier* (Steel Leap), which was produced in Paris by the Ballets Russes.

In opposition to the modernists there arose in Soviet Russia a powerful movement in favor of a special type of proletarian music. The Russian Association of Proletarian Musicians (RAPM) proclaimed the Principles of Proletarian Music in a manifesto issued in 1924, opposing all progressive trends of modern music and all types of Western urban art, including jazz, and favoring revolutionary themes, in the tradition of Beethoven's *Eroica*. At the same time, the RAPM attacked the old guard of Russian music for their nationalism and conservatism. After several years of strong propaganda activities, which threatened to bring Russian music to an impasse, the RAPM was dissolved by the Government decree of April 23, 1932, a date which became a landmark in the evolution of Soviet ideology in music.

In place of the discredited idea of proletarian music, Stalin's formula of Socialist Realism, within the framework of national art, was applied to music. A new crisis arose when, in January 1936, the Moscow newspaper *Pravda* published two articles severely criticizing the composer Dmitri Shostakovitch, first for the 'leftist deviation' and 'naturalism' in his opera *Lady Macbeth of the District of Mtsensk*, and then for the 'oversimplification' in his treatment of a Soviet theme in the ballet *Svetly Rutchey* (The Bright Stream). The articles posed a problem of defining Socialist Realism, and drawing a line of demarcation so as not to commit the fallacy of 'naturalism' or 'oversimplification'. The Shostakovitch case is particularly important in the annals of Soviet music, because of the stature of the composer and his place in Soviet art. Shostakovitch, born in Leningrad in 1906, was brought up entirely in the atmosphere of Soviet life, and the development of his talent paralleled the evolution of Soviet ideology in general esthetics. His early works were satirical in character. His opera *The Nose*, after Gogol's tale, featured such effects as drunken hiccups, imitated by harp and violins, and the sound of a razor on the face. The part of the principal character, the Nose, was to be sung by a performer with his nostrils stuffed with cotton wads. There was an octet of eight janitors singing eight different advertisements. The opera was produced as an experimental spectacle in Leningrad, on January 13, 1930.

In his ballets, Shostakovitch also pursued a satirical vein, as demonstrated in the discordant 'Polka' that illustrates the Geneva disarmament conference, in the ballet *The Golden Age*. A similar satiric strain is observed in Shostakovitch's symphonies. His First Symphony, written at the age of nineteen, has become a standard piece of orchestral repertoire in Russia and abroad. Less successful were the Second Symphony, entitled *October*, and the choral Third Symphony, surnamed *May First*. After the rebuke, administered to Shostakovitch in *Pravda*, he abandoned programmatic music, and returned to pure symphonic composition. His Fourth Symphony remained in manuscript, but his Fifth, performed at the Festival on the occasion of the twentieth anniversary of the Soviet Revolution, in October 1937, received tremendous acclaim, and Shostakovitch once more regained his place as a foremost Soviet composer. The Sixth Symphony was less successful, but the Seventh, written under dramatic circumstances during the siege of Leningrad, became a world sensation. This symphony depicts the struggle of the Soviet citizen against the invader, and its triumphant finale foretells the inevitable victory. In 1943 Shostakovitch wrote his Eighth Symphony, which also enjoyed an excellent reception. In recognition of his merit, the Soviet Government twice awarded to Shostakovitch the Stalin Prize of one hundred thousand rubles, for his Piano Quintet and the Seventh Symphony.

During recent years, the national element has been very strong in the works of Soviet composers. Sergey Prokofiev, returning to Russia in 1933, has written numerous compositions in a strongly national vein, among them the cantata *Alexander Nevsky* (after the film of the same name glorifying the repulse of the Teutonic Knights by the Russian Prince Alexander in the year 1242), and during the war, completed the opera *War and Peace*, after Tolstoy. He also wrote a suite entitled *1941*, and a *Ballad of an Unknown Boy*, concerning a young guerrilla fighter who gave his life for the country. Yuri Shaporin (born in 1890) has written two patriotic cantatas, *Na Pole Kulikovom* (On the Kulikov Field), commemorating the Russian victory over the Tatars in the fourteenth century, and *Skazanye o Bitve za Russkuyu Zemlyu* (Chronicle of a Battle for Russian Land), on the subject of the war against the Nazis.

Soviet composers of the older generation have successfully adapted themselves to the new themes. The most important names among them are Reinhold Glière (born in 1875), Sergey Vassilenko (born in 1872), Maximilian Steinberg (born in 1883) and Mikhail Gnessin (born in 1883). Glière excels in monumental symphonic and operatic subjects; Vassilenko cultivates romantic music; Steinberg, disciple and son-in-law of Rimsky-Karsakov, continued the tradition of the Russian National School; Gnessin writes music based on Hebraic motives.

A special case is presented by Nicolas Miaskovsky (born in 1881), the greatest symphonist of modern Russia. He has written 24 symphonies, of which the major portion were composed during the Soviet period. Despite his predilection for somber and individualistic moods, Miaskovsky's symphonies are highly regarded by Soviet musicians, and he is the acknowledged dean of Soviet composers.

The name of Aram Khatchaturian, an Armenian composer, born in 1903, is now in ascendance. He has written symphonies, concertos and chamber music, notable for a sincerity of emotional expression. Khatchaturian's wife, Nina Makarova, is one of the most talented women composers in the Soviet Union. Other important names in Soviet music are: Boris Asafiev (born in 1884), author of numerous operas and ballets, who writes music criticism under the name Igor Glebov; Leo Knipper (born in 1898), author of eight symphonies; Alexander Krein (born in 1883), composer of effective stage music; his brother Gregory Krein (born in 1880), and Gregory's son, Julian Krein (born in 1913), who has written instrumental music in a romantic vein; Vissarion Shebalin (born in 1902), an able symphonist; Alexander Veprik (born in 1899), who writes music inspired by Jewish folklore; Dmitri Kabalevsky (born in 1904), composer of several operas, symphonies, and concertos; Mikhail Starokadomsky (born in 1901), who writes in a neo-classical manner; Valery Zhelobinsky (born in 1912), who has written effective piano music; and Vano Muradelli (born in 1908), Caucasian-born composer who has attracted attention by his strongly individual style.

Popular music plays an important part in Soviet life. Folk-like ballads, marches, and even syncopated music classified as 'Soviet Jazz', are widely sung and played in the Soviet Union. The most successful among Soviet composers of light music is Isaac Dunayevsky (born in 1900), who is the recipient of a Stalin prize in recognition of his achievement. Soviet 'mass songs' have a strong flavor of Russian folk music, and some of them have become in fact folk songs, as, for example, 'Polyushko, Pole' (Meadowland) by Knipper; 'Katyusha' (Katherine) by Blanter, *Provozhanye* (Farewell) by Zakharov, and others. A marching song by the band leader Alexandrov, 'Gimn Partii Bolshevikov' (Hymn of the Bolshevik Party), was proclaimed, by the Government decree of March 15, 1944, the National Anthem of the Soviet Union, in place of the Internationale, and was furnished with a new set of words stressing the national and patriotic character of the country's credo.

No comprehensive history of Russian music exists in the English language. *A History of Russian Music* by M. Montagu-Nathan (1914) is sketchy in treatment. Gerald Abraham's book *On Russian Music* (1939) is limited to the discussion of nineteenth-century Russian composers. There are satisfactory biographies, in English, of individual Russian composers, notably Tchaikovsky, Mussorgsky, Rubinstein, Scriabin, Rachmaninoff and Shostakovitch. Rimsky-Korsakov's book of memoirs, *My Musical Life*, is available in English, too. Some information on later composers is found in Sabaneyev's book *Modern Russian Composers* (1927). There are scattered magazine articles on various aspects of Russian music, and accounts of Russian church music and notation are available in recent editions of music dictionaries. Literature on Russian music in the French and German languages is very scant, and the available publications in those languages are mostly out of date. As to music histories in Russian, the basic work is the two-volume edition *Otcherki po Istorii Musyki v Rossii* (Sketches in Russian Music History) by Findelson, published in 1929. It gives exhaustive information on old Russian music, ancient instruments, church music, notation, bringing the account up to the year 1800. The progress of nineteenth-century Russian music is synonymous with the creative achievements of the great Russian composers from Glinka to Tchaikovsky, and the period has been covered with great completeness in the recent publication. Not only detailed biographies and musical analyses of the works of Tchaikovsky, Mussorgsky, Borodin, Rimsky-Korsakov and others have been published, but their correspondence, note-books and minutiae of life have been brought to light in numerous authoritative editions by Soviet musicologists. No history of the Soviet period of Russian music has as yet been attempted, but there are concise dictionaries of Soviet composers, and ample information on Soviet music is found in the music periodicals, notably *Sovietskaya Musyka*. Thousands of orchestral scores, operas, chamber music works, piano compositions and songs by Soviet composers have been published by the State Music Publishing Edition, affording rich material for the student of Soviet music. Information on Soviet music in the Soviet Republics of the Caucasus, Central Asia and Siberia is found in special publications dealing with the progress of music in these Republics. Detailed bibliography of Russian music, up to 1935, is given in G. Orlov's compilation *Musikalnaya Literatura* (Leningrad, 1935).

2. RUSSIAN FOLK MUSIC

An analyst approaching the subject of Russian folk music should first of all fully comprehend the problems involved in the classification of folk melodies. Each popular song consists of three inseparable elements: the text, the tune, and the rhythm. The text determines the tune as much as the tune determines the word sequence, and the rhythm is the quotient of the text and the melody. The analyst's problem is to find the laws governing the relationship among the words, tones, and rhythms, and determine the implied harmony. The widest division of opinion exists among authorities on the subject of homophonic or polyphonic essence of the Russian song. The composer Serov, one of the first who urged a scientific approach to the popular melos, states dogmatically that Russian modes are not only similar but identical with the Greek modes. P. Sokalsky, in his monumental work *Russian Folk Music in Its Melodic and Rhythmic Structure and Its Differences from the Foundations of Contemporary Modern Music* (1880) agrees fully with Serov in the belief that Russian melos is homophonic by nature. Sokalsky goes even further; he maintains that the modes of Russian song had come directly from ancient Greek modes through the agency of Byzantine priests who penetrated Russia during the country's Christianization in the 11th century. It is needless to insist how unsupported such a theory is. In opposition to Serov and Sokalsky, two other notable theorists and collectors of Russian songs, Melgunov and Paltchikov, conclude that Russian songs are polyphonic, and that harmony is an integral part of their structure.

As a compromise it may be suggested that Russian songs began monodically, and then developed polyphonically, but, in absence of historical support, the controversy cannot be settled at the present time.

The analysis of modes of the Russian song reduces itself to the analysis of range and interval sequence. Sokalsky summarizes his views in the following clauses: 1. The prevalent movement in Russian folk song is descending. 2. The range of folk modes varies from a fourth to the eleventh, the older the song, the fewer tones it possesses. 3. The inner meaning of a mode is determined by groups of fourths and fifths, and the downward move of a fourth, changed to a downward move of a fifth, creates a melodic modulation. 4. In a tetrachord the upper tone assumes the role of the tonic, and the lower of the dominant; conversely in the pentachord, the lower tone is the tonic, the upper the dominant. 5. Inasmuch as each fourth or fifth possesses its own tonal center and its peculiar tendency of movement, downward, or upward, the alternation of these tonal centers imparts motion and inner life to the song. 6. A transition from one tetrachord to another represents a melodic modulation, for the mode is changed. Such a transition is usually effected by means of a move a fourth down from an intermediate tone of the original tetrachord. 7. In ancient Russian music we often find an incomplete tetrachord, or a trichord, with an interval of one-and-a-half tones. Often also an additional tone is present as an embellishment.

But more important than the consideration of modes, range, and movement, is the observation of recurrent note groups. It is not sufficient to indicate a typical cadence of a falling fourth. It is important to consider the interval that precedes that falling fourth. From groups of three notes, comprising two intervals, we pass to a group of four notes, comprising three intervals. Such groups are true idioms of the Russian musical language, and the understanding of idioms is prerequisite to the understanding of the language. But this work is still in the future.

The problem of rhythm in Russian music is that of syllabification, and consequently, an arithmetical one. Arranging the text in rhythmic lines, we add up time values in each line. The number obtained is the numerator of the time signature. Prime-number numerators (5, 7, 11) are frequent in Russian folk song. Glinka, Borodin, Mussorgsky, and Rimsky-Korsakov make frequent use of prime-number signatures, 5/4 (Glinka), 7/4 (Borodin), and 11/4 (Rimsky-Korsakov). Stravinsky intensifies the dynamism of Russian folk rhythms by constant alternation of meters and the use of "instantaneous" one-accent bars with small-unit time-signatures (2/16 in *Le Sacre du Printemps*).

The first collection of Russian folk songs was published in 1782 by Vasily Trutovsky, a priest who was a singer at the court of Catherine the

Great. His little volume contains 39 songs, arranged in 3 parts, and is entitled *Collection of Simple Russian Songs with Notes*. The original songs are arranged in square meters and furnished with a figured bass. In 1790 Ivan Pratch, a Russianized Czech, published a large collection of 150 songs, and this collection, despite its clumsy school-teacher harmonization, still remains the primary source-book. It is interesting to observe that the Russian themes in Beethoven's *Razumovsky Quartets* are note for note from the Pratch collection. Paltchikov established in 1896 that the songs published in Pratch's collection were gathered for him by one Nicolas Lvov, a Russian landlord and a dilettante who surrounded himself with amateur singers from his own class, a discovery which further questions the authenticity of Pratch's collection. Amateur singers are apt to be coached, and any coaching would rob the folk song of its natural essence. In his preface Pratch reports that Pansiello could not be brought to believe that these beautiful songs were creations of simple folks, and thought that they were composed by skillful musicians. This remark touches on an important question. How many folk songs are composed songs? A song by virtue of its universal popularity may acquire an air of anonymous spontaneity. Denza's song "Funiculi Funicula" was mistaken for a folk song by Rimsky-Korsakov who used it in his orchestral piece, entitled *Neapolitan Song* (1907), and Richard Strauss, who incorporated it in his early symphonic poem *Aus Italien*. One of the most popular Russian "folk songs" is the "Red Sarafan" by Varlamov. Wieniawski wrote variations on it in his well-known *Souvenir de Moscou*. In America, "Dixie" has become a popular folk song, although it was composed and published by Emmett. Russian city songs are mostly of Italian or German origin, yet they are as truly Russian songs as those of the countryside. Stravinsky uses one of these city songs in *Petruchka*. The well-known melody of the slow movement of Tchaikovsky's Quartet, op. 11, was heard by Tchaikovsky in a village carpenter shop, but the original words were of urban origin. The Russian Civil War song "Yablotchko" ("Little Apple") is of unknown authorship, but it has become a Soviet folk song. Glière in the "Sailor's Dance" in his ballet *Red Poppy* and Shaporin in his Symphony use "Yablotchko" as a main theme. The so-called gypsy songs of Russia are salon pieces composed by amateurs whose obscure names appear on the printed sheet. To some extent, they too are part of Russian folklore, although their popularity was confined to the semi-literate stratum of the Russian middle class.

In the 19th century, numerous collections of Russian folk songs were published. Artistically speaking, collections harmonized by Balakirev (1886), Rimsky-Korsakov (1877), Tchaikovsky, and Liadov are valuable, but for scientific examination of Russian modes and rhythms collections made by Melgunov (2 series, 1879 and 1882) and Paltchikov (1888) are fundamental sources. Melgunov was severely criticized by musicians at the time of the publication of his collection for his disregard of established rules of harmony. But this very non-conformity to rules, and fidelity to the actual harmony in choral singing of peasant Russia, makes Melgunov's, and after him, Paltchikov's collections so valuable. Trutovsky and Pratch smoothed down the asperities of the original song. Melgunov and Paltchikov set down the songs of the Russian countryside unembellished.

Early in this century the St. Petersburg Academy of Science organized an expedition for the purpose of recording the peasant songs of Russia with the aid of the phonograph. The results were published, in Russian and English, in two important series (1905 and 1912) under the general title *The Peasant Songs of Great Russia as They Are in the Folk's Harmonization, Collected and Transcribed from Phonograms by Eugenie Lineff.* In this collection the main object was to give a faithful reproduction of Russian songs as sung by peasants, with all the singularities of an uneducated but musically inclined singer. The transcription of the phonograph recording was also made as close to the original as possible, correcting only the deviations from the tempered pitch. The songs were gathered by the Academy Expedition all over Central Russia, and represent a better cross-section of Russian folk music than the previous collections. The Academy collection seems to support the belief of the essentially polyphonic character of Russian folk songs as enunciated by Melgunov and Paltchikov. According to the phonograms, each song starts with a solo. The chorus comes in later, and is entirely improvisational, each singer elaborating on the melody according to his own taste and ability. The number of independent voices is usually two, three, or four. The modern school of Russian folksong theorists follows the Melgunov-Paltchikov theory of the polyphonic character of Russian folk singing. Among the later treatises on the subject is Kastalsky's *Singularities of the Musical System of Russian Folk Song* (1923).

3. RUSSIAN MUSIC IN ART SONGS

Russian national music came of age on May 24, 1867. On that day, St. Petersburg, the capital of Russia, welcomed guests from Slavonic lands with a concert of works by Czech and Russian composers, conducted by Mili Balakirev. The program included a *Serbian Fantasy* by Rimsky-Korsakoff, an overture on Czech themes by Balakirev, Glinka's orchestral dance *Kamarinskaya*, and a Ukrainian dance, *Kazatchok*, by Dargomyzhsky.

On the following day, the famous Russian critic of literature, drama, art and music, Vladimir Stasov, an eloquent champion of all things Russian, wrote in the *St. Petersburg Dispatch*: "Let us hope that our Slavic friends will carry the memories for a long time of the poetic sentiment, talent and skill displayed by a small but already mighty company of Russian musicians."

Stasov did not list the members of this "mighty company" by name, but the reference was clearly to the so-called Balakirev Circle of young musicians who gathered in St. Petersburg at periodic sessions and passionately discussed the necessity of creating a true Russian art. The members of the Circle, besides Balakirev himself, were Borodin, Cui, Mussorgsky and Rimsky-Korsakoff. The oldest was Borodin, 33 years of age at the time of the Stasov declaration; the youngest, Rimsky-Korsakoff, was barely 23.

The performance of Russian works at a concert attended by foreign dignitaries was an event of no small importance at the time, for the

---

Ch. 3: originally published with the record album *Thirty Russian Art Songs*, Unicorn Records, date unknown.

Russians were quite unsure of their ability to match creative powers with acknowledged masters of the West. Some representatives of Russian culture were embarrassed by this exhibition of home talent. Turgeniev, the great novelist, who was present at Balakirev's concert, spoke angrily of the "shameful arrogance" on the part of these Russian composers whom he regarded as little better than amateurs. But Turgeniev was a Westerner in sympathies; Stasov, the critic, and his "mighty company" of friends were Slavophiles and believers in Russian genius.

The expression "mighty company" (in the original Russian, *Mogutchaya Kutchka*, literally "a mighty little heap") was picked up in derision by some of the opponents of the Balakirev Circle, but as the powers of the national group grew, the adjective "mighty" ceased to be ludicrous, and Stasov's felicitous description became indelibly engraved in the annals of music history. In articles and books published outside Russia, the designation "mighty five" is often used.

Who were these five, who shaped the destinies of Russian national music in the nineteenth century? Alexander Borodin, an illegitimate son of a Georgian prince, a student of science, and later a professor of chemistry, who regarded music as an avocation, and had great difficulty in finding time to compose; Cesar Cui, a learned writer on military science whose book on field fortification became a standard manual in Czarist Russia; Mili Balakirev, a genial mentor of his circle, a member of a well-to-do family, who had plenty of leisure for work, but could never sustain his creative effort, so that he would drag the composition of a single work through many years; Modeste Mussorgsky, the erratic genius, who served in the army and then was a government employee, and who regarded himself as insufficiently trained in music, and constantly deferred to his friends as undoubted superiors; and Nicholas Rimsky-Korsakoff, a young marine officer, who, like his friends, felt the deficiency of his musical education, but overcame his initial handicap and became the greatest master of the "mighty company," the only one who had the persistence of a professional composer and who produced one work after another in a steady flow.

The dominating ideal of the "mighty company" was Russian national art. They followed the example of Glinka, who produced the first truly Russian opera, *A Life for the Czar*, and who introduced the rich element of Russian musical orientalism in his *Russlan and Ludmila*. But Glinka was connected too intimately with the traditions of Italian opera to be the sole guide of a national school. He was concerned mainly with the proper flow of melody, and cared little for the perfection of Russian prosody. In fact, he often wrote the melody first, and then had a librettist fit the words to the vocal line. This procedure was followed even in such a profoundly Russian opera as A Life for the Czar. Much closer to the new ideas of Russian music was Dargomyzhsky, the proponent of realistic musical speech. "I want the sound to express the word," he declared. Much later, Mussorgsky wrote: "Whatever I hear spoken, and whoever speaks, whatever is said, my brain instantly works out the musical exposition of the words."

Dargomyzhsky and Mussorgsky carried the ideas of musical realism to such a degree that the traditional division of an opera into sections— arias, choruses, instrumental interludes—became no longer workable. The sacrosanct symmetry of the musical phrases was also abandoned in favor of complete freedom of musical speech. It should be emphasized that this was a purely Russian national development entirely unconnected with Wagner's ideas of vocal writing. In fact, the members of the "mighty company" were opposed to Wagner and his Germanic art, and believed that Wagner's influence on Russian music was pernicious. The slogan launched by Mussorgsky was "To the New Shores," but these shores were situated in Russia.

In performance, too, Russian nationalists emphasized the power and the significance of the words. Chaliapin used to say: "Vocal teachers employ vague terminology such as 'support the breath,' or 'lean on the diaphragm,' and the like. All this may be necessary, but it does not get to the core of the problem. It is not enough to teach a person to sing an aria or a serenade. One must teach the meaning of the words uttered by the singer, and the emotions that summon these words to life."

Stanislavsky was insistent on the esthetic importance of the spoken word. "Say Ocean," he once told a young singer. "According to the coloration of the vowel O, the ocean may be either calm or turbulent." To another singer he said: "What I want to hear are not the naked notes, but 'thinking notes.' The whole human being must sing in you, and not solely your vocal apparatus."

Not only the members of the "mighty company" and their spiritual descendants, but also romantic Russian composers accepted at least a particle of musical realism, as promulgated by the Nationalists. Tchaikovsky was not a militant nationalist, but he expressed repeatedly his love for

Russian folk songs. He wrote to Madame von Meck: "The Russian element in my music is ingrained in me from childhood, when I absorbed the fantastic beauty of folk melodies, and I have ever since become passionately enamored of Russian national themes."

Paradoxically, it was St. Petersburg, the most western city in Russia, that became the cradle of Russian national music, while Moscow, the ancient capital, remained the center of cosmopolitan musical culture, exemplified by Tchaikovsky. Of course, the music of the Moscow composers is full of Russian sentiment; but it is a subjective Russian quality, the notorious "Russian soul," suffused with melancholy and ridden by a sense of inexorable fate. On the other hand, the art of the national composers of the St. Petersburg group is Russian in an objective sense. In symphonic music, and in operas, the composers of the St. Petersburg group make use of Russian subjects from recorded history or poetic legends; in vocal works, the texts are typically Russian, and often nationalistic. A particularly interesting example is the remarkable song "Vision" by Balakirev, to the words by Khomiakov. Here the imagination of the poet carries him to a future Pan-Slavic commonwealth; in his dream he flies, like an eagle, to Prague, and hears the Greek Orthodox service in the cathedral, invoking God's blessings on all Slavic lands. In his musical characterization, Balakirev reaches great eloquence, and the sonorous conclusion, with a hymnlike chant and ringing church bells, is an apotheosis of nationalist aspirations of Russia.

The magnificence of Russian tone-painting in Borodin's song "The Sea" is no less impressive. Here he tells a story of a young sailor who takes to the sea with his beautiful bride, in a boat laden with treasure brought from conquered lands. Then the sea darkens, the relentless waves overwhelm the boat, and the young couple perishes in the abyss. The treachery of the sea is portrayed by Borodin in an alternating series of changing moods, from guileful calm to savage assault. When a Russian noblewoman spoke to Debussy in admiration of his symphonic poem La Mer, he observed: "If you want to hear a real masterpiece of the marine genre, listen to Borodin's song 'The Sea.'"

Borodin was not only a master of epic poetry and colorful characterization. He possessed a fine streak of humor. In this mood, he wrote the song entitled "Conceit," representing a pompous individual caring for no one but his own exalted person. In recitative-like phrases, he depicts every facet of the would-be hero. Here is the art of musical caricature at its best.

Grandeur and humor are reflected with equal penetration in the songs of other members of the Russian National school. The greatest master of both is Mussorgsky. He reaches the peak of dramatic power in his cycle *The Songs of Death*, and he is devastating in mockery of his musical antagonists, as portrayed in *Rayok*, a musical review of the Russian contemporary scene with sly references to local events, such as a banquet tendered to Berlioz during his visit to Russia, the adulation of Adelina Patti, and the obsequious currying of favors from the Grand Duchess Helen, who is portrayed as the Muse of joy and pleasure.

A highly developed sense of musical humor marks the songs of Dargomyzhsky. And yet his art, like that of Gogol, is "visible humor through invisible tears." Such is his song "The Worm," describing the state of mind of a humble government clerk, who prostrates himself before the mighty of the land.

Humor through tears animates also a song by Cui, named with stark immediacy "Hunger." This is one of Cui's cycle of songs to the texts by the poet Nekrasov depicting the hopeless lot of the Russian peasant. The song is unusual for Cui, who was at his best in gentle miniatures.

In the songs of Rimsky-Korsakoff, the distinguishing feature is eloquent dignity; there is a perfection of form, a mastery of the vocal line which are rarely matched even among the greatest songs of the age. Pathos and humor are alien to Rimsky-Korsakoff's Muse; but there is no mistaking the fine penetration of the meaning of the texts in his songs and in his operas.

Russian romanticism at its most poignant is expressed in the songs of Tchaikovsky. The poems which he chose for his songs were congenial to his besetting moods: unrelenting melancholy, surrender to fate, brooding remembrance of past happiness. It is a matter of verifiable statistics that the majority of Tchaikovsky's songs are cast in minor keys; but this tonal wistfulness does not preclude the frequent outbursts of inner joy, occurring even in the saddest of Tchaikovsky's songs. It is the universality of human emotion that makes Tchaikovsky still the most popular Russian composer, in and outside Russia. Sergey Rachmaninoff continued the tradition of Tchaikovsky both in selection of melancholy texts and in characteristic melodies and harmonies, with mournful cadences and emotional climaxes. Nicholas Tcherepnin belonged to Rachmaninoff's generation; his songs possess a fine romantic quality, with perhaps more cheerfulness in exposition of mood. The music of Alexander Gretchaninoff contains elements of Russian romanticism in equal measure; there are influences both of Tchaikovsky and Rimsky-Korsakoff. He had a natural instinct for the singing phrase, and several of his songs written in his youth remain perennially popular.

The impact of Russian music on the world is tremendous; its universality is proved by its penetration into the creative habits of composers in lands as different in their cultural history as France, Spain and Italy; England and Scandinavia. Russian national elements are transmuted into new melodic and rhythmic patterns, while the emotional essence is absorbed and rendered again in forms of expression characteristic of each of these many nations.

Part II

SOME MAJOR COMPOSERS

4. NIKOLAI RIMSKY-KORSAKOV: MUSCOVY'S MUSICAL MERLIN

When *Scheherazade* was first heard in America, the amazed correspondent of the *Musical Courier* exclaimed: "Rimsky-Korsakov—what a name! It suggests fierce whiskers stained with vodka!"

Several decades later, Hollywood's technicolor film makers portrayed the composer as a young marine officer enjoying himself in the Casbah. Inspired by the dancing of a sinuous Algerian maiden, he was shown quickly jotting down the third movement of *Scheherazade* on the back of a wine list; and later that same evening, according to the movie, a Casbah restaurant orchestra played the newly completed suite in highly creditable manner.

The real-life Rimsky-Korsakov was far from such an intriguing figure. His vodka consumption was moderate, although as a young ensign in the Russian Navy, he went to sea and did touch at various Mediterranean ports; but on the evidence of his *Chronicle of My Musical Life*, there were no known contacts with Algerian dancers. His personal life, as a whole, was utterly respectable and not at all conducive to dramatization in color, or even in black and white.

There was nothing in his appearance, manners, conversation, or correspondence to set him apart from the Chekhovian world populated by the Russian intellectuals of 75 years ago. He was a mediocre conversationalist with limited ability as a musical performer. He played piano badly, and as a conductor could give merely adequate presentation from a limited repertory of Russian symphonic works. He wore a professorial beard, used glasses, and lived practically all his life in St. Petersburg, with

---

Ch. 4: originally published in *HiFi & Music Review*, June 1958.

his wife, Nadezhda Nicolayevna, née Purgold, and growing children. He enjoyed moderately good health, and succumbed to a heart attack in 1908 at the age of sixty-four.

That Rimsky-Korsakov, typical figure of the St. Petersburg academician, could create music of electrifying vitality and brilliant color is not so paradoxical as it might seem. It is well known that writers of colorful and exciting stories are often sedentary and possess little personal kinetic force.

On March 6, 1844 (according to the Russian old-style calendar), Rimsky-Korsakov's father, a 60-year-old middle-class citizen from the small town of Tikhvin, in the Novgorod district, wrote down in his pocket almanac; "Nika, born at 4:53 P.M." The mother, Sophie, was an illegitimate daughter of a rich landlord named Skariatin.

As a child, Nika stuttered and his parents feared that he would never learn to talk normally. He was compulsively tidy and cried when he even dirtied his hands or fingers. He also had one overwhelming passion, a toy drum, which he pounded incessantly. From the drum to a real musical instrument was a natural transition, and before too long he was trying to play the piano.

His older brother was a naval officer and his sea duties fascinated the young boy. When he learned to read, his favorite books were stories of ocean voyages. He also liked astronomy, and at the age of twelve wrote to his mother: "I woke up during the night and to my great delight I saw Orion, Betelgeuse, Sirius, Castor and Pollux, and many other stars."

Rimsky-Korsakov's interest in music took a sharp upturn at the age of thirteen after he had seen his first opera in St. Petersburg. He wheedled fifteen kopeks from his parents to buy music paper, and because he adored Italian opera, made an attempt to arrange the sextet from *Lucia* for piano. Gradually his horizons broadened and he began to appreciate symphonic music; Beethoven's *Pastoral* Symphony became for him "the best in the world."

Music was not a career for a young man in old Russia. So he was trained for naval service, and in 1862 was sent on a three-year cruise aboard the clipper, *Almaz*. The ship reached the port of New York in 1864, while the Civil War was raging. The Russians were then regarded as dear friends of the North and on the occasion of the arrival of the *Almaz*, Longfellow wrote an ode of friendship to the Russian Czar.

The ship proceeded to Brazil, where the young ensign was enchanted with the tropical climate and naively expressed his amazement at winter in June. The voyage was planned to be around the world, but in Rio de Janeiro the Captain received orders to return to Russia. The trip back through Gibraltar and into the Mediterranean offered the chance for a brief visit to the Casino in Monaco, where several gold coins were lost at the gambling table. Then the ship turned back to the Straits of Gibraltar and by way of England and Norway returned to St. Petersburg.

This was the most exciting geographic event in Rimsky-Korsakov's life. He later made several visits in Germany and in France; but by that time his heart was with his work in St. Petersburg, where he had become professor at the Conservatory. In the meantime, history was being made in Russian music. Mussorgsky sounded the slogan, "To the New Shores," and the new shores were definitely of nationalist Russian configuration, as opposed to the Western European influences represented by Tchaikovsky and Anton Rubinstein.

Rimsky-Korsakov was only twenty-three when the critic Vladimir Stasov wrote the famous article in which he referred to "a small but already mighty company of Russian musicians." He had in mind the members of the so-called Balakirev Circle—of which Rimsky-Korsakov was one. It is impossible to say how Stasov's rather generalized and anonymous reference became crystallized in a definite number: "The Mighty Five." But thenceforward, Rimsky-Korsakov took up the banner of Russian nationalism, with Balakirev, the mentor and only trained musician of the lot; Cui, the music critic and military writer; Borodin, the chemistry professor; and Mussorgsky, the genius without a permanent occupation.

At first, Rimsky-Korsakov was quite militant in his nationalism, even using Russian indications of tempo and expression marks in his early manuscripts. For publication, however, he changed them to the traditional Italian. Like his colleagues of the Mighty Five, Rimsky-Korsakov felt a sense of inadequacy as a composer. He was self-taught and had avoided the rigorous training that in Germany or France was a matter of routine. When he was appointed professor of harmony at the St. Petersburg Conservatory, he had to teach and learn the rules at the same time. Even when internationally famous, he complained of his inability to work with professional dispatch: "I work inefficiently; I set down wrong notes on paper; I seem to be unable to fix a relatively simple rhythmic idea, and at times cannot find the right interval without trying out the melody on the piano. While copying the final draft, I cannot remember even a couple of bars correctly, and have to follow the original note for note. . . . Non-Russian composers work steadily to old age; consider, for instance, Wagner and Verdi. I am fifty-eight years old, and apparently for a Russian it is old enough."

This fatigue and self-proclaimed old age at fifty-eight was part of Rimsky-Korsakov's Russian moodiness; but as a matter of biographical fact, there was no slackening in his energies to the very end of his life. During the abortive Russian Revolution of 1905, Rimsky-Korsakov fought valiantly against the attempts of authorities to expel conservatory students for participation in political meetings, and found himself relieved of his duties as a result. Even during the last week of his life he was busily engaged in a fight with censorship officials who demanded the deletion of some allegorical lines in his operatic setting of Pushkin's text of *The Golden Cockerel*; for it came too close to satire on the Russian government of the last Romanoff. He refused to compromise, and as a result, the opera was not produced until after his death.

Russian composers have always felt a strong attraction to the Orient, not the fabled Orient of Cathay and Cipango, but the trans-Caucasian Persian East and the rich subcontinent of India, so full of bright sun and of dark mystery. *Scheherazade* was the earliest revelation from Rimsky-Korsakov's palette of this splendidly accoutered Orient. The culmination of his Oriental idiom was also his final masterpiece, the opera *The Golden Cockerel*, the work of a musical Merlin in its vibrant harmonic textures and serpentine scales.

Academician though he was, Rimsky-Korsakov was no stuffy conservative. Neither was he a wild-eyed innovator or experimenter with substances dangerous to euphony; but he did advance, slowly but surely, to the very border of the accepted science of his day—the Ultima Thule of justifiable dissonance. So long as he could find a rational explanation for a musical procedure, he was quite willing to try his skilled hand at it. His opera-ballet *Mlada* (1890) included in the score, for instance, an ocarina tuned in the scale of alternating whole tones and semitones—neither major, minor, nor chromatic! Here was a defiance of tradition at a time when Wagner was still regarded as a violent revolutionist. Modern composers of a later day, unaware of Rimsky-Korsakov's little ocarina scale, discovered it for themselves, and some explicitly claimed priority for its invention— Willem Pijper of Holland, Felix Petyrek of Vienna, Ludomir Rogowski of Poland, and, in America, Normand Lockwood and Robert Palmer.

Startling usages abound in *The Golden Cockerel*: here a scale of alternating semitones and minor thirds, harmonized by consecutive aug-

mented triads, and there an exceedingly bold superposition of di-
minished-seventh chords on a totally unrelated whole-tone row. Remarkable modernistic devices are found also in that least known of
Rimsky-Korsakov's operas, *Kaschey the Immortal.*

In the domain of rhythm Rimsky-Korsakov was not averse to departure from tradition. Russian folk music is based on asymmetrical
rhythms, 5/4 being particularly favored in some melorrythmic patterns. In
the first act of the opera *Sadko* (1896) he treated a whole choral episode
in a compound asymmetrical meter of 11/4. In order to master this
unusual beat, the choristers of the St. Petersburg Opera used to practice
it by chanting the 11-syllable Russian sentence *"Rimsky-Korsakov sovsem
sumasoshol"* (Rimsky-Korsakov is absolutely mad).

"Rimsky-Korsakov is absolutely mad" were words (in Russian) providing metrical
memory key for Sadko chorus.

While he had no belief in any mystical correlation between musical
sounds and ideas, he did have an instinctive feeling for a correspondence
of colors and keys. In his scheme, the major keys possessed these hues:

C	white
D-flat	warmly dark
D	golden
E-flat	somberly dark
E	dark blue
F	bright green
F-sharp	gray-green
G	golden brown
A-flat	violet
A	roseate, youthful
B-flat	strong and dark
B	steely dark

Among minor keys, Rimsky-Korsakov had definite associations only
for C minor, which was golden yellow, and C-sharp minor, which was pur-
ple-red. The key of A major was particularly dear to his heart because it

represented youthful emotion, and was connected in his mind with spring and with dawn. The theme associated with Spring in the opera *Snow Maiden* is cast in that key, and when his older colleague Balakirev suggested transposition a tone higher, for the sake of better singing *tessitura*, Rimsky-Korsakov rejected it outright; the "steely dark" key of B being quite contrary in his mind to the character of Spring.

These color associations are entirely subjective and the listener would have to possess absolute pitch to appreciate such esoterica. But no such guide is needed for enjoyment of the gorgeous instrumental timbres deposited in wonderfully proportioned layers throughout his scores—of which *Scheherazade*, the *Russian Easter Overture*, and *Capriccio Espagnol* are so typical. He was a master of orchestration, and believed that scientific musical perfection could be achieved by combining instruments in requisite super positions, and alternating solo passages in contrasting succession. In his treatise on orchestration, he selects, without false modesty, examples solely from his own works to prove each point of discussion.

The initial impact of Rimsky-Korsakov's Russian-Oriental music on non-Russian audiences produced a genuine shock reaction. Vienna's renowned and feared critic, Eduard Hanslick, protested against this dose of "Russian champagne, a little sour . . ." Yet this "sour champagne" proved intoxicating and creatively exhilarating to musicians of the Latin countries.

The orchestration of Debussy (who during his youth spent several summers in Russia as house musician to Tchaikovsky's patroness, Mme. Nadezhda Von Meck) owes much to Rimsky-Korsakov's imagination. Respighi's Roman pines could well have grown on the banks of the Neva River (he was a Rimsky-Korsakov pupil in 1901); and Manuel de Falla's three-cornered hat is cut coloristically from the same cloth as Rimsky-Korsakov's Russian cap. A music critic once wryly remarked that the best Spanish composer was Rimsky-Korsakov, for his *Capriccio Espagnol* breathes Iberian fire even more effectively than the native product.

America came last in the line of the international conquests won by Rimsky-Korsakov's highly colored music. As late as 1905, the Boston critic, Louis Elson, proclaimed, "The Russians have captured Boston! . . . The *Scheherazade* engagement began with a bombardment of full orchestra, under cover of which the woodwinds advanced on the right. The violins now made a brilliant sortie on the left flank of the main body. It was a magnificent charge; at one time the concertmaster was quite alone, but his cavalry soon rallied around him. A furious volley of kettle-drums followed. . . . At this the entire audience—including some very big guns— surrendered."

The surrender of Boston to Rimsky-Korsakov was nothing in comparison to the abject submission a generation later of Hollywood and Broadway. This conquest was accomplished by infiltration. A goodly contingent of excellent Russian musicians came between 1905 and 1920 to seek their fortunes on these shores and in so doing colonized first Broadway and later Hollywood. With the advent of talking pictures, their services as skilled arrangers and composers were soon in heavy demand. The film industry was still under the spell of sheiks, odalisques, and suchlike Oriental characters, and music à la Rimsky-Korsakov, fragmentized and diluted, suited these subjects perfectly. Thus, under jejune palm-trees, sufficiently tropical to create the illusion of luxuriance, Rimsky-Korsakov's pristine muse became transformed into a Jezebel-like courtesan, redolent of aromatic oil from Makassar, and adorned with tinkling ankle bracelets.

On Broadway, too, public taste of the day demanded exotic spectacles, painted with Oriental colors. By watering down Rimsky-Korsakov's Russianized Orientalism, the composers of New York could arrive at the right formula for success. Many a popular hit of the 1920s derived melodic and harmonic turns from Rimsky-Korsakov and other Russian composers. Even cowboy songs began to sound like the "Song of India" from *Sadko*, with a pentatonic scale for its melodic foundation.

Last, not least, sound tracks of virtually all movies set in Casablanca, Cairo, Tangier, etc., to say nothing of those for the sumptuous travelogues across Oriental lands, vibrate with Korsakovian chromatics. These are amply supported by luscious Kostelanetz-type harmonies, with every interstice of seventh- and ninth-chords filled in to saturation—all this arranged for the most glutinous combination of strings, woodwinds and brass, forming at climactic points a vast and all-pervasive plasma of sonority. Rimsky-Korsakov would probably have shuddered at this lateral offspring of his creative imagination. But the genealogy cannot be denied, despite its monstrous mutation.

In the half century since his death in June of 1908, Rimsky-Korsakov has become an object of veneration throughout his native land. His operas are standard repertory on all Russian stages; his symphonic works, and his songs are as greatly loved as they ever were. But there is a decided shift in the appreciation of his art outside Russia, and particularly in the United States. *Scheherazade*, once a mainstay of symphonic programs (the operas have never gained a real foothold here), has now moved into the less elevated locale of summer concerts or the "Pops," has been arranged for small instrumental ensembles, and further degraded by indiscriminate jazzification. The once mysterious and exotic art of Rimsky-Korsakov is now in public domain, not only juridically (for there is no American copyright on Russian music), but also esthetically. The rainbow of Korsakovian hues has faded, largely through the abuse of these colors by imitators and unintentional traducers. Whether the thrill of the original impact can ever be restored, with or without "high-fidelity," is a question. In the meantime, the pale ghost of Rimsky-Korsakov flits through bits of popular music, in would-be exotic ballads, in the booming sound tracks of the movies, in the very flavor of popular-styled modernism. This transmutation of Russian Orientalism continues unabated. The final product may bear no visible—or audible—resemblance to the original Korsakovian seed, but the great Russian has effected a sea-change of tremendous proportions, spread over an astonishing area of chronological time and geographical space.

5. ALEXANDER GLAZUNOV: KEEPER OF RUSSIAN TRADITION

The cause of Russian national music received a great impetus when a six-teen-year-old boy, in the uniform of the Technical High School of St. Petersburg (all schoolboys wore uniforms in old Russia), appeared on the podium in the concert hall of the Nobility Assembly. He acknowledged the warm applause that greeted the first performance of his Symphony in E Major, conducted by Mily Balakirev. The boy's name was Sascha Glazunov, or more formally, Alexander Konstantinovitch Glazunov.

The event took place in the spring of 1882. Not quite two years before that, Glazunov had begun serious study with the great Rimsky-Korsakov. He was a private pupil, and he came to Rimsky-Korsakov's apartment on Sundays. In a single lesson, Glazunov could absorb more material than a regular conservatory student in a month. It was sufficient merely to indicate to him the method of handling concerted voices in counterpoint, the best ways to modulate from one key to another, the effective use of various instruments in a symphonic work, and he would instantly catch the idea, apply it to his own problems in compo-sition, and produce a score already possessing elements of mastery.

Not only was Glazunov a fantastically talented student, but he endeared himself to Rimsky-Korsakov's heart by another quality, rare among beginners in composition: a wonderful tidiness in writing notes on manuscript paper. This gift of penmanship is often underestimated by teachers and pupils alike, and negligent students are apt to excuse them-selves by saying that Beethoven's handwriting was almost illegible.

Ch. 5: originally published in *The Christian Science Monitor*, January 4, 1957.

Glazunov's working habits were as methodical as his penmanship. As a pupil, he never failed to prepare his lessons and bring in the required number of pages of music. As a mature master, he attended to every detail of a new work before allowing it to be performed. When he himself became a great teacher, he urged his students to be methodical above all. He never believed that a great musical talent excused sloppiness.

The music critics faced the task of reporting the youthful symphony of Sascha Glazunov with something like awe. Cesar Cui, himself a composer, wrote "Glazunov's first symphony is an astounding work, almost frightening in its precocious mastery." The Russian critic Stasov nicknamed him "young Samson."

Glazunov accepted these extraordinary tributes with becoming modesty. He continued to study diligently. He learned to play on the violin, then the French horn, trumpet and trombone, and clarinet. He played piano fairly well. His goal was not to become a virtuoso, but to acquire enough knowledge of instrumental technique to score for the orchestra with precision and effectiveness. In his symphonic works, this sympathetic understanding of instrumental playing makes the music sounds naturally, effortlessly. Not that Glazunov simplified the technical problems. Far from it. His scores are rich in sonority, and every instrument is given an important part in the complex contrapuntal design. Succession of tranquil and turbulent passages is calculated with a fine regard to the progress of musical thought. Orchestral players in Russia used to remark jocularly that Glazunov rarely used long stretches of rests for any instrument, because he believed that no player should stay idle while others work. But Glazunov's insistence on doubling instrumental groups had a more artistic explanation. He wished to insure the effectiveness of the ensemble, and he succeeded without producing opaque sonority. He instructed his students to do likewise. He said that there were three ways of scoring for orchestra: (1) so that any fairly efficient ensemble could play the music after a reasonable amount of rehearsing; (2) so that only a virtuoso orchestra, with an expert conductor, could make it sound; and (3) so that no conductor and no orchestra could possibly attain satisfactory results. He urged young orchestrators to adopt the first method.

Glazunov found an enthusiastic supporter in the person of the Russian musical Maecenas, Mitrofan Belaiev, founder of the famous publishing firm that printed thousands of works by Russian composers. When Glazunov was only eighteen, Belaiev arranged in St. Petersburg a concert of his works, and he began to publish Glazunov's music. The great European master Liszt heard about Glazunov and expressed a desire to see him. Belaiev took the young composer to Weimar, where they visited Liszt; the Weimar orchestra performed Glazunov's Symphony. This visit left a profound impression on the future development of Glazunov's musical style; Lisztian harmonies are in evidence in many of Glazunov's works. Belaiev took him also to Bayreuth where he heard Wagner's operas, but Glazunov resisted the intrusion of Wagnerianism, and adopted only external color effects from Wagner's music. Perhaps this inner antagonism to Wagner made Glazunov avoid the theatrical musical genre; he never wrote an opera.

Like all Russian composers, Glazunov was fascinated by the splendor and exoticism of oriental music; many of his vocal and instrumental works reflect the sinuous melodic patterns of the East. His study of medieval modes inspired his orchestral suite entitled *From the Middle Ages*. He wrote a festive march for the Columbian Exposition in Chicago; he conducted his own works in Paris and London. He continued to compose in a steady flow; in twenty years he wrote eight symphonies and a great number of vocal and chamber works. Then he called a halt on his tireless endeavors. Rumor had it that he did not want to undertake a ninth symphony because he felt that no composer ought to try to equal Beethoven even in the sheer number of symphonies. But there is another, more plausible explanation for Glazunov's decision. He was called upon to teach orchestration and composition at the St. Petersburg Conservatory. In 1905 he became its director, and gave all his energies to his work as pedagogue and administrator.

He led the famous conservatory through a perilous political period, when the Czarist government took measures to subdue the revolutionary agitation among Russian students. Glazunov never took part in politics, but he protected his students who participated in various public manifestations, and politely but firmly resisted the encroachment of the political police on the affairs of the Conservatory.

He was a mild man of infinite humanity. The Russian laws under the Czars forbade the settlement of Jewish people in the large cities unless they belonged to a restricted number of professional or commercial categories. Talented young musicians of the Jewish faith who flocked to the St. Petersburg Conservatory stood in the danger of deportation. On numerous occasions, Glazunov sheltered these applicants in his own home, or provided other places of temporary residence for them during entrance examinations. Glazunov, the most law-abiding of musicians, broke an unjust law, but the authorities never called him to account.

The music of Glazunov suffered an eclipse during the turbulent age of modernism. To the end, Glazunov remained faithful to the ideals of nineteenth-century art. He refused to compromise with dissonant music; but he was unfailingly fair to students of his Conservatory who indulged the passion for modernistic discords, provided they fulfilled their academic requirements. When Sergey Prokofiev, the most gifted alumnus of the St. Petersburg Conservatory, played his piano concerto at commencement, Glazunov left the hall as inconspicuously as he could, but his departure was noticed by all. It was symbolic of his artistic probity that he made no objections to the granting to Prokofiev of the first prize (a grand piano) for a work so completely at variance with Glazunov's own ideals.

6. REINHOLD GLIÈRE

Reinhold Glière belongs to the generation of Russian composers who even before the Revolution occupied a solid place in the history of Russian music. The Soviet period of Glière's creative work is marked by a change of subject matter rather than of musical texture. His music can, therefore, be taken as a fair example of a composer's transfiguration in the light of new revolutionary events. In this process of self-adaptation, Glière has been brilliantly successful while remaining true to his musical self, and now he can be classed among Soviet composers who express the inner essence of Soviet music: socialist realism in a national frame. The word *national* must be understood in an enlarged sense, and should include all the minorities of the component republics of the Soviet Union. Although Glière is primarily a composer of Russian music, he is the author of the opera *Shakh-Senem*, based on the folklore of the Turkic peoples of the Caucasus. In its orchestral score are introduced some native instruments, the *Tar*, which is a sort of guitar, and the *Kemancha*, a sort of violin played like a cello, on the knee. This opera was first produced in Baku in 1926.

Glière was also one of the first qualified Russian composers who contributed to the music of the masses, in his topical orchestral *Fantasy for the Festival of the Comintern* and *March of the Red Army*.

Glière was born on January 11, 1875, new style, in Kiev. In 1894, he entered the Moscow Conservatory. He studied composition with Arensky, Taneiev, and Ippolitov-Ivanov, and graduated in 1900 with a gold medal. In 1905, he went to Berlin for two years to complete his musical educa-

---

Ch. 6: originally published in *The American Quarterly on the Soviet Union*, July 1938.

tion. At that time he was already the composer of two symphonies and numerous compositions for chamber music, piano, and voice. His style was chiefly derived from the great national school of nineteenth-century Russia plus a surface layer of impressionism which was beginning to be a fashion at that time. As to form, Glière always clung to the classical sub-division of movements and logical development of themes within each movement. Impressionism in form was never a temptation to him. It is in Glière's harmony that one may find a chord expansion that definitely places him among twentieth-century composers. There is a certain kin-ship with Scriabin, and the profusion of orchestral color with a prolixity of arpeggiated passages is characteristic of both composers.

The high point of Glière's pre-war music is reached in his Third Symphony, surnamed after the hero of the Russian epic, *Ilya Murometz*, which was first performed in Moscow in 1912. It is a grandiose work, one of the longest in symphonic literature.

In 1913, Glière became professor of composition at the Kiev Conservatory and was elected director in 1914. In 1920, he moved to Moscow and was engaged as professor of composition at the Moscow Conservatory. He was elected President of the Union of Soviet Composers in April 1938. It was during this post-revolutionary period that he became interested in the ethnological material of the Soviet Orient. In the Proletcult, and later in the Communist University of the Workers of the Orient he performed valuable work on collecting authen-tic melodies of minority nations. In 1923, he was asked by the Commissariat of Education of Azerbaidzhan to codify the melos of Caucasian tribes, the material which he used in his opera. During all this time, Glière never ceased to compose. His symphonic compositions of the post-revolutionary period include the symphonic poem *Cossacks of Zaporozh*, conducted for the first time by the composer himself in 1924 in Moscow. Inspired by the well-known painting of Repin (the Cossacks writing a defiant letter to the Turkish Sultan), it is a symphony of boister-ous joy, effectively scored.

But perhaps the greatest glory of Glière is his ballet *Red Poppy*, writ-ten in 1926–1927, and first performed in Moscow on June 14, 1927. The story of the ballet may be described as a Soviet melodrama. A Soviet ship arrives in a Chinese port of call. A beautiful Chinese dancer watches the Soviet sailors as they help the Chinese coolies in their exhausting toil. The simplicity of the Soviet captain, so different from the Chinese bosses, attracts her. The villain of the melodrama is her unscrupulous fiance who leads a plot against the Soviet crew. When his designs are uncovered, he retreats. Harboring double hatred of the captain, as a rival in affection and a danger to his political ambitions, he forces the dancer to hand the captain a cup of poisoned wine. But the dancer knocks the cup out of the captain's hands at the last moment, and saves his life. For this, she is shot by her fiance, and before her death, she hands a red poppy to the leaders of Chinese rebels as a symbol of the eventual victory of the Chinese working class.

The Soviet sailor's dance from *Red Poppy*, based on the tune "Yablochko" ("the little apple"), has become popular all over the world, and one hears it over the radio in America and in Europe.

Thus, Glière has combined the new Soviet thematics with Russian national folk music, and in this he has accomplished what Soviet composers consider their most important task, and what has been described as socialist realism in music.

7. ALEXANDER SCRIABIN

The star of Scriabin, which once burned with the splendor of a supernova, has now inexplicably fallen to a low order of magnitude. In the firmament of modern composers Scriabin appears as an opaque luminary, and is slightingly described as an epigone of Wagner. True, there is a considerable amount of Wagneromantic rhetoric in Scriabin's symphonies, and his chromatic harmonies have a Tristanesque quality, but these are extrinsic matters that should not obscure the inherent individuality of Scriabin, which is unique.

Scriabin was a mystic, a product of the twilight culture of the *fin de siècle*, when solipsism and pantheism could cohabit in the same mind without a sense of self-contradiction. In Scriabin's philosophy, music was not merely an art of pleasurable sounds; his aims transcended esthetics. He dreamed of an ultimate consummation, a *mysterium*, in which all arts, all sciences and all religions would be brought together in a hyper-Hegelian synthesis by a volitional act, with Scriabin himself as demiurge, mystagogue and supreme artificer. Scriabin had sketched out the text of this mystery play, but he died too soon to make progress on the actual composition of the score.

Mystical elements pervade the programmatic designs of Scriabin's works. His symphonic "poem of fire," *Prometheus*, is melodically and harmonically derived from a six-note chord, which Scriabin called "Mystic Chord," even though to more prosaically minded musicians it may be no more mystical than the old familiar dominant-ninth chord with two unresolved suspensions. Modern listeners miss the presence of divinity in

---

Ch. 7: originally published in the Boston Symphony Orchestra program book, 1969.

Scriabin's *Poème divin*, and fail to respond to the ecstasies of the *Poème de l'extase*. The ebullient piano rhapsody *Poème satanique* has lost its demoniacal élan, and the sensuality of the piano vignette entitled *Désir* is unconsummated in its evanescent ending on an arpeggiated dissonance.

Many composers felt a strong association between tonalities and colors. Scriabin made an earnest attempt to combine light and sound in the score of *Prometheus*, in which he includes a special part, *Luce*, symbolizing the fire that Prometheus stole from the gods. It is notated on the musical staff as a *clavier à lumières*, a color organ intended to flood the concert hall in a kaleidoscope of changing lights, corresponding to the changing harmonies of the music. Unfortunately, the task of constructing such a color keyboard was beyond the technical capacities of Scriabin's time. Serge Koussevitzky, the great champion of Scriabin's music, had to omit the *Luce* part at the world première of *Prometheus* which he conducted in Moscow in 1911. Poor Scriabin! It would be a child's play for an electrical engineer today to set up a switch of multicolored neon lights flicking off and on according to Scriabin's specifications. The experiment is well worth trying, perhaps to mark the centennial of Scriabin's birth in 1972.

Scriabin was born on Christmas Day of 1871, according to the old Russian calendar (corresponding to January 6, 1872, Gregorian style), and this coincidence with Nativity made an extraordinary impact on his Messianic mentality. Conscious of the frailty of the human form, he separated the Messiah within him from the outer shell of his physical self. "I treasure the devotion you feel for the One who dwells within me," he wrote to his wife Tatiana. "You have faith in Him, because He is great, even though I myself am often meek, small, weak and exhausted. I am not yet He, but I will soon become that which is He!"

Scriabin felt this mystical identity with overwhelming self-intoxication during the process of composition: "I am carried aloft to extraordinary heights by the immense wave of my inspiration!" he wrote. "I suffocate! I am in a state of blessedness! I write music that is divine!"

Even divinely inspired persons need food and shelter. Scriabin was not endowed with profitable talents. As a pianist, he played mostly his own music, and could not command large audiences. Like many composers before him, he had to depend on the aid of wealthy patrons of art to keep body and soul together. His first benefactor was Belaieff, the famous publisher of Russian music.

A man of considerable professional knowledge of music (he often read proofs of the music he published), Belaieff was impressed by Scriabin's talent and offered him a publishing contract. Apart from the stipulated amounts for Scriabin's compositions, Belaieff periodically supplied him with extra money and partly financed his appearances in Europe as pianist and composer.

Belaieff died in 1904 and Scriabin had to look for other sources of supplementary funds. Relief came from Margarita Morozova, a wealthy Moscow merchant woman who gave Scriabin an annuity of 2,400 rubles without any obligations. This bounty enabled Scriabin to undertake an extensive trip abroad. In 1906, at the invitation of the Russian conductor Modest Altschuler, founder of the Russian Symphony Orchestra in New York, Scriabin went to America. He gave piano recitals of his works and appeared as soloist with the Russian Symphony Orchestra in New York and with the orchestras of Chicago and Detroit. But there arose unforeseen complications. Scriabin was joined in New York by Tatiana, to whom he was not legally married, since his first wife refused to give him a divorce. Scriabin was warned by friends that he might be evicted from his hotel and deported on a charge of moral turpitude. There had been a famous precedent, when Maxim Gorky, travelling in the United States with his common-law wife, was expelled from the country. Fearful of a similar scandal, Scriabin decided to leave America. As usual he was short of funds. He cabled to Glazunov, who was in charge of the Belaieff Edition with which Scriabin had continued arrangements for royalties and for new works: "Indispensable quitter Amérique immédiatement Prière envoyer télégraphe 600 roubles New York Expédierai six compositions." Glazunov sent the necessary money, and Scriabin took the next boat back to Europe.

Despite this contretemps, Scriabin felt kindly towards America and Americans. "I think that the opinions commonly held in Europe about America are prejudiced and unfair," he wrote. "Americans are far from being inartistic, and they are not devoid of talent."

In the meantime, a certain chill developed in Scriabin's relationship with his benefactress Margarita Morozova. Scriabin resented her lack of enthusiasm towards his affairs. He poured reproaches on her for missing a performance of the *Poème divin* in St. Petersburg. "Time will come," he wrote her, "when people will travel from the South Pole to the North Pole to hear a single pause of my music. Yet a friend like you would not make an

overnight trip in a comfortable sleeping car to hear my best work! It hurts!"
Morozova soon discontinued her contributions to Scriabin's welfare.

At this juncture, a knight in shining armor appeared on Scriabin's
horizon in the person of Serge Koussevitzky. He went to see Scriabin in
Lausanne, where the Scriabins were staying, and offered him a most generous contract with the Edition Russe de Musique, which had just been
founded by him. The terms, 5,000 rubles annually, with a five-year guar-
antee, were so exceptional that Koussevitzky even warned Scriabin not to
tell Rachmaninoff, who was also under contract with the Edition Russe de
Musique, how much he was getting.

Koussevitzky was, of course, not only Scriabin's publisher, but an
inspired interpreter of Scriabin's symphonic music. Koussevitzky's marriage to Natalie Ouchkoff, heiress to a tea fortune, gave him almost unlimited resources for the promotion of his career as conductor. He organized
a magnificent series of symphony concerts in Moscow, emphasizing works
of Russian composers. In 1910 Koussevitzky launched a fantastic musical
voyage down the Volga River, on a chartered steamer, and engaged
Scriabin to join him on the trip as soloist in his Piano Concerto. There
were many in the audiences of Koussevitzky's Volga concerts who had
never seen or heard a symphony orchestra in operation before, and the
whole enterprise had a character of exploration and discovery.

No more mutually beneficial and artistically exalted collaboration
could be imagined than that existing between Scriabin and Koussevitzky,
both in their mature thirties, and both animated by high ideals in art.
Tragically, it came to a grinding end. Scriabin had regarded Koussevitzky
as an apostle whose mission was to serve the cause of his music. Riding
high on a wave of relative prosperity, assured of a regular annual income,
he slackened the tempo of his output. There was no written contract, and
Scriabin apparently thought that the lucrative sums dispensed by
Koussevitzky were unconditional contributions, similar to the ones he had
been receiving from Morozova. He therefore experienced an unpleasant
shock when Koussevitzky notified him that he was 13,000 rubles in
arrears on his obligations towards the Edition Russe de Musique. A most
disagreeable exchange of claims and counterclaims ensued, until the
break became irreparable. Scriabin, now a well known figure in Russian
music, had no difficulty in finding another publisher, Jurgenson, and
securing a satisfactory contract. Despite total severance of personal relations, Koussevitzky continued to perform Scriabin's music.

On April 27, 1915, at the age of forty-three, Scriabin died of blood-poisoning induced by a trivial abscess. Profoundly grieved, Koussevitzky extended an offer of financial assistance to Scriabin's family, which was accepted. When in 1924 Koussevitzky became conductor of the Boston Symphony Orchestra, his opening program featured the *Poème de l'extase*. But even Koussevitzky was eventually affected by the inexorable shift of musical tastes, away from the mystical emotionalism represented by Scriabin's type of music. During the last years of Koussevitzky's tenure as conductor of the Boston Symphony Orchestra, Scriabin's name all but disappeared from his programs.

When Stravinsky was asked in a recent interview to evaluate Scriabin's position in music, he observed cruelly that while he regretted Scriabin's early death, he was horrified to think what kind of music Scriabin would have written had he lived to a ripe old age. But has this art, which Scriabin believed to be of divine inspiration, irretrievably fallen into historical desuetude? The avant-garde of today may yet discover in Scriabin's orgiastic exudations and solipsistic revelations a psychedelic source of singular attraction in the new brave musical world.

The thorniest problem of re-evaluation of Scriabin's music was posed in Soviet Russia. Ideologically, Scriabin's astral mysticism, his eschatological visions, his sublimated eroticism were completely alien to a socialist society guided by the doctrine of dialectical materialism. Scriabin's early piano pieces continued to figure on the programs of Soviet pianists, but his symphonic works, overladen as they were with mystical overtones, had to be rationalized before they could be incorporated in the Soviet symphonic repertory. This rationalization was effected by divesting Scriabin's scores of all extraneous associations and judging the music on stylistic and technical grounds only. After this ideological exuviation, Scriabin's mystical works were finally rehabilitated. A performance of *Le poème de l'extase* was given in Moscow after a hiatus of some twenty years in 1938 with excellent success. As a part of the "legacy of the past," Scriabin's letters, meticulously annotated, have been published in a large single volume. Articles dealing with various aspects of Scriabin's career continue to appear in the Soviet musical press.

Historically speaking, Scriabin remains an isolated figure in modern music. Not a single composer, in Russia or elsewhere, has picked up the musical thread of Scriabin's unique art. A tragic exception was Scriabin's son Julian, who at the age of eleven wrote piano preludes that were direct continuations of his father's last opus numbers, with their characteristic chromatic convolutions and unresolved but euphonious dissonances. In 1919 Julian took private lessons in composition with Glière in Kiev. His mother, Tatiana Scriabin, was away in Moscow on business, when one Sunday afternoon in June, Julian with a group of other children went on an excursion to the central island in the Dnieper River, accompanied by a woman school teacher. None of the children could swim, and Julian, shy in the presence of girls, waded alone to a small bay by the shore, where there was a sudden drop in the depth of the water. When at dusk the guide began gathering the children to take them home, Julian was missing. His body was discovered when it was quite dark.° His mother was in transit and could not be reached. She did not arrive in Kiev until several days after Julian was buried. Her words in a letter written when Julian was eight years old, turned out to be prophetic. "I live by memories," she wrote, "by past joys and sometimes even by hopes for the future. This happens particularly when I watch the spiritual and musical development of my little Julian, who begins to resemble his father more and more, in soul and body, with every passing day. He is my hope, my joy, and also my constant worry. It is terrifying to have to take care of such a fragile boy!"

The evolution of Scriabin's musical idiom, from Chopinesque beginnings to the "Mystic Chord," may be described as a growth of harmonic suspensions. In the early works of Scriabin such suspensions, while protracted, are eventually resolved. In his more advanced compositions, the process became "a suspension of a suspension." Auxiliary melodic notes were suspended indefinitely, and the resulting dissonances became, in Scriabin's estimation, consonances of a higher order. Dabbling in physics—and metaphysics—Scriabin related the dissonant components of his chord formations to the upper overtones of the natural harmonic series. A further subtilization of Scriabin's musical language led to a dissonant coalition of major and minor tonalities. Yet Scriabin never abandoned the use of key signatures, even when his music acquired a decidedly atonal character. He preserved the time signature as well despite the extraordinary degree of rhythmic differentiation of asymmetrical patterns.

° It is an unforgettable memory that I, as a friend of the Scriabin family and Secretary of the Scriabin Society of Kiev, had to accompany a professional team of seamen who dragged the bay and found Julian's body, which they towed on a rope from a rowboat to the shore. N.S.

The programmatic titles of Scriabin's works are descriptive of his own state of mind during the process of composition, and this subjective correspondence extends also to expression marks, which are intensely psychological, and always written in French: "avec une noble et joyeuse émotion," "avec une ivresse toujours croissante," and "presque en délire." Scriabin's first two symphonies have no descriptive titles. The Third Symphony is the *Poème divin*; the fourth, *Le poème de l'extase*; the fifth, *Promethée, Le poème du feu*.

The Second Symphony is the most "symphonic" of the five. It is in five movements that are easily reduced to a classical scheme. The key is in C minor, with the finale in C major, a symphonic "tierce de Picardie," identical with the tonal scheme of Beethoven's Fifth Symphony. The first movement, *Andante*, is cyclic in structure, with a brief interlude, *Allegro giocoso*, in euphonious C major, separating the exposition from the recapitulation. The contrast between a spacious opening theme, marked *serioso*, and a nervous palpitating second motive is expertly drawn. The second movement, *Allegro*, in 6/8 time, in E-flat major, is an ecstatic scherzo, presaging the syncopated effusions of Scriabin's later works. The third movement, *Andante*, in 6/8, in B major, is a bucolic eclogue, opening and closing with the presentation of a veritable aviary in the flute part. This may be the only instance of ornithological, or any other kind of onomatopeia found in any of Scriabin's scores.

The fourth movement, *Tempestoso*, in 12/8, gravitating towards the key of F minor but modulating freely through a number of enharmonically related keys, possesses the melorhythmic élan that was to become Scriabin's distinguishing mark, a "glacial flame" burning in all of his music. The transition from this tempestuous movement to the finale, effected by the classical application of a sustained dominant pedal point, is without pause. The finale is marked *Maestoso*, set in symmetric 4/4 time, in the clearest C major, self-asserting and triumphant. The music moves on without a halt to its conclusion in triple forte.

Scriabin's Second Symphony is relatively conservative in its technical aspects. There is a sensible balance between diatonic and chromatic elements in the score; cumulative dissonant agglomerations are invariably dissolved into harmonious concords. The cadences, in particular, are formally strong and almost redundantly grandiloquent in their sonorous reiterations of tonic triads. It is all the more puzzling why the work affected professional musicians and Russian music critics as being an apotheosis of dissonance.

The Second Symphony was first performed in St. Petersburg on January 25, 1902, under the direction of Anatole Liadov. When Liadov received the score, he found the music horrendous. He wrote to Belaieff, who published the score: "Some symphony! Scriabin might well join hands with Richard Strauss! Compared with this, Wagner is a mere suckling infant mumbling sweet nothings. Help! I am going crazy!" Liadov's outburst may have been a jocular exaggeration, but there was no jocularity in the reaction by Arensky, who denounced the work in a letter to Taneyev: "The program of the last concert of the Russian Symphonic Society included the Second Symphony by Scriabin. This must have been a gross error. The program should have announced the performance not of a Symphony but of Cacophony, because in it there are no consonances whatsoever. For thirty or forty minutes the peace is disturbed by a senseless piling-up of dissonances. I cannot understand why Liadov agreed to conduct such nonsense. I went to the concert only to amuse myself. Glazunov never showed up at all, and Rimsky-Korsakov, whom I asked what he thought of it, said that he could not understand how any composer could depreciate the value of consonances to such an extent as Scriabin."

The reviews were none too favorable. *The Russian Musical Gazette*, the foremost Russian music periodical of the time, which all musicians were in the habit of reading, conceded that Scriabin had talent but berated him for "flaunting his dissonances at the public to the point of saturation, so that they begin to offend the ear."

Despite the ambiguous reception of the Second Symphony in St. Petersburg, Safonov performed it in Moscow on April 3, 1903. There was some hissing in the audience, immediately drowned by demonstrative applause. Julius Engel, the knowledgeable critic of the Moscow newspaper *Russkyie Vedomosti*, wrote a long article in Scriabin's defense. He pointed out that Scriabin's works had already attracted serious attention in Europe, and that booing and hissing is not the proper response to his music. "True, Scriabin's music," he continued, "is an art of the upper crust, far from the healthy spaciousness of fields and meadows, an art raised in the sophisticated and nervous atmosphere of a large city without fresh air. Strife, passion, caprice—these are the typical traits of Scriabin's musical personality, reflected in such designations as *tempestoso, appassionato*, etc., which are strewn on the pages of his scores. . . . It may seem that the composer is trying to attain the unattainable, that he is jumping

above his head, that he is struggling to portray the unimaginable, to con-
jure up the figure of a Superman. Even though his triumphant pronouncements appear inflated and bombastic, there is a breath of life in his
music, intensely propulsive, fresh, looking inquisitively into the future,
and not an impotent melancholy, giving up the struggle. In this lies the
contemporary merit of Scriabin's achievement."

Another Moscow newspaper, *Russkoye Slovo*, continued the already
established line of attack against Scriabin as a discord-monger. "The
Second Symphony is a work of great intricacy. The first aim of the young
composer is to stun the public by incessant modulations, deceptive
cadences and other harmonic ingenuities. The second aim is to embroi-
der these harmonies with a number of auxiliary notes, resulting in dissonant combinations that would startle even the most uncompromising followers of the school of César Franck. But Scriabin is merciless. He
continues to swim in a sea of harmonic morbidities, and in the end one
feels defeated, crushed, unable to protest, to listen, to think. After the
concert, in a state of exhaustion, with a heavy head, one is glad to have a
moment of rest, relieved to wait for the violinists to tune up their instruments and to hear at last a perfect fifth in pure intonation." It is interesting to note that this review was written by a former classmate of Scriabin
in the piano department.

8. NIKOLAI MIASKOVSKY: THE MAN OF TWENTY-THREE SYMPHONIES

Nikolai Miaskovsky is the only contemporary composer who writes symphonies in such numbers that comparison with the prolific eighteenth-century composers is in order. Ever since Beethoven, nine has been considered the limit of numerical achievement in writing symphonies. It is said that prolific romantic composers such as Bruckner and Mahler had a superstitious feeling about exceeding the number nine and felt that the composition of a tenth symphony would be interrupted by death. Miaskovsky, living in a country where superstitions are not in vogue, has gone merrily along, and refused to interrupt his symphonic production even when Hitler's hordes menaced Moscow. The latest symphony reported was No. 23.

In order to understand Miaskovsky's creative evolution, it is necessary to know the circumstances of his early life. He was born April 20, 1881, in the fortress of Novo-Georgevsk, near Warsaw, and spent the first seven years of his life there. The only musical inclination he showed at that time was in the form of crawling under the piano when somebody played. Then the family moved to Orenburg and from there to Kazan. His first teacher was an aunt, a high-grade neurotic who could hardly succeed in implanting a love for music. But musical impressions from the outside poured in, various summer operettas, and—Miaskovsky's first overwhelming musical experience—Glinka's *Life of the Tsar*. Soon he entered the cadet school in Nizhny-Novgorod and then in St. Petersburg. He graduated in 1899 and was automatically pushed into a military career, traditional in his family. He selected the least obnoxious of the higher military schools, the Engineers' School. His musical studies continued under the tutorship of various teachers, but, on coming to Moscow, he finally decided to take up composition seriously. He wrote Rimsky-Korsakov in

St. Petersburg, asking him to recommend a teacher in Moscow. Rimsky-Korsakov replied with a cordial letter, advising him to see Taneev. Taneev looked over Miaskovsky's first attempts and turned him over to Glière, with whom Miaskovsky took an entire course in harmony in six months' time.

In 1904, Miaskovsky went to St. Petersburg. Glière recommended him to Kryzhanovsky, with whom he studied counterpoint, fugue, form, and a little orchestration. There he met the literary and musical modernists of that era and wrote his first serious works, songs to the texts of the poetess Z. Hippius. In these songs Miaskovsky already established his characteristic style, free tonality and a subtle rhythmic melodic line. Finally, he entered the St. Petersburg Conservatory and joined the classes of Liadov in counterpoint and Rimsky-Korsakov in orchestration. At that time he already showed that he was modernistically inclined. In 1908 he received a scholarship, and, in 1911, graduated from the conservatory, a full-fledged composer. Among his classmates were Serge Prokofiev, Boris Asafiev, and Lazare Saminsky.

Miaskovsky is a symphonist by nature. A glance over the list of his compositions reveals no operas, oratorios, ballets, or any other type of applied form. But it does not mean that Miaskovsky creates in terms of "absolute" music. Every one of his symphonies has an implied program, whether implied or expressed, and he may well be called a true romantic composer, a Mahler of Russia. His symphonic output may be subdivided into four periods, from the first to the sixth symphony, from the seventh to the twelfth, from the thirteenth to the eighteenth, and from the nineteenth to the twenty-third. The first period is typical of his pre-revolutionary moods, introspective and at the same time mystical. The Sixth Symphony is the culminating point of these individualistic moods, although it was conceived in 1922 when Miaskovsky began to revise his intellectual outlook in the direction of a more realistic scheme of composition. In his extraordinarily frank "Autobiographical Notes," published in the June 1936 issue of *Sovetskaia Muzyka*, he writes concerning this period:

> Despite my instinctively correct ideological direction, the absence of a theoretically confirmed intellectual outlook produced in me a neurotic and sacrificial conception of the revolution and the then raging civil war; this state of mind naturally found its reflection in the first sketches of the

Sixth Symphony which I conceived about that time. The first impulse was given to me by the singing of the French revolutionary songs "Ça Ira" and "Carmagnole" by a French artist who sang them exactly as they do in the workers' districts of Paris. I made notes of his version, which was different from the printed versions, and I was particularly impressed by the rhythmic energy of "Carmagnole." When in 1922 I started my Sixth Symphony, these themes naturally found their place in the symphony. The confused state of my world outlook at that time had inevitably resulted in a conception of the Sixth Symphony which sounds so strange to me nowadays, with the motives of a "victim," "the parting of the soul and body," and a short apotheosis symbolizing "beatific life" at the end; but the creative ardor of this symphony which I felt during its composition makes this work dear to me even now. Apparently, it still has a power to move the listener, as far as I can judge from performances here and frequent hearings abroad, particularly in America.

Miaskovsky's second symphonic period, from the Seventh to the Twelfth Symphony, symbolizes a path from the "subjective" to the "objective" or, in other terms, from the individual to the collective. Without trying to be literal in programmatic descriptions of the life in the Soviet Union of that period, he nevertheless went for inspiration to the fields and factories of the country. Between symphonies he tried his hand at mass songs, among which the "Wings of the Soviets" and the "Lenin Song" are the more successful. In the autumn of 1931, he conceived the plan of the Twelfth Symphony, known also as the *Collective Farm Symphony*, although this subtitle is not used by Miaskovsky himself. The inception of this symphony coincided with the first plans for collectivization of agriculture, an idea which appealed to Miaskovsky as having definitely symphonic material in it. The three movements of the symphony symbolize three stages of collectivization: the old order, the struggle for the new plan, and the accomplishment of the plan.

The third period of Miaskovsky's symphonic cycle, from the Thirteenth to the Eighteenth Symphony, represents a synthesis of subjective moods and the objective realistic ideas. Miaskovsky himself considers his Thirteenth Symphony a highly pessimistic work. "This Symphony," he states, "was the result of an insuperable urge to find an outlet for the accumulated subjective moods," which, he bitterly adds, "have always been in my make-up, and are ineradicable at my age."

Thanks to this emotional discharge, in the following Fourteenth Symphony, Miaskovsky succeeded in creating a dynamic and stimulating work. The Fifteenth Symphony is lyrical, but its lyricism is not somber, and its directional impulse is optimistic. Still nearer to the contemporary ideals are the Sixteenth and Seventeenth Symphonies. Finally, the Eighteenth Symphony is a joyful symphonic postscript, a summing up of materials stored up at an earlier date, with themes and melodies of a general Russian type, in mass-song style.

The Nineteenth Symphony was the beginning of a new phase, almost utilitarian in character. Miaskovsky's symphonic writing became more compact, more directly addressed to the masses. The Nineteenth Symphony is written for the military band, and its composition was prompted by the arrangement which the Moscow conductor Petrov made of Miaskovsky's Eighteenth Symphony. Miaskovsky liked the idea and accepted Petrov's suggestion to write a new symphony scored for the band. Miaskovsky writes in *Sovietskoyo Iskusstvo* of February 14, 1939, on the eve of the first performance of the Symphony by Petrov's ensemble over the radio station Comintern:

> My Symphony is in four movements, and is written according to all the requirements of symphonic conception. But the special character of the medium has brought about alterations in my musical language and methods of expression in the direction of greater clarity. The first movement of the Symphony is built on the juxtaposition of solemn themes on one hand, and dancing folk-like motives on the other. The second movement is a symphonized waltz. The third is meditative and lyrical and the fourth movement is in precipitous motion. If my new work results in heightening the interest for serious music in the broad masses of the warriors of our valiant Red Army, and if, at the same time, the Symphony will prove useful in building up Soviet military bands, I feel that my task has been largely successful.

The Twentieth Symphony did not produce a noticeable stir in the Moscow music world. But Symphony No. Twenty-one, performed on November 16, 1940, when the war clouds were already gathering, produced a profound impression. The Moscow musicologist Gregory Schneerson wrote to the author these lines: "The success was enormous. Miaskovsky was called to the stage three times. There were shouts, *Bis*, a demand for a repetition, a rare case in the symphonic annals." In the program note for the Moscow premiere, Schneerson characterizes Miaskovsky's Symphony No. Twenty-one as "one of his most noble works." He continues:

> The great quality of this composition lies in the combination of impressive beauty of conception with a plasticity of musical images, profundity of content, perfection of form and integrity of structure. This Symphony, permeated with philosophical reflection, leaves an ennobling impression. In this relatively small work, there is concentrated an enormous life-asserting force, which receives its magnificent expression in the powerful culmination in the development section. The formal structure of the symphony is distinguished by great originality. The symphony is in one movement, but the introduction acquires here a separate and individual station. Broadly developed, this introduction contains in itself, as in a seed the entire cycle of main concepts of the Symphony. The initial theme, given out by the clarinet, determines the mood. This is the fundamental musical thought, from which grow other thematic elements of the Symphony. A closely related theme is the one in A minor, active, excited, precipitous. The dynamic and progressive development of this subject leads to the second theme in C major, folk-like, broad, luminous in its mood and color. It is on this motive that, after a tense fugal development of the principal subject, is built the festive and triumphant culmination. The recapitulation, which repeats successively the first and the second subject, arrives at a greatly enhanced coda, based on the material on the introduction. It is as though the composer returns to initial mood of lyric reflection, which has now acquired a deeply transfigured character.

Then the war came, but it was not loud enough for Miaskovsky's symphonic inspiration. Miaskovsky describes the circumstances of the composition of the Twenty-second and Twenty-third symphonies in these dramatic lines:

> When the war began I was in Moscow, where I had spent a quarter-century of creative work. I lived in a quiet corner of Moscow, in the intellectual quarter. I remember the first air alarms. Buildings and ancient memorials were camouflaged, anti-aircraft guns set up on roofs. Then the bombings began, and they did not spare our quiet street.

I worked intensely in those days, even during stretches in bomb shelters. After completing three songs and two military marches, I conceived the idea of a symphonic ballad. It was finished in October, during the stern days of the Hitlerite offensive against Moscow. The symphony, my Twenty-second, consists of three movements: the first tells of happy life and work, overshadowed by forebodings of impending storm; the second depicts violence and brutality—I wanted to convey the feeling of the unforgettable, heroic autumn of 1941. Judging by its press reviews, the symphony was accepted by the public just as I conceived it.

Late autumn found me in Kabardino-Balkaria, a small Caucasian republic whose people has a wealth of wonderful songs and dances. Here, in the town of Nalchik, I wrote another symphony in three parts, the Twenty-third, whose theme was inspired by Kabardino-Balkarian national music.

Now I am completing a string quartet in three movements, dedicated to the bright memory of those who perished for my country. It reflects one thought—the blood which has been spilled has not been in vain. We saved Moscow, we saved the country, and victory will be ours.

9. ALEXANDER TCHEREPNIN— SEPTUAGENARIAN

Sasha Tcherepnin, a tall boy for his age, was a familiar figure at the St. Petersburg Conservatory fifty-odd years ago, as he was seen walking down the corridors accompanied by his father Nicolas Tcherepnin, professor of composition and conducting, teacher of a generation of Russian composers, and himself a composer of stature. Paradoxically, it was Sasha's mother, not his father, who gave him his first music lessons. As soon as he learned to manipulate the piano keys, he began making up tunes of his own. There was so much music lying around the house that he picked up the rudiments of notation intuitively. He learned notes and the Russian alphabet at the same time. Now, at seventy, he cannot even remember when he could not read Russian words or musical notes.

The Tcherepnin household in St. Petersburg was the crossroads for musicians, writers and artists. Sasha's maternal grandfather was the French painter Albert Benois, whose brother was Alexandre Benois, stage designer for Diaghilev's Ballet Russe and the author of the scenario for Stravinsky's *Petrushka*, as well as that of the ballet *Le Pavillon d'Armide* by Tcherepnin-pére. Among Tcherepnin's maternal ancestors was the Italian composer Catterino Cavos, who settled in Russia early in the nineteenth century and identified himself with the cause of Russian music. His position is of historical importance, for he anticipated Glinka by twenty years in writing an opera on the story of Ivan Susanin, and it was Cavos who conducted the first performance of Glinka's opera *A Life for the Tsar* on the same subject. Another maternal ancestor was Johann Friedrich Kind, the author of the libretto of Weber's *Der Freischutz*.

Ch. 9: originally published in *Tempo*, winter 1968-69, issue 87.

Through the Benois branch of the family Tcherepnin is related to the actor Peter Ustinov, whose maternal grandmother was a Benois. Ustinov often comes to see Tcherepnin in Paris, in London or in New York, to discuss and play music.

Alexander Tcherepnin's life is exceptionally well documented. Since the age of six, he has kept a diary, punctiliously recording events of his life, personal and professional. Miraculously, all of its bulk has been preserved, packed away in trunks in Paris, in New York and in other places. At some future time this diary will provide an inexhaustible fount of intimate information on artistic life during the first two thirds of the twentieth century. There are delightful vignettes in this monumental manuscript. At the age of fourteen Sasha was busily engaged in the composition of a grand national opera *The Death of Ivan the Terrible*, improvising on the family piano. To imitate the sound of a huge bell, which he needed for the last act, he got hold of a sheet of iron, throwing it on the floor with a tremendous clatter.

It so happened that the apartment below was occupied by Hippolytus Tchaikovsky, brother of the composer, an elderly man unaccustomed to such un-Tchaikovskian noises. One day Tcherepnin found a carte de visite slipped under the door of his apartment, with an imploring message, 'Dear Sasha, please have pity on a sick old man. I can endure your piano exercises with equanimity but not your improvisations.' Tcherepnin complied, and a few days later there came another message from Tchaikovsky's brother: 'I have now recovered from my illness, and you are free to resume your practicing, and even your improvisations.'

Tcherepnin-père became aware of his son's musical experiments rather late in the game. As he looked over Sasha's scribblings, he observed with a sigh, 'Alas, you are bound to be a composer!' He used to call his son's pieces 'bloshki,' little fleas, because their melodic leaps were so wide and so unpredictable. One of these 'fleas,' composed in 1913, and eventually published as No. 4 in a piano album, *Pièces sans titres*, op. 7, is a specimen of bitonal harmonies rather bold for the period.

Like all Russians born in the nineteenth century, Tcherepnin has three different birthdays. He was born on January 8th, 1899, according to old Russian style, which corresponded to January 20th of the Gregorian calendar. The year 1900 was a leap-year in Russia but not in the West, and as a result the difference between the two calendars increased to 13 days in the twentieth century, so that the 8th of January now corresponded to the 21st of January. This is the date on which Tcherepnin celebrates his birthdays, but is he justified in doing so? The incontrovertible fact is that he was born on a day which was the 20th of January in the civilized world. Is there any reason to condone the vagaries of the Russian Orthodox Church in retaining the antiquated Julian calendar?

Composing and keeping a diary became an almost physiological necessity for young Tcherepnin, like food and drink. In fact, he continued to write music even when food gave out in icebound Petrograd (Russianized from St. Petersburg during the German war) in the year of the Revolution. The Petrograd winter of 1917–18 was the most severe since Napoleon's armies invaded Russia in 1812. People used furniture for fuel and went to bed wrapped up in furs. Daily bread rations were reduced to a quarter of a pound, and even for that the emaciated Petrograders had to stand in line. A Russian music critic bartered his grand piano for twelve pounds of black bread. Malnutrition began at birth, and babies, few of whom survived, were fed frozen potatoes. Obesity became an unknown condition. Glazunov, the beloved director of the Petrograd Conservatory, whose corpulent figure was a sightseeing landmark in Russian musical circles, lost half of his imposing avoirdupois in a single year. Sasha Tcherepnin, who was tall but not broad and had little excess fat to expend, was stricken with scurvy. It was in this state of bodily distress that he wrote his funereal 13th piano sonata, which opens in the nethermost regions of the keyboard with a theme from the Russian Mass for the Dead. 87 opus numbers and 41 years later, Tcherepnin used the same subject as the cantus firmus of his Fourth Symphony. This 'Hunger Sonata' as it might well be called, was eventually published under the redeeming title 'Sonatine romantique.'

Amazingly, concert life was still going on in Petrograd under the siege of cold and hunger. Some lucky artists were paid in kind, receiving a few pounds of bread, horsemeat and sometimes such luxuries as butter, flour and sugar. When cats and dogs began to disappear from the streets of Petrograd, and dogmeat sandwiches were sold openly near the closed food markets, the Tcherepnins made plans to leave. Like most people fleeing the doomed city, they headed south. Nicolas Tcherepnin received an offer to assume the directorship of the Conservatory of Tiflis, the capital of the then independent republic of Georgia in the Caucasus. In the fall of 1918, travelling with the greatest difficulties through the land ravaged by war and revolution, the Tcherepnins finally arrived at their destination. Sasha resumed his musical studies at the Tiflis Conservatory, but was struck down by the epidemic of Spanish flu and typhoid fever. Fortunately, Tiflis had food, medicine and a warmer climate, and he recovered. Their stay in Georgia was not long, however. The waves of civil war reached the Caucasus, and the family was once more on the move. They crossed the Black Sea to Constantinople and from there proceeded to Paris, which had already become a Russian cultural centre, with a populous colony of Russian artists, among them such luminaries as Diaghilev and Koussevitzky.

Tcherepnin-père had been associated with Diaghilev, as composer and conductor, in the years preceding World War 1, and was no stranger to other artistic enterprises abroad. With his father's aid, the young Tcherepnin, by then a full-fledged composer, established fruitful contacts. He received his first big chance in London, where he gave a piano recital of his own music in 1922. In the following year he was commissioned to write a ballet for no less a celebrity than Anna Pavlova. She gave him the choice of a scenario on an Oriental subject, so that she could use costumes which she had brought with her from India. Tcherepnin selected the legend of the Prince Gautama, who became Buddha. Pavlova herself acted the part of the princess, Gautama's wife, before his renunciation of the world. Tcherepnin was now twenty-four years old, and his career was auspiciously launched. There was no lack of concert opportunities, no dearth of publishers. He needed only the continued impetus of invention and realization. An event of sentimental importance was his appearance in 1913 as soloist in his first piano concerto in a concert in Monte Carlo, with the orchestra conducted by his father.

The time had come for young Tcherepnin to outline his larger goals, to ask himself what direction he was going to take as a creative artist. Retrospectively, he muses on the biographical and musico-epistemological aspects of his pursuits. His conspectus of these has ten points:

1. Instinctive period
2. How do I do it?
3. Piano practice
4. Theoretical study of Beethoven's works
5. The formation of a sui generis 9-note scale
6. The theory of Interpunctus
7. Escape from the mousetrap of Cultural Music into the world of natural art, that is folklore.

8. Journey to the East
9. Return to the West
10. Synthesis

Elaborating on these ten points, Tcherepnin equates the instinctive period with his early youth. The question, 'How do I do it?' reflects the first period of self-examination. Intuition was not enough; he had to find the rationale for his music. Piano study and the analysis of Beethoven's works were pragmatic occupations.

The invention of a 9-note scale, however, represents the response to an intellectual impulse. Ever since his first attempts at serious composition he had been conscious of the ambivalence of homonymous major and minor tetrachords and triads, which also fascinated Stravinsky. But to Stravinsky the duality of the major and minor was *res per se*, sufficient unto itself. To Tcherepnin it was the point of departure for a new modality. By building another major-minor triadic complex on the major mediant of the original dual triad, he obtained a six-note scale of alternating minor thirds and minor seconds, identical with the one used by Rimsky-Korsakov in his opera *Le Coq d'Or* for 'oriental' effect. Melodic inversion of this scale generates three more notes. Superimposition of both scales results in a scale of nine notes. It consists of three conjunct tetrachords, each containing a whole tone and two semitones.

The scale is used by Tcherepnin also as a matrix for contrapuntal and harmonic sets. This melodic-harmonic convertibility is analogous with the usages of classical music or, for that matter, of Schoenberg's method of composition with twelve notes related only to one another. The scale has come to be known as the 'Tcherepnin Scale', and is classified as such in the august *Musik-Lexikon* of Hugo Riemann. It can be analysed in many various ways, for instance as the evolute of three mutually exclusive augmented triads at the distance of a semitone and a whole tone respectively. Or else it can be described as a chromatic 'lipogram', in which the second, the sixth and the tenth notes (or the third, seventh and eleventh) of the chromatic scale are excised. In my own compendium, *Thesaurus of Scales and Melodic Patterns,* the Tcherepnin Scale is tabulated under No. 184, and defined as a double interpolation of the division of the octave into three equal parts. Permutations of the component intervals produce two basic modes, which, of course, can be transposed to any note of the chromatic scale.

Tcherepnin is not a slave to his own system, however, as some composers are to theirs. The eight-note scale of alternating whole tones and semitones, for example, has captured and held in thrall a number of composers, who use it to the exclusion of all other tonal progressions. Among them, the Dutch Willem Pijper earnestly believed that it was his own invention, 'Pijper's Scale', as it is often called by his disciples. In point of historical fact, it was Rimsky-Korsakov (whose imaginative modernism is grossly underrated) who cultivated the eight-note scale as a medium of exotic tone-painting. It is described as such in Russian reference works. Just as Rimsky-Korsakov did not limit his musical vocabulary to the scale that bears his name, so Tcherepnin does not keep his imagination chained to the Tcherepnin Scale. In harmony especially, he employs a variety of structures—diatonic, pandiatonic, pentatonic. Although his melodies often assume atonal shapes, Tcherepnin has never been tempted to join the growing cohorts of dodecaphonic composers. Here and there, surreptitiously, he inserts passages containing all the twelve notes of the chromatic scale, but he has never written an explicit piece in the twelve-note idiom—a remarkable abstention, considering that even such intrinsically undodecaphonic composers as Walton and Britten, and Stravinsky himself, have all adopted modified serial procedures in some of their works. Perhaps, being a free spirit, Tcherepnin instinctively recoils from the rigidity of the Schoenbergian doctrine.

The theory of 'Interpunctus' is simple in its schematic plan, but infinitely varied in its applications. It posits a lemma that a coupled contrapuntal set may enter the vacant interior of another coupled contrapuntal set, provided that the first can be placed within the second without overlapping. The resulting four-part set may in turn enter, as an integral entity, the gaping maw of yet another coupled contrapuntal set, forming a polyphonic edifice of six parts. As far as instrumental, or vocal, ranges can reach, the resulting six-part set can be absorbed in the stomatic cavity of a still more voluminous two-part set, and so on and so forth. The concept of Interpunctus may well be illustrated by Swift's famous quatrain:

So, naturalists observe, a flea
Hath smaller fleas that on him prey;
And these have smaller still to bite 'em;
And so proceed ad infinitum.

Interpunctus can be represented geometrically by the diagram below. An instructive example of Interpunctus is found in the third movement (Andante) of Tcherepnin's Symphony in E, Op. 42. In it the paired horn and trumpet are encapsulated by the duo of the clarinet in high register and the timpani; the resulting four-fold complex then enters the wide expanse between the high notes in the violin solo and a passage in the low register of the double-bass solo. Numerous subaltern interpuncti supervene, compounding the polyphony in a series of intricate developments.

Tcherepnin was never a folkloric composer by intent and purpose, but he needed, as he himself phrased it, the fresh air of ethnic modalities to 'escape from the mousetrap of cultural music'. This he proceeded to accomplish by a study of folk music of many lands. In 1934 he was given an opportunity to travel to China and Japan. He gave master courses at the Conservatory of Shanghai. There he met a young Chinese pianist Lee Fisien Ming, who later became his wife. He edited publications of pieces by Chinese and Japanese composers, most of them his own pupils. These editions were the first in the Orient to propagandise works by native composers writing in a modern idiom.

Tcherepnin's father died shortly after the end of the European war in 1945; his mother died in 1958. With his wife and two small sons, Tcherepnin settled in the United States, and on April 1, 1958, became an American citizen. In 1967, at the invitation of the Union of Composers of the Soviet Union, he undertook an extended concert tour in Russia, after nearly fifty years away from his native land. He revisited the city of his birth, which had in the meantime changed its name twice—St. Petersburg, Petrograd, Leningrad. His recitals in programs of his music were thoughtfully praised in the Soviet press, and Russian music lovers extended cordial welcome to him, with traditional bouquets of fresh flowers as a tribute to his artistry.

At mid-century, during his 'American' period, Tcherepnin reached Point 10 of his categorical tabulation, Synthesis. This consummation was achieved in his Second Symphony in 1951 and culminated with the *Symphonic Prayer* of 1959, which embodies styles and techniques that he had found useful and effective. In recent years he has become interested in electronic music. He has incorporated an electronic part in the score of his musical fairy tale, *Story of Ivan the Fool*, after Tolstoy, written for a BBC broadcast on Christmas Eve 1968. Tcherepnin's lifetime has coincided with an unprecedented change in musical styles, from the innocent ecstasies of Scriabin to the unhinged exhibitions of the latest avant-garde—possibly the most revolutionary half-century in music history. Tcherepnin himself has contributed his share to this cavalcade of sound, revelling in auto-genetic dissonances and twisting tonal melodies out of joint. Among his innovations is a symphonic movement for pitchless percussion in his Symphony in E of 1927, ante-dating by several years a similar percussive interlude in Shostakovitch's opera *The Nose*. The experimental character of this symphonic movement is compounded by special effects in the string section, with players instructed to strike the bodies of their instruments with the back of the bow. Also of interest are Tcherepnin's essays in laconic musical utterances, dating back to the 'little fleas' of his adolescence. His Trio, Op. 34, is probably among the shortest compositions written for piano, violin and cello. It is in three movements, and its total duration is only eight minutes.

Personal impressions sometimes furnish a stimulus for a composer's fancies. Smetana in his first string quartet has a high E in the violin part to illustrate the persistent note buzzing in his ears before he lapsed into insanity. One of Schumann's symptoms of approaching madness was an auditory hallucination of someone tuning middle A. A similar, but fortunately passing perturbation happened to Tcherepnin as a result of a temporary failure of the cabin pressurization system during an aeroplane flight. It upset the equilibrium between his inner and outer ears with a curious effect: he began hearing not one, but two notes, an obsessive motive D-E, in a nervous syncopated rhythm. Being practical minded, he put this intrusive motive to use as a recurrent theme in his Second Piano Sonata, Op. 94.

He faced a crucial test of tolerance for new-fangled auricular bombination when his sons Ivan and Serge, both of whom have ineluctably become composers, joined the avant-garde. Serge, born in France in

1941, investigates the constructivistic potentialities of stochastic parameters in musical composition. The titles of his pieces are indicative of his preoccupation with surrealistic abstractions: *At Baech, Addition and Subtraction, Cone, Piece of Wood, Piece of Wood with Weeping Women, Morning after Piece*. Tcherepnin's younger son Ivan, born in 1943, pursues the chimera of multimedia presentations with the aid of digital computers. His non-aleatoric works reveal an interest in the formal aspects of music: *Reciprocals, Four Pieces from Before, Work Music, Cadenzas in Transition*. One is tempted to telescope two scenes in the fourth dimension of time: Nicolas Tcherepnin, looking over the shoulder of his adolescent son Alexander and marvelling at his free treatment of unresolved dissonances, and the septuagenarian Alexander surveying with curiosity and pride the manuscripts, in graphic optical notation, of his own sons, and certain that somehow this brave new music signalises the emergence of a new means for the sonic art of the future. Tertium non datur, proclaims an old scholastic rule of logic. But in esthetics a tertium may well be found in a viable coalition of seemingly incompatible concepts. Alexander Tcherepnin has opted for electronic music just as his father had to reconcile himself to the prevalence of dissonance. In turn, the youthful advanced guard finds utilitarian merit in the formal symmetry of the language of the classics. The three generations of the Tcherepnin family, extending through a whole century, demonstrate the historical truth that music is an art in flux, forever returning to its sources to replenish the energies spent in the pursuit of novelty.

10. IGOR STRAVINSKY

Stravinsky's influence upon the development of contemporary music has been so potent that the changes in his style were often followed by minor revolutions among creative musicians. He was named Igor because he was born on St. Igor's day according to the Russian calendar. His father was a bass singer of the Imperial Opera. Thus Stravinsky was reared in a musical atmosphere. He was not a child prodigy however. It was almost by accident that at the age of 19 he met Rimsky-Korsakov in Heidelberg and played for him some of his compositions; Rimsky-Korsakov found his harmonic sense insufficiently developed and recommended him to go for preparatory work to one of his experienced students, Kalafati. Rimsky-Korsakov accepted Stravinsky only in 1907, and gave him private lessons in orchestration and free composition. Stravinsky did not study at the Conservatory and so holds no Conservatory diploma or any other certificate of graduation.

During 1905–07, Stravinsky composed his First Symphony, which is marked opus I (a piano sonata, written in 1903–04, remained unpublished, and without an opus number). This curious work, entirely academic in essence and Brahmsian in style, did not show any influence of Rimsky-Korsakov or other members of the group of Mighty Five. The second opus, *Le Faune at la bergère*, suite of songs for mezzo-soprano and orchestra, to Pushkin's words, is much more characteristic and contains elements of impressionism in Debussy's manner. The real Stravinsky begins to emerge in the Fantastic Scherzo, op. 3. With the first performances of Stravinsky's works, the First Symphony January 22, 1908, and *Le Faune et la bergère* on February 29, 1908, given in St. Petersburg, his name as one of Rimsky-Korsakov's talented pupils began to be known in musical circles. For the occasion of the marriage of Maximilian Steinberg and Rimsky-Korsakov's daughter on June 17, 1908, Stravinsky wrote a dedicatory symphonic poem, *Fireworks,* which is marked opus 4. Four days after the marriage ceremony, Rimsky-Korsakov died. Stravinsky wrote a memorial work for him, *Chant funèbre,* op. 5, which remains unpublished.

The loss of his teacher and adviser caused a momentary cessation in Stravinsky's creative work: that year, 1908, he wrote only 3 songs, op. 6, and 4 piano Etudes, op. 7 (the last work marked with an opus number). The new stimulus came in the person of Diaghilev, who was at that time organizing his Ballets Russes in Paris. He happened to hear the performances of *Fantastic Scherzo,* and decided to commission Stravinsky to arrange for orchestra 2 pieces by Chopin, the *Nocturne* and the *Valse brillante,* to be used in the ballet *Les Sylphides.* Stravinsky gladly accepted, and thus entered into a relationship with Diaghilev which has in large measure determined the course of his creative work. Having done the orchestrations for Diaghilev, Stravinsky returned to the work on his opera *Le Rossignol,* begun before Rimsky-Korsakov's death. The first act was finished when Diaghilev gave him another commission, this time for an original work to the subject of the Russian fairy-tale, *The Firebird.* Stravinsky completed the score on May 18, 1910, and the ballet was produced by Diaghilev in Paris on June 25, 1910.

The Firebird is Stravinsky's first masterpiece. In its music we can trace the influence that Rimsky-Korsakov had on his most famous pupil. There are passages that forcibly remind us of Rimsky-Korsakov's opera *Kastchev the Immortal.* The musical idiom is entirely in the tradition of the Russian national school, and the orchestration follows the general lines of Rimsky-Korsakov's.

Stravinsky's second ballet was *Petrouchka.* The genesis of *Petrouchka,* is described by Stravinsky in his autobiography. It was to be an orchestral piece with an important piano part, a *Konzertstuck.* The dialogue between the piano and orchestra conjured up in Stravinsky's mind the picture of an exasperating puppet. The title *Petrouchka,* the pathetic hero of the Russian Marionette Show, came naturally to Stravinsky's mind, and soon he showed Diaghilev the first sketches. Stravinsky completed the score on May 26, 1911, in Rome, exactly three weeks before his 29th birthday, and the ballet was produced by Diaghilev in Paris on June 13, 1911. The significance of *Petrouchka* in modern music could not be appreciated at the time, when it was regarded merely as an extremely effective ballet score. But the music soon overshadowed the ballet.

Probably for the first time two keys were put together to produce a poly-tonal effect. This combination of C major and F sharp major, the "Petrouchka chord," has in time become a base for new complex tonality, created out of the elements of two opposite major keys. This bitonal chord may have originated from a purely *pianistic* arrangement of white keys versus black keys, but the implications of this accidental discovery (if it was accidental) were far-reaching, and started a vogue of polytonality.

But even more far-reaching was the production of *Le Sacre du Printemps*, the score of which Stravinsky completed on March 8, 1913. From the initial bassoon solo to the final frenzy of the sacred dance, *Le Sacre du Printemps* relentlessly moves on, creating musical values so new that the musical world was faced with the alternative either to reject this music as a freakish exhibition of an unbalanced young man, or accept it as a revolu-tionary innovation. The scandalous scenes that took place during the first performance of *Le Sacre du Printemps* on May 29, 1913, in Paris, have been described many times, and that date holds truly a revolutionary significance.

Shortly before the War Stravinsky made his last voyage to Russia. He returned full of ideas about works typically Russian in character based on Russian folk songs. These Russian songs he used in three compositions, the short *Pribaoutki*, for voice and 8 instruments; *Berceuses du Chat*, vocal suite for female voice and 3 clarinets; and the grandiose Cantata, *Les Noces*, scored for the unusual ensemble of voices, solo and in chorus, 4 pianos, and 17 percussion instruments. The War, which found Stravinsky in Switzerland, interrupted the composition of *Les Noces*, the score of which was not completed until 1923. In Switzerland his main source of inspiration continued to be Russian folklore, and in 1916–17 he composed a burlesque chamber opera, *Renard*, founded on Russian folk songs, and 4 choruses for female voices and Russian peasant melodies. About the same time he wrote 3 little songs for children, also in Russian style.

The Russian Revolution found Stravinsky in Rome, and he was called upon by Diaghilev to write a substitute for the imperial Russian hymn. Stravinsky chose to orchestrate the Volga Boatmen's Song, and it was played in place of the Russian hymn at the Diaghilev Production in Rome on Apr 9, 1917. The War, the Revolution, and the subsequent collapse of the economic world convinced Stravinsky that the time of large-scale orchestral works was past; that the composer had to return to the minstrel show ideal, and write theater music of small dimensions requiring few instruments and few actors. Still deeply absorbed in Russian folklore, he selected a tale about a deserting soldier and the devil. The cast of this tale was indeed economical: a narrator, who told the story, and an instrumental ensemble of 17 instruments: clarinet, bassoon, trumpet, trombone, percussion, violin, and double bass. The combination was astutely chosen; the clarinet and bassoon gave the entire range in wood-wind; the trumpet and the trombone made available the complete range of brass instruments; the violin and the double bass covered the string range; and the assorted percussion manned by one player provided the strong rhythmic background. The first performance of *l'Histoire du Soldat* took place in Lausanne on September 28, 1918.

Stravinsky now went in search of new musical resources. On the morning of the Armistice he wrote *Ragtime* for 11 instruments, an attempt to recreate the spirit of early American jazz. An important *pièce d'occasion* was the little suite of 3 pieces for clarinet without accompaniment. Some critics attach a significance to these pieces which seems exaggerated, but the contrast between the multitudinous *Le Sacre du Printemps* and the monodic clarinet pieces may be symbolical of Stravinsky's change.

The success of Tommasini's ballet on Scarlatti's music gave Stravinsky an idea to write a ballet on the music of Pergolesi. This set another problem, that of stylization. Stravinsky, in his use of thematic material from other composers, is never a mere arranger; his ballets after Pergolesi or Tchaikovsky are either perversions or recreations, depending on the viewpoint. The Pergolesi ballet was finally materialized in the form of the suite *Pulcinella*, which was produced by Diaghilev in Paris on May 15, 1920. The post-War period is marked in Stravinsky's music by a new austerity, a deliberate divestment of all inessential details. The reorchestration of the *Firebird* made in 1919 is typical of Stravinsky's new ideals of artistic economy. The reorchestration was ostensibly designed to make the score more accessible for smaller orchestral ensembles. But orchestra conductors seem to prefer the original version of 1909–10 to the restrained and less colorful second version. In 1921–22 Stravinsky composed a one-act opera buffa, *Mavra*, after Pushkin, significantly dedicated to the memory of Pushkin, Glinka, and Tchaikovsky. At this time Stravinsky had abandoned all ultra-tonal elaborations; the idiom of *Mavra* is diatonic, with frequent superpositions of the tonic and the dominant—a bitonality profoundly different from the Petrouchka chord. *Mavra* was his last work based on Russian themes. His interest from 1923 on turned in the direction of absolute music in the classical manner. The Octet for wind instruments (1923) is written along the lines of economy, but the imagery of the *l'Histoire du Soldat* is entirely absent. The impetus of post-War neo-classicism is usually regarded as due to Stravinsky's change of styles as exemplified in his works of the period. In April 1924 he completed the composition of his Concerto for piano and orchestra of wind instruments. This concerto, written with the practical purpose of creating a vehicle for a forthcoming American tour discloses the typical traits of new Stravinsky. The Serenade for piano, written in the following year, is couched in this new style. The ideological negation of the esthetic code of the luxuriant pre-War period is further emphasized in the oratorio *Oedipus-Rex*, the full score of which was completed on May 10, 1927, and was performed under the composer's direction in Paris on May 30, 1927. In search of the least temporal and most universal verbal means of expression, Stravinsky had the French text translated into medieval Latin. This was an outward sign of a new direction: towards religious medievalism.

Early in 1925 Stravinsky went on his first American tour. His first appearance in America was in the capacity of conductor of his own works with the New York Philharmonic Orchestra, and his first American appearance as pianist took place with the Boston Symphony Orchestra on Jan 23, 1925, when Stravinsky played the piano part of his Concerto. In America Elizabeth Sprague Coolidge commissioned him the composition of a ballet suite. Stravinsky entitled his new work *Apollon Musagète*. It is entirely in the classical tradition, in strict form of an ancient dance suite, and the chastening harmonic and orchestral color is evident. *Apollon Musagète* was produced for the first time in Washington on April 27, 1928. A new ballet, *Le Baiser de la Fée*, "ballet-allegory inspired by the Muse of Tchaikovsky," was written during the same year, 1928, with Stravinsky conducting the orchestra. In it Stravinsky used Tchaikovsky's actual melodies as he used Pergolesi's melodies in *Pulcinella*. But the ballet is far from being in Tchaikovsky's style, and one had better not speculate what Tchaikovsky would have thought of the treatment. But as long as elaboration on borrowed themes is at all thinkable, *Le Baiser de la Fée* has its justification. In 1929 came Capriccio for piano and orchestra. Once more Stravinsky reasserted his belief in the perpetually young forms of old music, and once more he filled the old form with new ideas. The first performance of Capriccio took place on Dec. 6, 1929, in Paris. On August 15, 1930, Stravinsky completed his *Symphony of Psalms*, written for the 50th anniversary of the Boston Symphony Orchestra, and characteristically dedicated "à la gloire de Dieu." The score is for chorus and orchestra without violins or violas, which suggests intentional elimination of expressive quality in tone-color. The tempi are indicated only by metronome marks, and the 3 component movements are a Chorale, a Fugue, and a rhythmic Finale. Due to change of dates, the world premiere of the *Symphony of Psalms* took place at Brussels on Dec. 13, 1930, and the Boston performance followed on Dec. 19, 1930. *Oedipus Rex* and the *Symphony of Psalms* express a religious aspect of Stravinsky's later period, with "neo-classical" works preceding and following them.

A meeting with the violinist Samuel Dushkin, and friendly suggestions of a publisher, gave Stravinsky the idea of writing a violin concerto. It was composed in 1931, and performed for the first time with Dushkin as soloist in Berlin on October 23, 1931. On July 15, 1932, he completed the composition of a suite for violin and piano, which he entitled *Duo Concertant*. The music is pastoral, and the 5 movements of the *Duo* reflect the spirit of bucolic airs and dances of Lully.

Early in 1933 Stravinsky was asked by Madame Ida Rubinstein to write music for her ballet *Perséphone,* to a poem by André Gide. He consented, and between May 1933 and Dec. 1933 completed the score which, besides the chorus and orchestra, included also a narrator. The premiere of *Perséphone* was given in Paris on Apr. 30, 1934, with Stravinsky conducting, Shortly afterwards, on June 10, 1934, Stravinsky became a French citizen. He had made his home in France since the War, and his greatest successes were connected with Paris, so there should be nothing remarkable in the fact that a most profoundly Russian composer should be a citizen of France. Nonetheless, Stravinsky's action was symbolic in its professed abandonment of Russian national heritage.

In 1935 Stravinsky wrote a Concerto for 2 pianos, without orchestral accompaniment, and performed it with his son, Sviatoslav, at a concert of his music in Paris on November 21, 1935. For his 1937 American tour he wrote a ballet on an "American" subject, a poker game. The ballet, under the title of *Card Party,* "a ballet in 3 deals," was produced at the Metropolitan Opera House in New York on April 27, 1937, with Stravinsky conducting the orchestra. In 1938 he wrote a Concerto for 16 instruments, which represents a further step in reducing the musical scheme to the bare necessities of motion and form. It was first performed in Washington under the title of *Dumbarton Oaks,* the name of a private estate of a Washington music lover.

11. SERGE PROKOFIEV:
HIS STATUS IN SOVIET MUSIC

The music of Serge Prokofiev is probably the greatest single influence in Soviet music. Prokofiev belongs to the middle generation, standing between the composers who, like Glière and Vassilenko, were well known before the Revolution, and composers like Shostakovich, whose formative years were spent under the Soviet Regime. While pre-Revolutionary composers had to be "naturalized" as Soviet musicians, Prokofiev's music fitted without strain into the scheme of "socialist realism," as the Soviet catch-word describes the essence of Soviet music. The evolutionary catalogue of Prokofiev's works shows an extraordinary constancy of purpose. There are no sudden changes of style, no incursions into self-denying classicism or sweeping modernism. There are no recantations, no "returns to Bach." Instead, there is a creative self-assertion. In the early years of the Soviet Republic, musicians were apt to speculate on whether this or that composer was "consonant" with the spirit of the new nation born of revolution. Of contemporary composers, there were few who were as close in spirit to the new music of the masses as Prokofiev's cheerfully lyrical muse. Yet Prokofiev was a Westerner. He went eastward around the world in 1918, and he did not revisit Russia until 1927. As a concert pianist and conductor of his own works, he was a familiar figure in Paris, Berlin, London, and New York. Diaghilev, acting entirely outside of Russia, has produced the majority of Prokofiev's ballets. Prokofiev's first Soviet composition, *Le Pas d'Acier*, was largely a Westerner's conception of the march of industrial life in Soviet Russia. It was "pro-Soviet" music, if music can be pro or con, but it touched only on the external life of the Soviet Union. But in the same

Ch. 11: originally published in *The Quarterly on the Soviet Union*, April 1939.

year when *Le Pas d'Acier* was produced by Diaghilev in Paris, Prokofiev went to Russia on a concert tour. The reception accorded to him was unmistakable: Prokofiev was accepted as a truly Soviet composer, even though working in France. In 1934, Prokofiev settled permanently in Moscow, without abandoning his annual visits to Europe and America.

Throughout this period, between his first tour in Russia and his final settlement in Moscow as a Soviet composer, Prokofiev's music underwent subtle changes in a direction away from the constructivist ideal of the European theater and towards the self-sufficient design of romantic realism, the realism of human emotion. Distilling the three chief ingredients of his musical essence, dynamism, lyricism, and sarcasm, Prokofiev has formed a style with less sarcasm than in early works, while enhancing the lyric power, and leaving his youthful dynamism undiminished.

Prokofiev's creative biography starts at a very early age. He attempted to write an opera at the age of nine. The title was *The Giant*, and it was in three acts and six tableaux, the libretto by the composer. It was written in piano score, and the vocal line followed the melody of the right hand. His second juvenile opera, *Desert Island*, was partly scored for the orchestra by the ten-year-old Prokofiev, who by now was already taking regular lessons from Glière. At twelve he wrote a complete score of *Feast During the Plague* to Pushkin's story. Soon he entered the Petrograd Conservatory, where he studied composition with Rimsky-Korsakov and Liadov, piano with Essipova, and conducting with Cherepnin. He graduated in 1914, winning the grand prize, a Bechstein piano. As a pianist, however, he did not pursue an independent career and has appeared almost exclusively in recitals of his own works. In the field of conducting, too, he has been the interpreter of his own music in his public appearances. After his graduation, he appeared on the Petrograd and Moscow stage as a new *enfant terrible*, scaring his old professors with novel devices, and stimulating the young comrades-in-arms by his daring. There was an element of mischief in Prokofiev's early piano pieces, a boyish defiance of rules and regulations. Counterpoint for counterpoint's sake and the entire stock of pedantic scholarship had little appeal for Prokofiev. In fact, he has never composed a straight-forward fugue outside of the classroom, and the fugal element is practically absent from his symphonic works.

His first work of major importance is his *Scythian Suite* (1914). The inspiration of this suite derives from pre-Slavic Russia, and there is an overabundance of rhythm and flowing melody. Of course, the work was extremely "modern" for the time, and Prokofiev, as all modernists, came in for a share of violent opprobrium. One Moscow critic, himself a composer, in his desire to squelch Prokofiev, made a fatal blunder: without attending the scheduled concert in Moscow, he delivered a blast in his daily paper against the atrocities of the new work, and concluded his review by saying: "The composer himself conducted the work with barbaric abandon." The misfortune of the critic was the fact that the performance had been cancelled at the last moment, due to the stringencies of wartime. The only manuscript score was in the hands of the composer, so the critic could not plead an earlier acquaintance with the work. This episode, which illustrates the danger of condemning new music without a hearing, did much to arouse interest in Prokofiev's work in wartime Russia. A few years later, during the early days of the Revolution, Prokofiev wrote his *Classical Symphony*, a work which adheres to the classical form and the classical tonality, but in which the humor, the dynamic power, and the lyric quality are typically Prokofiev's. The popular Gavotte from this symphony has twentieth-century charm, and the deceptive modulations add tinge to the old form. During the same period that the *Classical Symphony* was composed, Prokofiev wrote the powerful incantation *Seven, They Are Seven*, to the ancient Sumerian legend. Scored for a large orchestra, chorus, and tenor solo, it can be cited as Prokofiev's most "leftist" work, if we take the word "leftist" as signifying extreme modernism fed on dissonance. Obviously Prokofiev was in search of a style. He had already proved that he was capable of expressing himself along the entire range of harmonic idioms, from the classical to the ultramodern. Now it was a question of synthesis. In his symphonies subsequent to the *Classical Symphony*, he made his choice plain. His style was to be what we have called romantic realism. The harmonic idiom, as now established, was tonal and modal, with chromaticism only as a useful adjunct, never an extension into post-Wagnerian atonality. It is curious that Prokofiev shuns impressionism and prefers literal pictorialism, often with an ironic twist. Prokofiev's ballets, which are the product of his Paris period, are often literal in illustrating the action, but never vaguely impressionistic. At the same time, the musical material of the ballets is rich enough to be used symphonically, without the theater. In his Fourth Symphony, Prokofiev uses themes from his ballet *The Prodigal Son* as subjects in the classical sonata form. Also, the symphonic suites from his ballets and operas lose little from the absence of stage action.

In his five piano concertos, Prokofiev has created a new type of virtuoso style, percussive and lyrical at the same time. The pianoforte technique in these concertos occupies the intermediate position between the classical concerto and the modern use of piano obligato. But even in his symphonic compositions the piano plays a prominent part among the instruments of the orchestra. Prokofiev was equally successful in his two concertos for the violin. While the First Concerto still reflects the style of Russian academicism, the Second Violin Concerto embodies the best traits of Prokofiev's new style, characterized by a perfect proportion of lyrical and dynamic power. A concerto for cello and orchestra was presented for the first time during the decade of Soviet music in Moscow in November, 1938.

The recent trend in Soviet music towards the formation of a style, national in its inspiration, has moved Prokofiev to write an *Overture on Russian Themes*. His music to the film *Alexander Nevsky* also belongs to the category of the new national period. Prokofiev has made a symphonic suite from this music. He has also made a symphonic suite from the music to the film *Lieutenant Kizhe*. The story is about the mad Tsar Paul, who misread a Russian expletive, and conferred on that part of speech a military order, an imperial slip which could not be revealed by the courtiers without incurring a possible disgrace. So, the loyal henchmen created a mythical personage to be endowed with all the properties of a living subject of the Tsar, i.e., the passport and a record of faithful service. The music is satirical and Prokofiev here finds an occasion to use his best extravaganza style.

Perhaps the most novel of Prokofiev's later work is his Symphonic Fairy Tale for children, *Peter and the Wolf*, written for production at the Children's Theater in Moscow in 1936. It introduces a narrator, telling the story of the Red Pioneer, Peter, who, over the objection of a grouchy grandfather, sets forth on the adventure of conquering the Russian equivalent of the Big Bad Wolf. Peter is aided by a bird, a cat, and a duck, but while using them as allies, he has to be on the lookout for the cat, who has designs on the bird. The duck eventually falls victim of the wolf, but remains alive even in the wolf's belly, while the wolf is being triumphantly carried off to the zoo. The interesting feature of this work is the use of instrumental leitmotivs, so that the grandfather is portrayed by a bassoon, the bird by a flute, the cat by a clarinet, the wolf by horns, and Peter by a romantically adventurous theme in the strings. The principle of literal illustration is here carried to its ultimate clarity. In fact, the device is elementary, and no attempt is made to Wagnerize the procedure. The narrator tells the story, and with every mention of the principals, an instrument plays the corresponding motive. Naturally, the music finds great favor among Russian children. It is even more remarkable that it has become an outstanding success with the sophisticated symphony audiences in America.

At forty-eight, Prokofiev is in a fortunate position among composers of the day. His music is accepted, not only by the sophisticates of the modern world, but by a great majority of listening audiences, both in Russia and abroad. In his native land, he holds no academic courses and teaches at no conservatory, but his influence on young Soviet musicians is profound. There is a sense of mental health that pervades Prokofiev's music, which makes him a factor in the movement towards musical optimism.

12. DMITRI DMITRIEVITCH SHOSTAKOVITCH

Dmitri Shostakovitch has reached the age of thirty-six, and, from the middle of the road, can now look back on a career full of dramatic episodes. Not since the time of Berlioz has a symphonic composer created such a stir. In far-away America, great conductors vie with each other for the *jus primae noctis* of his music. The score of his Seventh Symphony, the symphony of struggle and victory, has been reduced to a roll of microfilm and flown half-way across the world, from Russia to Persia, from Persia to Egypt, from Egypt to Brazil, and from Brazil to New York, to speed the day of the American première. How the old romantics would have loved to be the center of such a fantastic adventure! But Shostakovitch is a product of another age, realistic and collectivist, rather than romantic and egocentric, an age that takes airplanes and microfilms for granted. He is proud of his status as a Soviet composer, and he understands the responsibility that all artistic expression entails in collectivist society.

In Soviet Russia it is not merely a question whether the music is intrinsically good or bad. It is also a question of directional method. The most revolutionary subject matter will not help a Soviet composer who tepidly writes in an imitative manner. On the other hand, music written in a style that is purely experimental cannot find its way to the people, and no Soviet composer can work isolated from the rest of Soviet society.

In an interview with an American correspondent, Shostakovitch stated his conviction in this way:

Ch. 12: originally published in *The Musical Quarterly*, 1942.

I consider that every artist who isolates himself from the world is doomed. I find it incredible that an artist should want to shut himself away from the people, who, in the end, form his audience. I think an artist should serve the greatest possible number of people. I always try to make myself as widely understood as possible, and, if I don't succeed, I consider it my own fault.

This necessity of being understood by the people explains the extraordinary ups and downs suffered by Shostakovitch as a symphonic and operatic composer. Take for instance Shostakovitch's opera *The Nose*, after Gogol's fantastic story, dealing with a clerk whose nose vanishes mysteriously from his face after a visit to the barber shop, to be metamorphosed into a self-important government official. The opera is expertly contrived, and its innovations are many. Under the influence of Western European modern opera, the speaking voice is introduced in the recitative. The part of the Nose is sung with the nostrils stopped, so as to produce a muted nasal effect. The instrumentation is full of special effects, and there is an interlude written entirely for instruments of percussion.

The opera was written in 1928, and was produced in Leningrad on January 13, 1930. The artistic political council of the State Little Opera Theatre, playing safe, announced the opera as "an experimental spectacle." The program book carried a questionnaire to be filled in by the audience:

1. Did you like the opera as a whole?
2. Is the music understandable?
3. Do you approve of the form of presentation?
4. Did you like the performance of the singers?

In the program note, Shostakovitch declared his conviction that "in the current conditions of Soviet life, the most timely subjects are satirical." The Soviet music critic Ivan Solertinsky explained that, by translating Gogol into current language, Shostakovitch had created a Soviet opera, even though the idiom might be influenced by the Western modernists.

Shostakovitch was twenty-two years old when he wrote *The Nose*, and his curiosity for new forms of musical expression is easy to understand. In a contemporary biographical note, Shostakovitch's music was summarized as "a denial of all mystical (*à la* Scriabin) and hopelessly somber (*à la*

Tchaikovsky) moods, restriction of the sphere of refined subjective lyricism, an urge for vigorous and pointed rhythms expressive of the spirit of industrialism, and individual orchestration full of effective contrasts of orchestral colors."

Writing about the same time, Solertinsky finds a "paradoxical parallel" between Shostakovitch and Tchaikovsky:

> Despite the difference of their socio-philosophical roots, neither of the two has a trace of feudal dilettantism, which by virtue of some historical atavism has even affected some, if not many, Soviet composers. As a creative character, Shostakovitch is far removed from the romantic ideal of an artist who works only when he is inspired, possessed, or plunged into the state of divine folly. Above all, he is a professional who has the command of the technique in any *genre*. He is even inclined to emphasize the artisan quality of the musical profession. He works a great deal and writes rapidly, often without rough drafts. He composes in full score without preliminary sketches for piano. Like a trained chess-player, who can play simultaneous games on several chess-boards, Shostakovitch can work on several musical compositions, at times on contrasting psychological planes.

In 1930, the attitude of Soviet musicians towards Tchaikovsky was uncertain, but, as the years went by, Shostakovitch emphasized his desire to emulate Tchaikovsky's spirit of universal humanity. Writing on Slavonic music in an article published in 1941, Shostakovitch states: "The philosophical profundity of Beethoven's symphonic style is supplemented by Tchaikovsky with passionateness of lyrical utterance and with that concrete quality in expressing the innermost human emotions, which have made his symphonic art accessible and comprehensible to the masses." The Soviet line of symphonic succession has thus become crystallized: from Beethoven to Tchaikovsky to Shostakovitch.

Shostakovitch's talent for musical satire found its expression at an early stage, in caricaturing the decadence of the capitalist West and unregenerate bureaucracy at home. His satirical ballet *The Golden Age*, produced in Leningrad on October 27, 1939, was accompanied on the stage by a pantomime picturing life in a big capitalist city. The famous discordant "Polka" appears in Act III, and caricatures the Geneva Disarmament Conference.

Polka "Once in Geneva" from the ballet "The Golden Age"

The program of this ballet is characteristic of the Soviet theatre of the time, and is worth reproducing in full:

ACT I
INDUSTRIAL EXPOSITION

PROCESSION OF GUESTS OF HONOR — REVIEW OF WINDOW
DISPLAYS — DEMONSTRATION OF EXHIBITS — BARKER —
PRESTIDIGITATOR — PRIZE-FIGHTING FOR PUBLICITY — RIOT AT THE
BOXING MATCH — DANCE OF FLAMING YOUTH — DIRECTOR'S
APPEARANCE WITH DIVA — ADAGIO DANCE — ARRIVAL OF THE SOVIET
FOOTBALL TEAM — DIVA'S VARIATIONS — SOVIET DANCE — SOVIET
WORKER INVITES DIVA TO A DANCE — DIVA DANCES WITH THE
FASCIST — DANCE OF THE NEGRO AND TWO SOVIET FOOTBALL
PLAYERS — WALTZ: ALLEGED BOMB PLOTTERS ("THE HAND OF
MOSCOW") — CONFUSION AMONG THE FASCISTS — A RARE CASE OF
MASS HYSTERIA — FOXTROT.

ACT II

Pantomime: Sleuthing by an *Agent-provocateur*, and an Arrest —
Workers' Procession to the Stadium — Pioneers' Dance —
Reception of the Soviet Football Team — The Football
Game — Interlude.

ACT III
MUSIC HALL

Tap Dance: Shoe-shine of the Best Quality — Polka: "Once in
Geneva" (Angel of Peace) — Touching Coalition of Classes,
Slightly Fraudulent — *Cancan* — Liberation of Prisoners —
General Exposure — Finale: Solidarity Dance of Western
Workers and the Soviet Team.

Shostakovitch's second ballet, *The Bolt*, was written on a Soviet theme. It was produced in Leningrad on April 8, 1931. Later, Shostakovitch expressed his dissatisfaction with the stage.

My first two ballets, "The Golden Age" and "The Bolt," I consider highly unsuccessful from the dramatic standpoint. It seems to me that the principal error was that the authors of the scenario, attempting to show current Soviet life on the stage, have disregarded the peculiar art of the ballet. To interpret socialist life in the form of a ballet is a very serious task, and one must not approach it frivolously. Such episodes as the "Enthusiasm Dance" in "The Bolt," or the pantomime of the labor process (the hammer struck on the anvil), betray a superficial treatment of a realistic ballet designed to represent Soviet life.

In 1932, Shostakovitch wrote a remarkable opera after a story of the Russian nineteenth-century writer Leskov, entitled *Lady Macbeth of the District of Mzensk*, dealing with a woman who, in collusion with her lover, kills her husband. It was produced in Leningrad on January 22, 1934, and later in Moscow and other Russian cities under a new title, *Katerina Izmailova*, after the name of the heroine. The opera met with great enthusiasm among Soviet musicians. The Russian opera conductor Samosud wrote in the program book: "I nominate 'Lady Macbeth' a work of genius, and I am convinced that posterity will confirm this estimate. One cannot help feeling proud that, in a Soviet music theatre, an opera has been created that overshadows all that can possibly be accomplished in the operatic art of the capitalist world. Here, too, our culture has indeed not only overtaken, but surpassed, the most advanced capitalist countries."

Analyzing the score, the Soviet music critic Ostretsov described Shostakovitch's method of musical satire as "debasement of the material"— that is, grotesque presentation of musical forms characteristic of a given period. Shostakovitch himself explained the use of an old story for the subject of his opera by stating that it was necessary to give a revolutionary interpretation of the old régime. From the technical standpoint he reaffirmed the importance of the singing voice as the primary medium of operatic art:

> Opera is above all a vocal form, and the singers must attend to their primary duty, which is to sing, and not to talk, declaim, or intone. All my vocal parts are based on broad *cantilena*, making full use of the resources of that richest instrument, the human voice. The musical development progresses according to a symphonic plan, and, in this respect, "Lady Macbeth" is not a mere imitation of the old type of opera, consisting of separate arias and choruses. The musical *entr'actes* continue and develop the preceding musical thought, and serve the purpose of supplying commentary to the stage action.

Lady Macbeth enjoyed a successful run of two years. And then the lightning struck. On January 28, 1936, the Moscow newspaper *Pravda* came out with an article entitled "Confusion instead of Music", in which Shostakovitch's opera was condemned as expressive of petty-bourgeois sensationalism.

> While our music critics swear by the name of socialist realism, the stage serves us, in Shostakovitch's opera, the coarsest kind of naturalism. The predatory merchant woman, coming into possession of wealth and power through murder, is pictured as a victim of the régime. . . . The music quacks, grunts, growls, suffocates itself in order to express the amatory scenes as naturalistically as possible. "Love" is smeared all over in the most vulgar manner. The merchant's bed occupies the central place on the stage. On it, all "problems" are solved. . . . Some critics call this glorification of merchant lust a satire. But there is no satire here.

The suggestive trombone *glissandi* in the bedchamber scene had been eliminated in early Soviet productions, but they were allowed to shock the select top-hat audience at the New York performance on February 5, 1935. It is probably with reference to that performance that *Pravda* wrote: "Is not the success of 'Lady Macbeth' abroad explained by the fact that this opera tickles the perverted tastes of the *bourgeoisie* with its fidgety, screaming, neurotic music?"

Calamity never comes singly. On February 6, 1936, another article, entitled "The False Ballet", appeared in *Pravda*, accusing Shostakovitch of the frivolous treatment of a Soviet subject in his new ballet *The Sparkling Brook*. (The title is the name of a mythical collective farm in the Caucasus.) This second blow hurt even more than the first. For, while *Lady Macbeth* was a satire on the old régime, *The Sparkling Brook* was a picture of Soviet life, and so carried a greater responsibility. Shostakovitch was fully aware of that. In the preface to the program book he wrote: "To create a ballet on a Soviet theme is a difficult task entailing a great responsibility. But I am not afraid of difficulties. It would have been simpler to follow the trodden path, but it is also less interesting; it is fruitless, tedious. . . . My music for this ballet is, in my opinion, gay, light, entertaining, and, above all, suitable for dancing."

The librettists, too, gave an account of their intentions: "The authors are convinced that life on a collective farm can and should be shown not only in the light of irreconcilable class struggle, but in colorful and sunny beauty, in a festive spirit, and with youthful joy, which is the essence of the new socialist society."

The *Pravda* articles unloosed a wave of comment all over the country. Resolutions and letters poured in, proclaiming solidarity with the ideas expressed in the *Pravda* articles. The headlines were characteristic: "Down with Formalist Confusion in Art"; "Down with *Bourgeois* Esthetes and Formalists"; "Long Live Music for the Millions"; and finally, "Down with Advocates of Confusion in Music". The last was directed against Shostakovitch's champions, who, the papers said, were not sufficiently self-critical.

The fortnightly review, *The Worker and the Theatre* gave a concise summary of the whole controversy: "Shostakovitch appears as the most prominent representative of tendencies harmful to Soviet art: pathological naturalism, eroticism, and the formalistic grotesque (as in 'Lady Macbeth') or else primitivistic schematicism (as in 'The Sparkling Brook')." Then *The Worker and the Theatre* proceeded to attack its own music critic, Solertinsky, for articles in praise of Shostakovitch: "In his writings, published mainly in the pages of our magazine, Ivan Solertinsky has disorientated our young composers, pushing them towards the most perilous paths of formalistic trickery and emasculated *virtuoso* play."

It looked for a while as though Shostakovitch's career was ended, and that he would never be able to rise again. To be sure, there was no ban on Shostakovitch's music, and even the offending *Lady Macbeth* continued in the repertoire of the Soviet opera houses. Shostakovitch kept his post as instructor at the Leningrad Conservatory. He continued to enjoy all the social and economic privileges of a Soviet composer. But psychologically his position became extremely difficult. Time was out of joint for Shostakovitch. His satirical talent had outlived itself, and was no longer consonant with the new stage of the Revolution.

The story of Shostakovitch's return to grace is as dramatic as the story of his temporary fall. His ultimate rise was not due to his theatrical music, but to his symphonies. In order to tell the full story of Shostakovitch as a symphonist, we shall revert to the beginning of his career, and trace the facts of his early life.

The antecedents of Shostakovitch's family were these: his father, a businessman, was born in Siberia, as was his mother, Sophia, née Kokovlina. Early in the century his parents moved to Leningrad, where Shostakovitch was born on September 25, 1906. Both parents were very musical: the mother studied at the Leningrad Conservatory in her youth, and the father had a pleasing tenor voice and played the piano. One of Shostakovitch's two sisters is a laureate of the Leningrad Conservatory. Dmitri Shostakovitch married Nina Varzar in 1933. They have two children—a girl, Galya, and a boy, Maxim.

Shostakovitch received his primary musical education from his mother. He composed his first piece, a theme with variations, at the age of nine. At the age of eleven, shortly after the Revolution, he wrote a "Hymn to Liberty" and a funeral march for the victims of the Revolution. He studied at the Glasser School of Music in Leningrad, and later entered the Leningrad Conservatory. His teachers were Maximilian Steinberg in composition and Leonid Nikolaev in piano. During the difficult years after the Revolution, Shostakovitch had to eke out the family finances by playing piano in the moving picture houses.

Shostakovitch's First Symphony, so popular in Russia and abroad, was a graduation piece, composed at the age of nineteen. It was performed by the Leningrad Philharmonic under the direction of Nicolas Malko, on May 12, 1926. There are four movements, and the Symphony follows the standard form with this difference: not the third, but the second movement is a Scherzo (as in Beethoven's Ninth).

Shostakovitch has remained faithful to this form in all his symphonies, and in the great majority of his other compositions. But within each movement there are deviations and striking individual touches that make for unmistakable originality. In the recapitulation he usually reverses the order of the first and second subjects of a Sonata Allegro. The instrumentation is individualized, and Shostakovitch likes to open a symphony with an instrumental solo. From the metrico-rhythmic standpoint, there is a remarkable insistence on duple time. The rhythmic figure of an eighth-note and two-sixteenths is particularly frequent. When, as in the first movement of the First Symphony, there are episodes in 3/4 time, they often take the form of a caricature of a waltz. This prevalence of duple time in Shostakovitch's music is not peculiar to Shostakovitch alone among Soviet composers, and it has something to do with a general, if unformulated, feeling that the marching duple time expresses healthy optimism, while the languid dactylic 3/4 time suggests laxity of spirit, out of keeping with the revolutionary times. It is also characteristic that in Shostakovitch's music, as in the music of other Soviet composers, passages in 3/4 time are usually in minor modes. A notable exception to this is the Shostakovitch type of rapid Scherzo. But such Scherzos are invariably *a quattro battute*, and are simply masked bars of 13/4 or 13/8.

The following characteristics of Shostakovitch's technique in the First Symphony have become his trade marks, and are found in virtually the entire repertoire of his symphonic and chamber music. (1) A highly rhythmic opening subject, fundamentally diatonic, but embellished with chromatics. This theme is usually given to the clarinet or bassoon.

Principal Subject of the First Symphony

(2) Individualized instrumentation with frequent division of the strings, and special effects, such as violin *glissandi*. (3) Exploitation of the lowest and highest registers, particularly the low reaches of the brass and high notes in the strings. (4) Independent role of the percussion. There is a kettle-drum solo at the end of the First Symphony. (5) Inclusion of the piano in the orchestral score. (6) Inverted pedals in tremolos in the violins. In the second movement of the First Symphony, the high E in the second violins is repeated 576 times at a stretch, for the total duration of one minute and thirty-eight seconds. (7) Extensive scale runs. (8) Sudden modulations, directly into the tonic.

Shostakovitch's Second Symphony belongs to the period when Soviet music was under the influence of Western modernism. It is "formalistic" in the Soviet meaning of the word—that is, abundant in formal devices, such as polytonality and polyrhythmy. There is a canon of nine wood-wind instruments playing a descending chromatic scale, with entries spaced at intervals of sixteenth notes, so that the progression results in parallel chords of nine different notes. There is also an interesting application of polyrhythmic polytonality, the basses playing in quarter-notes; the cellos in eighth-notes; the violas in triplet eighth-notes; the second violins *divisi* in sixteenth-notes, and in groups of five notes; and the first violins in groups of five and six notes. Several keys are touched upon simultaneously.

Polyrhythmic Polytonality in the Second Symphony

A factory whistle is included in the score, with an indication that it may be replaced by four horns, three trombones, and a tuba, blowing in unison.

The Factory Whistle in the Second Symphony

The Second Symphony marks the high tide of "industrial music". It is compressed into one movement, with a choral ending, and is dedicated to October, the month of the Soviet Revolution according to the old-style Russian calendar.

The concluding chorus of the Second Symphony is written to the words of the Soviet poet Bezimensky:

> *O, Lenin! You have forged the will of the sufferers.*
> *You have forged the will of the calloused hands.*
> *We have understood, Lenin, that our destiny*
> > *Carries*
> > *The Name:*
> > *Struggle.*
> *Let everyone be young and brave in that struggle.*
> *for the name of victory is*
> > *October.*

October!—the harbinger of the awaited Sun,
October!—the will of the rebel centuries.
October!—labor, joy, and the song.
October!—the happiness of fields and working tables.
It is the banner of living generations.

October,
The Commune,
And Lenin.

The Second Symphony was performed for the first time in Leningrad on the tenth anniversary of the Soviet Revolution, November 6, 1927. Its Moscow première followed on December 4 of the same year, and it shared the program with the celebrated *Iron Foundry* of Alexander Mossolov, in which a sheet of steel joins the orchestra to give a realistic touch to the music.

The Third Symphony is dedicated to the festival day of international labor, May First. Like the Second Symphony, it is compact, in one movement, with a choral ending. The text of the chorus is an appeal to revolutionary uprising in all lands.

In a statement, published in the *New York Times* of December 5, 1931, Shostakovitch gave his reasons for composing music of political significance:

> I am a Soviet composer, and I see our epoch as something heroic, spirited, and joyous. . . . Music cannot help having a political basis—an idea that the *bourgeoisie* are slow to comprehend. There can be no music without ideology. The old composers, whether they knew it or not, were upholding a political theory. Most of them, of course, were bolstering the rule of the upper classes.
>
> We as revolutionists have a different conception of music. Lenin himself said that "music is a means of unifying broad masses of people." For music has the power of stirring specific emotions in those who listen to it. Good music lifts and heartens and lightens people for work and effort. It may be tragic, but it must be strong. It is no longer an end in itself, but a vital weapon in the struggle.

Melodically and rhythmically, we find in the Third Symphony many a pattern familiar from the First Symphony. Again the principal theme is given to the clarinet; this instrument opens the Third Symphony unaccompanied. There are some curious episodes, such as the passage for two horns in unison against the accompaniment of the snare-drum.

Horns and Percussion in the Third Symphony

There is the familiar waltz-caricature, played by the violins, in the high register, and the piccolo. As in the First Symphony, there is a slow section before the conclusion. The choral part is patterned after a marching song, with some odd syncopations.

Choral Ending of the Third Symphony

The Fourth Symphony has never been publicly performed, and is one of the works that Shostakovitch has repudiated as unsatisfactory. It was written in that, for Shostakovitch, catastrophic year 1936, when he tried to redeem himself in the eyes of Soviet society. The Symphony was put in rehearsal by the Leningrad Philharmonic in December 1936, but the reaction of those present at the rehearsals and of the orchestra members was not encouraging. Shostakovitch withdrew it from performance, and resolutely set to work to write another symphonic work, his Symphony No. 5. It was performed in Leningrad on November 21, 1937, and turned the tide for Shostakovitch. On the day following, the *New York Times* carried a wireless dispatch with these headlines: "Composer Regains His Place in Soviet. Dmitri Shostakovitch, Who Fell From Grace Two Years Ago, on Way to Rehabilitation. His New Symphony Hailed. Audience Cheers as Leningrad Philharmonic Presents Work."

Not only professional reviewers, but even an aviator, burst into print in praise of Shostakovitch. The influential music critic Ostretzov welcomed Shostakovitch's "liberation from individualistic chaos and formalistic experimentation." The writer of historical romances, Alexei Tolstoy, reviewed the performance of the Fifth Symphony in the government organ, *Izvestia*, and noted Shostakovitch's departure from "the decadent spirit of 'Lady Macbeth of the District of Mzensk', with its misdirected irony and estheticizing naturalism." "Glory be to our people, which procreates such talents", exclaimed Tolstoy. "Today we have ten masters, tomorrow there will be hundreds. Soviet art is world art, it must be world art!"

The aviator Gromov, hero of the non-stop flight from Moscow to America over the North Pole, set down his impressions in the pages of the monthly *Sovietskaya Musica*: "Shostakovitch's Symphony captivates the listener's imagination from the very first, and holds him in a state of joyful tension to the end. . . . Shostakovitch revives the philosophical symphonism of the Russian classics."

In a letter to the author of this article, Gregory Schneerson, the Moscow musicologist, wrote after the performance of the Fifth Symphony: "This is Shostakovitch's day of triumph! The Symphony is a work of extraordinary profundity, by a mature artist who has successfully overcome the childhood disease of leftism. This is, indeed, a joyous occasion!"

The Fifth Symphony bears all the familiar traits of Shostakovitch, but there are some significant abstentions, testifying that the composer was proceeding with caution. The form is academic: four movements, an opening Moderato in sonata form, a rapid Scherzo, a slow movement, Largo, and a boisterous Finale. The Fifth Symphony has no program. Apparently, after the dubious success of the "October" Symphony, No. 2, and the "May First" Symphony, No. 3, Shostakovitch had resolved to abandon explicit revolutionary programs, and had also decided to dispense with a choral ending.

The opening phrase of the Fifth Symphony gives a clue to the intent of the entire work. It is a canon in the octave between the lower and upper strings, and the thematic structure, whose intervals are given a dramatic rhythmical context, immediately suggests the Beethoven of the last Sonatas.

Beethovenian Opening of the Fifth Symphony

It must be recalled that, from the early days of the Revolution, Beethoven was held up as a model of a revolutionary composer. Soviet musicians were urged to find a musical idiom that would be as expressive of the Russian Revolution as Beethoven's *Eroica* was of Napoleonic times. Shostakovitch had heeded this suggestion: his Fifth Symphony comes nearest to being a translation of Beethoven into the language of present-day Russia.

Otherwise, the physiognomy of the music presents the familiar traits. The dash-dot-dot figure is used, in a slow tempo, as the rhythmic background for the second subject of the opening movement. The same figure appears later in diminution, in the trumpets. *Glissandi* of the violins are applied in the playful Scherzo.

Glissandi of the Violins in the Scherzo of the Fifth Symphony

There is a characteristic flute solo in the Largo.

Flute Solo in the Largo of the Fifth Symphony

The movement ends *pianissimo*; this is virtually the rule in a Shostakovitch Largo. The Finale, Allegro non troppo, is more Tchaikovskian than Beethovenian. The music plunges *in medias res* in the brass, with a theme whose tonality is curiously ambiguous.

Finale of the Fifth Symphony

A dramatic solo of the kettle drums leads to a blindingly brilliant ending. A *tremolo* on the dominant in the strings and wood-winds cuts, like an acetylene torch, through the fanfare of the brass. This dominant, A, is repeated exactly 252 times in rapid eighth-notes, for a total duration of one minute and twenty seconds, favorably comparing with, if not quite reaching, the endurance record set by the high E in the second movement of the First Symphony.

The difficulty Shostakovitch found himself in after the success of the Fifth Symphony was that he had to live up to that success in his later works. For years he had been considering a monumental symphony on the subject of Lenin. In an interview in the *Sovietskoyo Iskusstvo* of November 20, 1938, he made the following statement:

> I have set myself a task fraught with great responsibility, to express through the medium of sound the immortal image of Lenin as a great son of the Russian people and a great leader and teacher of the masses. I have received numerous letters from all corners of the Soviet Union with regard to my future Symphony. The most important advice contained in these letters was to make ample use of musical folklore.

This reference to the paramount importance of folklore is interesting. Although Shostakovitch's music is recognizably Russian, it does not draw upon the wealth of Russian folk-song as much as, for instance, does the music of Tchaikovsky. Shostakovitch must have felt the necessity of establishing a closer contact with that element of which Pushkin said: "The breath of Russia is there, it smells of Russia." Through the symbolic figure of Lenin, Shostakovitch hoped to connect Russia with the Revolution. But once more he was frustrated in an attempt to create a work, national in spirit and revolutionary in content. When the new symphony, the Sixth, was performed, Lenin's name was not attached to it.

E-flat Clarinet Solo in the Scherzo of the Sixth Symphony

Exceptionally, the Sixth Symphony has only three movements. There is no opening Allegro. Instead, the Symphony begins with an extremely slow movement, marked Largo, which is Shostakovitch's favorite indication for a slow tempo. The second movement corresponds to a symphonic Scherzo, but it is much less rapid than a typical Shostakovitch Scherzo. Here, for the first time in Shostakovitch's symphonic music, the E-flat clarinet is introduced, and is assigned an important solo.

The third (and last) movement is a lively rondo

Finale of the Sixth Symphony

The reception accorded the Sixth Symphony at its first performance was not conclusive. It was presented on December 3, 1939, in Moscow, in the course of the Festival of Soviet Music. At the same Festival three politically important cantatas were given: Prokofiev's *Alexander Nevsky*, glorifying the rout of the Teutonic Knights on frozen Lake Peipus on April 5, 1242; Shaporin's *On the Kulikov Field*, commemorating the Russian victory over the Tartar chieftain Mamay in the year 1380; and Koval's *Emelian Pugatchov*, illustrating the story of the rebel of that name who was executed by Catherine the Great on January 11, 1775. These cantatas, on the theme of national defense, overshadowed the programless Sixth Symphony of Shostakovitch. As a result, it received scant attention in the press. The analysis of it, published in *Sovietskaya Musica*, pointed out deficiencies and inconsistencies of style. Later on, however, it gained somewhat, and its performances became frequent.

Then came the thunderous Seventh. The circumstances under which it was created relate to high drama. One can imagine a play written half-a-century hence, in which one of the scenes takes place in a northern city, under siege, during the coldest winter in the memory of man. There, a young musician takes part in the civil defense of the city in the fire-fighting brigade at the Conservatory of Music. In his hours off duty, he meditates on a new symphony, dedicated to his city, to its heroic citizens.

This would accurately describe Shostakovitch in Leningrad during the winter of 1941. True, Shostakovitch had laid out plans for his Seventh Symphony before the outbreak of hostilities. In a press release of December 1940, he announced his plans for the following year: "In 1941, I hope to complete my Seventh Symphony, which I shall dedicate to the great genius of mankind—Vladimir Ilyitch Lenin." Once more the Lenin Symphony! But the war gave Shostakovitch an even greater subject, the nation, survival, victory.

Shostakovitch describes the impact of the fateful event thus:

> On that peaceful summer morning of June 22, 1941, I was on my way to the Leningrad Stadium to see my favorite Sunday soccer game. Molotov's radio address found me hurrying down the street. . . . Our fruitful, constructive existence was rudely shattered! At the Leningrad Conservatory, where I was head of the pianoforte department, vacations begin on July 1. But this was not the usual vacation time. Professors and students remained to form a local air-raid defense unit. I served as a fire-fighter. I had already applied as a volunteer in the army, but, although my application was accepted, I was not called for duty. Instead, I was asked to join the theatre section of the People's Volunteer Army. . . . Meanwhile, in the first hot July days, I started on my Seventh Symphony, conceived as a musical embodiment of the supreme ideal of patriotic war. The work engrossed me completely. Neither the savage air-raids nor the grim atmosphere of a beleaguered city could hinder the flow of musical ideas. . . . I worked with an inhuman intensity. I continued to compose marches, songs, and film music, and attended to my organizational duties as chairman of the Leningrad Composers' Union, and then would return to my Symphony as though I had never left it.

The first movement of the Symphony was completed on September 3, 1941. On October 1, Shostakovitch flew from Leningrad to Moscow. When the Government moved to the temporary capital in Kuibishev on the Volga, Shostakovitch followed. It was there that the Seventh Symphony was finished, on December 27, 1941. The first performance took place in Kuibishev on March 1, 1942, at a noontime concert, by the evacuated orchestra of the Bolshoi Theatre of Moscow. It was an extraordinary occasion. Members of the diplomatic corps, Red Army officers, and notables of rank and brain were present. The Soviet newspapers devoted columns to Shostakovitch's work. Alexei Tolstoy described the music as "The Seventh Heaven of Symphony". Accounts of the concert were cabled to England and America.

Samuel Samosud, the conductor of the première, gave these details of the preparation for the performance:

> The Symphony takes one hour and twenty-six minutes to play. In Kuibishev we had forty rehearsals, and some passages were gone over one hundred and fifty to two hundred times. The composer himself attended the rehearsals regularly. He insisted that the orchestra follow the directions in the score to the letter, particularly as regards tempo. During these rehearsals, we hit on some happy ideas. For instance, in the concluding section of the first movement, where the war theme returns once more, the sound of the trumpet warns, as it were, that war is not over, that dangers are still threatening. The trumpet in the orchestra could not produce the necessary impression of distance, and so we decided to place the trumpet player behind the curtain to achieve the required effect. The composer warmly approved of this idea.

The Symphony quickly made the rounds of all major cities of the Soviet Union. At the Moscow performance on March 19, an air-raid alarm was sounded, but so absorbed was the audience in the music that it refused to move until the last chords were heard. Shostakovitch received an ovation lasting twenty minutes.

Leningrad, still besieged, still cut from the rest of Russia, except for perilous airplane flights or, during the winter, for an uncertain trek over frozen Lake Ladoga, heard the Seventh too. Shostakovitch wrote in *Izvestia* of April 12, 1942: "Music does not cease in besieged Leningrad. Art, which in any other country would be relegated to the background at such a time, has in our land become a weapon against the enemy. From the inspirational sound of symphonies, songs, oratorios, and marches, the Soviet people draw new strength for the battle."

The Seventh Symphony bears the unmistakable imprint of Shostakovitch's style and technique. But it is Shostakovitch on a loftier plane. The harmony is purified; major triads are employed with unabashed candor, free of extraneous admixtures. There are undertones of solemnity which, in the music of another symphonist, might be called religious. Definitely, there is, at climactic points, an affinity with the bell-like music of the apotheosis in Rimsky-Korsakov's opera *The Invisible City of Kitezh*. Perhaps the image of that legendary city, which went under the surface of the lake to conceal itself from the invading hordes of the barbaric enemy, has conjured up, in Shostakovitch's creative memory, a parallel with the immediate present.

The first movement opens with a vigorous C-major theme, in powerful unisons, punctuated by the rhythmic spurts of the trumpets and kettle-drums.

Opening of the Seventh Symphony

This is the theme of the Leningrad citizen, who has become the hero of the siege. The tonality darkens when an E-flat is introduced in the melodic ascent. The music softens; there is a moment of lyrical lassitude. Suddenly, out of nowhere, a little puppet-like tune is heard in the strings *pizzicato* and *col legno*, against the steady beat of the drum.

The War Theme from the Seventh Symphony

Relentlessly, it grows, takes on body, spreads all over the orchestra, magnified, yet unchanged in its melodic pattern. A Soviet writer described it as a "psychological portrait of the enemy." Alexei Tolstoy saw in it "a sudden outbreak of war, the patter of iron rats dancing to the tune of a rat catcher." The theme of the citizen-hero struggles through, integrated, from melodic allusions, into a powerful restatement. But the "iron rats" leave a path of destruction in their march. The victims are mourned in a threnody intoned by a bassoon solo.

Threnody from the First Movement of the Seventh Symphony

The second movement, Moderato poco Allegretto, is a Scherzo, a rather unusual one for Shostakovitch. It opens with a simple modal subject in the second violins, in 4/4 time.

Opening of the Second Movement of the Seventh Symphony

The Scherzo proper gives prominence to a solo for E-flat piccolo clarinet, played against a contrasting subject in the lower wood-winds. Shostakovitch describes the Scherzo as "recalling glorious episodes of the recent past." The third movement, Adagio, portrays, according to Shostakovitch, "the thrill of living, the wonder of nature." After a choralelike introduction in full chords, the music swims into clear D major. A nervous, gipsy-like dance is heard, a recollection of carefree gaiety, and the movement is concluded in optimistic clarity. The finale, Allegro non troppo, follows the slow movement without pause. It begins with a broad descriptive melody.

Opening of the Finale of the Seventh Symphony

Imperceptibly, the music comes to rhythmic life, becomes fugal, and increases its dynamic energy. If the war theme of the first movement grew by arithmetical addition, the last movement grows by spherical expansion. The first movement depicts the mortal struggle; the fourth expresses the will to victory. To convey this determination, the Finale summons all the resources of the orchestra, ending in a crushing C major. Shostakovitch has said, in grim jest, that in reply to Hitler's Blitzkrieg he would write a "Blitz" Symphony. The extraordinary impact of this music on its listeners in Russia, in England, where the Symphony was played on June 29, 1942, and finally at the radio première in America on July 19, when Toscanini interpreted the music *urbi et orbi*, has justified Shostakovitch's quip. It is a symphony to kill Hitler.

Shostakovitch's knack for writing music that appeals to the largest audience does not stop with his symphonies. He is equally successful as a composer of chamber music. It does not often happen that a piano quintet produces a sensation, but Shostakovitch's Quintet has done just that. In form and substance it is once more a projection of Shostakovitch's fundamental formula, except that to the familiar four movements there is added an academic but extremely effective fugue. The Quintet opens with a slow introduction for piano solo.

Opening of the Piano Quintet

The main body of the first movement is slow Scherzo, and is akin to a similar section of the Sixth Symphony. Then comes the fugue, and a fast Scherzo. The slow movement, Intermezzo, leads to the Finale, in rondo form.

The first performance of the Quintet took place at the Moscow Festival of Soviet Music, on November 23, 1940, with Shostakovitch playing the piano part. It made a deep impression. *Pravda*, which does not often devote space to chamber music concerts, published a lengthy review of the work: "It is music created in full maturity of power, a work that opens new vistas to the art. . . . Shostakovitch's Quintet is not only the most significant of his accomplishments; it is unquestionably the best musical composition of the year 1940." The Quintet brought Shostakovitch a more tangible reward. On March 15, 1941, a number of special prizes were awarded by the Soviet Government to artists, musicians, and creative writers. Shostakovitch received a special Stalin prize of 100,000 rubles, certainly the highest honorarium ever paid to any composer in any country at any time, for a piece of chamber music.

Of other chamber music by Shostakovitch, his Sonata for 'Cello and Piano and his String Quartet deserve special mention. The 'Cello Sonata, written in 1934, adheres to the familiar four-movement form. It is more Russian in its inspiration than Shostakovitch's symphonic music. The second subject of the first movement reflects the melodic outline of a Russian urban romance.

Second Subject of the First Movement of the 'Cello Sonata

In the last movement, there is a remarkable display of running scales, which sound like Czerny gone berserk.

Shostakovitch's String Quartet, written shortly after the Fifth Symphony, was first performed in Leningrad on October 10, 1938. Its formal structure shows slight alterations in the usual four-movement plan. The first movement, in triple time, suggests a Sarabande, and the second is a theme with variations. A Scherzo follows, and then the Finale, which latter is in sonata form.

Of chamber music of the early period, a string Octet has been published. It is interesting because it contains, as in a nutshell, all of Shostakovitch's technical idiosyncrasies—*glissandi* of the violins, dash-dot-dot rhythms, etc.

Shostakovitch is a professional pianist. He won an honorary mention at the International Piano Contest held in Warsaw in 1927. In his writing, he treats the piano as a percussion instrument, and likes to explore the extreme registers of the keyboard. His early piano Sonata opens with a rumbling noise in the lowest octave. In some instances, the right and the left hand are placed at a distance of six octaves. Shostakovitch's most effective piano pieces are his Preludes in the twenty-four major and minor keys. As a rule, these Preludes begin and end on tonic triads, while the body of the composition is embellished with frills and turns, and the modulatory plan is marked by extreme fluidity.

Prelude No. 1

Prelude No. 24

Shostakovitch has written a Piano Concerto, for the solo instrument, trumpet, and strings. The order of the two middle movements that is usual for him is here reversed: the slow movement is the second; the quicker third movement serves as a brief introduction to the Finale. The Concerto ends in a breath-taking galop, with a trumpet blaring the bugle notes against the full C major chords of the piano and the strings. The piano writing is of the familiar quality, exploiting widely separated registers.

First Movement of the Piano Concerto

Shostakovitch played the piano part at the first performance of the Concerto, in Leningrad on October 15, 1933.

Being a utilitarian composer, Shostakovitch does not neglect the applied art of cinema music. He clearly understands the specific requirements of the medium. In an article published in the *Literaturnaya Gazeta* of April 10, 1939, he has this to say on the subject:

> To compose music for the cinema without theoretical and practical experience amounts to about the same thing as orchestrating without the knowledge of instrumental sonorities. Cinema music is often regarded as merely illustrative, supplementary to the screen. In my opinion, it should be treated as an integral part of the artistic whole.

When jazz came into its own in Russia and was ideologically accepted as the authentic expression of American city folk-music, a jazz band was organized in Leningrad. Shostakovitch wrote a short suite for the band, duly performed on November 28, 1938.

Between symphonies and jazz suites, Shostakovitch found time, mostly working at night, to reorchestrate Mussorgsky's *Boris Godunov*. His expressed intention was "to bring the orchestration into affinity with the Soviet epoch", to provide "a more symphonic development of the opera, and make the rôle of the orchestra more than a mere accompaniment for the singers."

In the midst of the war, Shostakovitch has continued to work at his multiple tasks. He has written music for the Tass Windows, an organization of artists, poets, and musicians, banded together for the purpose of furnishing commentary on current events. In Kuibishev, he has kept up his teaching activities, giving three lessons a day. As chairman of the Kuibishev Composers' Association, he has conducted regular Wednesday evening meetings. Every week, he has taken part in a Defense Day Concert. These tasks may seem humble for a composer who has just shaken the world with a symphony, but for Shostakovitch all work, useful for his art and for his country, is important. In a statement, published on the first anniversary of the Russian war, Shostakovitch said: "My energies are wholly engaged in the service of my country. Like everything and everyone today, my ideas are closely bound up with the emotions born of this war. They must serve with all the power at my command in the cause of art for victory over savage Hitlerism, that fiercest and bitterest enemy of human civilization. This is the aim to which I have dedicated my creative work since the morning of June 22, 1941."

LIST OF WORKS BY DMITRI SHOSTAKOVITCH

This list was compiled by Shostakovitch for the writer of this article. Works marked with asterisks have been repudiated by the composer as unrepresentative of his present ideals in music.

Opus

1 Scherzo in F-sharp minor for orchestra (1919)* Ms.

2 Eight Preludes for piano (1919–1920)* Ms.

3 Theme with Variations for orchestra (1920–1922)* Ms.

4 (1) *The Grasshopper and the Ant* (2) *The Jackass and the Nightingale*, for voice and orchestra, text by Krylov (1922)* Ms.

5 Three Fantastic Dances for Piano (1922). Published by the Music Section of the State Publishing House, 1926.

6 Suite for Two Pianos (1922)* Ms.

7 Scherzo in E-flat major for orchestra (1923) * Ms.

8 Trio for piano, violin, and 'cello (1923) * Ms.

Opus

9   (1) Fantasy (2) Prelude (3) Scherzo for 'cello and piano
(1923–1924) * Ms.

10 Symphony No. 1 in F minor (1924–1925). Published by the
Music Section of the State Publishing House, 1926. First performance: Leningrad, May 12, 1926.

11 Two pieces for string octet (1925)
(1) Prelude (2) Scherzo. Published by the Music Section of the
State Publishing House, 1927.

12 Sonata for piano (1926). Published by the Music Section of the
State Publishing House, 1927.

13 *Aphorisms* (Ten pieces for piano). Published by Triton,
Leningrad, in 1928.

14 Symphony No. 2, *Dedication to October* (1927). Published by
the Music Section of the State Publishing House, 1927. First
performance: Leningrad, November 6, 1927.

15 *The Nose*, opera in three acts after Gogol (1927–1928).
Lithographe*** First performance: Leningrad, January 13,
1930.

16 *Tahiti-Trot*. (Orchestral transcription, 1928.) Ms. lost.

17 Two pieces by Scarlatti for a wood-wind ensemble. (Orchestral
transcription, 1928.) Ms. lost.

18 Music for the film *The New Babylon* (1928–1929) Ms.

19 Incidental music to Mayakovsky's comedy *The Bedbug* (1929)
Ms.

20 Symphony No. 3, *May First*. Published by the Music Section of
the State Publishing House in 1932. First performance:
Leningrad, November 1930.

21 Six Songs to words by Japanese poets, for voice and orchestra.
(1) *Lot* (2) *Before the Suicide* (3) *Immodest Glance* (4) *For the
First and Last Time* (5) *Love* (6) *Death* * Ms.

22 *The Golden Age*, ballet in three acts (1929–1930). A suite from
this ballet was published by the Music Section of the State
Publishing House in 1936. First performance: Leningrad,
October 27, 1930.

23 Two pieces for orchestra (1929) * Ms.
(1) Entr'acts (2) Finale

24 Music to Bezimensky's comedy *The Shot* (1929) Ms.

Opus

25 Music to the drama by Gorbenko and Lvov *The Virgin Soil* (1930)°°°

26 Music to the film *Alone* (1930) Ms.

27 *Bolt*, ballet in three acts (1930–1931). First performance: Leningrad, April 8, 1931. Ms.

28 Music to Piotrovsky's play *Rule Britannia* (1931) Ms.

29 *Lady Macbeth of the District of Mzensk*, opera in four acts (1930–1932). The piano score published by the Music Section of the State Publishing House, 1935. First performance: Leningrad, January 22, 1934.

30 Music to the film *Golden Mountains*. A suite from this music published by the Music Section of the State Publishing House, 1935.

31 Music to the play *Conditionally Killed*, by Voevodin and Riss (1931) Ms.

32 Music to *Hamlet* (1931–1932) Ms.

33 Music to the film *Passerby* (1932) Ms.

34 Twenty-four Preludes for piano (1932–1933). Published by the Music Section of the State Publishing House, 1933.

35 Concerto for piano and orchestra (1933). Published by the Music Section of the State Publishing House, 1934. First performance, with composer at the piano: Leningrad, October 15, 1933.

36 Music to the film *Tale of a Priest and His Dumb Hired-Man* (1934) Ms.

37 Music to *The Human Comedy*, after Balzac (1933–1934) Ms.

38 Suite for jazz orchestra (1934) (1) Waltz (2) Polka (3) Blues. First performance: Leningrad, November 28, 1938. Ms.

39 Ballet, *The Sparkling Brook*, in three acts (1934). First performance: Leningrad, June 4, 1935. Ms.

40 Sonata for 'cello and piano (1934). Published by Triton, Leningrad, 1935.

41 Music to the film *Girl Companions* (1934) Ms.

42 Five Fragments for orchestra (1935) ° Ms.

43 Symphony No. 4 (1935–1936) °. Put in rehearsal by the Leningrad Philharmonic in December 1936, but withdrawn by the composer. Ms.

Opus

44 Music to Afinogenov's play *Salute to Spain* (1936) Ms.

45 Music to the film *Maxim's Return* (1936–1937) Ms.

46 *Four Songs* to Pushkin's texts (1936) Ms.

47 Symphony No. 5 (1937). Published by the Music Section of the State Publishing House, 1939. First performance: Leningrad, November 21, 1937.

48 Music to the film *The Days of Volotchaevo* (1936–1937) Ms.

49 String Quartet (1938). Published by the Leningrad Music Section of the State Publishing House, 1940. First performance: Leningrad, October 10, 1938.

50 Music to the film *Vyborg District* (1938) Ms.

51 Music to the film *Friends* (1938) Ms.

52 Music to the film *A Great Citizen*, first series (1938) Ms.

53 Music to the film *The Man with a Gun* (1938) Ms.

54 Symphony No. 6 (1939). Published by the Music Section of the State Publishing House, 1941. First performance: Moscow, December 3, 1939.

55 Music to the film *A Great Citizen*, second series (1939) Ms.

56 Music to the film *Silly Little Mouse* (1939) Ms.

57 Quintet for piano and string quartet (1940). Published by the Union of Soviet Composers, 1941. First performance: Moscow, November 23, 1940.

58 Orchestration of Musorgsky's opera *Boris Godunov* (1940) Ms.

59 "Song of the United Nations" (1942). Published by Am-Rus, New York.

60 Symphony No. 7 (1941–1942). First performance: Kuibishev, March 1, 1942. First American performance, NBC Orchestra, Arturo Toscanini conducting.

NS with Dmitry Kabalevsky, 1959

l to r: Igor Blazkov, NS, Leonid Grabovsky, and Eugene Machavariani at the entrance of the Conservatory Great Hall, Moscow, November 30, 1962

NS walking with Lina Prokofieva at the House of the Creative Arts at Staraya Ruza, November 8, 1962. She told him Prokofiev never divorced her and that his second marriage to a young Comsomol girl was illegal.

l to r: NS, Lina Prokofieva, Daniel Lesur, and Tikkon Khrennikov at Staraya Ruza, House of the Creative Arts, near Moscow, November 8, 1962

NS with his nephew, Soviet composer Sergei Slonimsky, at Peter the Great statue in Leningrad, 1962

Three generations: Electra Slonimsky Yourke, NS, Katharine Yourke, at Catherine's Palace, near St. Petersburg, April 1992

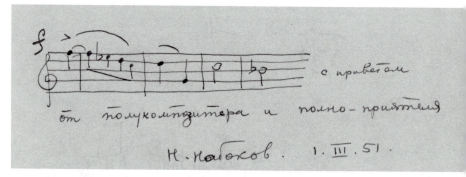

Prokofiev entry in NS's guest book, February 1938: "To hell with grannies, let's write music!"

From Nicholas Nabokov: "with greetings from a half-composer and a whole friend. N. Nobokov. 1 March 1951"

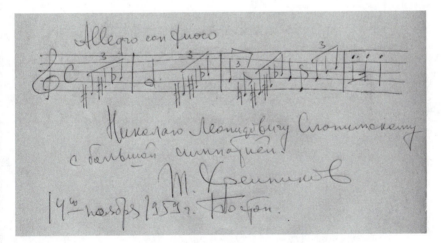

From Shostakovich: "To Nicolai Leonidovich Slonimsky in fond memory. D Shostakovich. 14 November 1959. Boston"

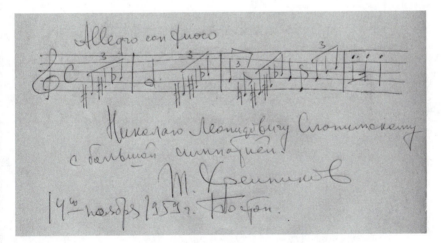

Khrennikov says: "To Nikolai Leonidovich Slonimsky with great sympathy." T. Khrennikov. 14 November, 1959. Boston"

13. SHOSTAKOVITCH'S WAR SYMPHONY

Oftentimes in history, a book, a poem, or a song becomes the symbol of national achievement. But never before has an orchestral work, a symphony, become a people's Marseillaise during a mortal conflict. This extraordinary accomplishment was achieved by the Russian composer, Dmitri Shostakovitch. There was enough in the story of the Symphony to stir imagination. It was written in Leningrad during the siege. Shostakovitch served as fire warden in the unit of the Leningrad Conservatory, and was in constant peril from air raids.

Shostakovitch dedicated the Seventh Symphony to the Leningrad citizen who has become a hero of the war. The sweeping melodic theme of the citizen opens the Symphony. Contrasted with it, there is a robot-like marching tune which expresses the mechanical relentlessness of the Nazi drive. This Nazi theme grows by the process of multiplication of the instruments employed. But a symphony is an orchestral sonata, and in a sonata there is a recapitulation, when the main theme comes back. War itself is in sonata form. So in Shostakovitch's Symphony, the Russian citizen returns in full glory, leaving of the Nazis nothing more than a melancholy trumpet off-stage, repeating its tune to the beats of an ineffectual drum.

When the Leningrad Orchestra was evacuated to Siberia, Shostakovitch flew out of Leningrad, over the German lines, to Kuibyshev. There, on March 1, 1942, the Seventh Symphony was given its first performance. It produced an overwhelming impression. Alexi Tolstoy called it "The Seventh Heaven of Symphony." The score of the symphony was reduced to a microfilm and flown across three continents to America.

Ch. 13: originally published in *The Christian Science Monitor*, December 26, 1942.

It aroused enthusiasm in New York, where Toscanini presented it in the radio premiere. All major American orchestras announced the performance of the Seventh Symphony for the current season.

The Seventh Symphony marked the culminating point to a dramatic career. Shostakovitch's name was familiar to the American concertgoers. His First Symphony, which he wrote as a graduation piece at the Leningrad Conservatory, had long been in the symphony repertoire in America. Some years ago, Leopold Stokowski startled the subscribers of the Philadelphia Orchestra with the performance of Shostakovitch's "May 1" Symphony. True, the choral conclusion, glorifying the word revolution, was left out, but the playing of a Bolshevik symphony stirred comment. Shostakovitch's opera *Lady Macbeth of the District of Mzensk*, received a luxurious production at the Metropolitan Opera House in New York, attended by a large concourse of people, among whom high society predominated.

Shostakovitch, when I met him in Leningrad in August 1935, was already a luminary of the first magnitude on the Russian horizon. The Intourist Soviet Agency listed Shostakovitch among sightseeing attractions: "Come to the Soviet Union, see the Kremlin and hear Shostakovitch." So I was eager to see Shostakovitch.

One of the few remaining old-fashioned *izvostchiks* took me, for the sum of seven rubles, to Dmitrovsky Pereulok, No. 5, where Shostakovitch lived with his widowed mother and his wife. I did not know which was Shostakovitch's apartment, and there was no janitor of whom I could inquire. But suddenly I heard someone play the piano. It was an unusual sort of playing, and it was unusual music, rhythmic, simple in outline, but adorned with considerable dissonance. There could be no mistake; it was Shostakovitch playing his own music. I ascended the stairs toward the source of that music, and soon found myself in front of Shostakovitch's door on the third floor. I rang the bell. The door opened, and there was Shostakovitch, a bespectacled young man looking a little like a picture of Schubert. He led me to the studio, where a grand piano stood, and almost immediately plunged into a discussion of musical affairs in Russia and in America.

On the piano I noticed the score of Stravinsky's *Symphony of the Psalms*. Shostakovitch told me that he admired the structural perfection of the work, and had even arranged it for four hands.

Shostakovitch, I observed, was a very accurate sort of person. On the table there was a leather-bound book in which Shostakovitch noted the time of composition of each of his works, the year, month, and day, and sometimes the hour. There was nothing amateurish about the man. He was not given to temperamental outbursts, and was always glad to accept suggestions from his interlocutors, from his colleagues, from his correspondents.

After an hour or so of musical discussion, Shostakovitch's mother announced that tea was served. We went to another room, not very spacious, but homelike, with flowerpots on the window sill and a bird in a cage. Shostakovitch introduced me to his wife. As I learned afterward, Shostakovitch's mother was a musician, and a graduate of the Conservatory in the piano department. She eagerly discussed her son's music, and wanted to know in detail what they think of Shostakovitch in America.

We returned to the studio. At the piano I tried over some of Shostakovitch's Preludes which I was going to play in America. Then we went over the piano part of his 'Cello Sonata. There is one passage in that sonata which sounds like exercises in scales, and I wanted to know how Shostakovitch plays them, straightforwardly, or with humorous exaggeration. I was surprised to find that Shostakovitch was not a humorist by nature, and that the satirical strain in his music was not meant to be witty, but constructively critical of the subject. For instance, the scene at the police headquarters in *Lady Macbeth of the District of Mzensk* was not intended to be grotesque, but served the purpose of exposing the rottenness of the regime of Czar Nicholas I. The celebrated "Polka" was originally a satire on the Disarmament Conference in Geneva. Shostakovitch has always considered himself a practical musician writing functional music, whether in satire or in glorification.

At a concert in Leningrad I heard Shostakovitch play all of his 24 preludes, his Piano Sonata, and the piano part in the 'Cello Sonata. His playing was clear, accurate, percussive. The piano was of Soviet manufacture.

The following year, 1936, was a dark period for Shostakovitch. His opera *Lady Macbeth of the District of Mzensk* was condemned in devastating terms in a semiofficial article in *Pravda*, as a work of tendencies contrary to the ideals of Soviet art. The success of the opera abroad was interpreted in that article as indication that Shostakovitch unconsciously played up to bourgeois tastes, and the very element of satire on the Czarist regime was deprecated as being an excuse for the glorification of a middle-class murderess, the Lady Macbeth of the title. A few weeks later, Shostakovitch's ballet *The Sparkling Brook* was similarly condemned in an even more violent article in *Pravda*. That was serious, for *The Sparkling Brook* treated a Soviet theme, the life on a collective farm.

From Shostakovitch's Seventh Symphony: The Russian Freedom Theme [top] and The Nazi War Theme [bottom]

Shostakovitch made two unsuccessful tries to stage a comeback, in his Fourth Symphony and in Five Fragments for Orchestra. The Fourth Symphony was put in rehearsal by the Leningrad Philharmonic, but was withdrawn by the composer himself. The Five Fragments were never even tried.

The return of Shostakovitch reads like high drama. He earned his rehabilitation by his Fifth Symphony, a work of Beethoven-like intent, without a definite program, and conceived as straight music. After its performance in Leningrad in November 1937, and later in Moscow, the Soviet press burst into enthusiasm. Shostakovitch was welcomed back into the fold like a prodigal son, and since then his star has been rising steadily. He received the special prize of 100,000 rubles for a Piano Quintet in 1940, and the self-same *Pravda*, in a special article, welcomed this Quintet as the greatest Russian composition of the year.

Shostakovitch is now 36. One would have to go back to the great 19th-century romantics to find a composer who enjoyed a similar success. Mendelssohn was acclaimed in England; he was not only a composer, but a pianist, and a brilliant conductor. When Toscanini and the trustees of the New York Philharmonic Orchestra cabled Shostakovitch an invitation to come to conduct and offered to set aside a number of dates to select from, he cabled back regrets, saying that he is not a conductor.

This has been an offer without precedence, and the regretful rejection on the part of Shostakovitch is also probably the first in the century-long existence of the New York Philharmonic. Russian artists have a strong feeling of social loyalty in normal times, and even more so in the times of war. Shostakovitch regards it as his primary duty to serve his people, as a fire fighter if necessary, as a musician, if he can. Immediately after completing his Seventh Symphony, he turned to more prosaic tasks, working in the propaganda agency called the Tass Windows, which supplies posters, leaflets, songs, and marches for the Red Army.

14. SHOSTAKOVITCH AFTER THE SEVENTH

Shostakovitch continues to be the darling of the musical world. Every new piece that comes from his prolific pen, be it an hour-long symphony or a song, is eagerly pounced upon by performers, particularly in America. This success is without precedent in music history, considering that Shostakovitch's music is difficult to play, and to untrained ears difficult to perceive. Those who believe that the Shostakovitch craze is the result of super-pressagentry on a planetary scale are most certainly mistaken, for no amount of ballyhoo could create an eager audience for such a bulky piece of merchandise as a symphony.

No, Shostakovitch's rise to Olympus is a genuine phenomenon of the as yet unfounded science of musical sociology. His Seventh Symphony has even become the subject of a learned paper by Sebastian de Grazia, entitled "Reactivity: Speed and Its adaptiveness in Musical Symbols" and published in the *Journal of the Biology and Pathology of Interpersonal Relations*.

The Seventh Symphony possesses the glamour of drama. Even though only the opus number appears on the title page of the original manuscript, Shostakovitch has himself connected the symphony with the heroic resistance of Leningrad during the siege, and so the Symphony has acquired the sobriquet "Leningrad." Now here comes a new symphony, the Eighth, which has no such dramatic program. Yet the interest for this new work is as great as for the Seventh. There are eager bids for the right of first performance in the United States, and cables are sent from Moscow with tantalizing descriptions of the imposing dish to be served

---

Ch. 14: originally published in *Musical America*, December 1943.

shortly to musical audiences here. And imposing it certainly is, for it takes over an hour to play: Shostakovitch is uncompromising in his symphonic expansiveness.

The Soviet music scholar Z. Zhitomirsky wirelesses the following description of the Eighth Symphony: "This intricate and extensive score is in five movements. The first movement is a philosophical Adagio. The second, third and fourth movements are conceived as three marches; a heroic march in short rhythms, gradually changing into a Scherzo-March, and reaching the grotesque in its relentless motion, and then a funeral march, similar in mood to the first movement of the Symphony. The Finale is dominated by bright pastoral tones. Such is the structure of this unusual work. The Eighth Symphony is extremely modern in its ideas, and means of expression. Shostakovitch himself characterizes the Symphony in these words: 'I can describe the philosophical concept of my new Symphony very briefly: Life is beautiful. All that is dark and igno-minious will perish. All that is beautiful will triumph.' Although the gen-eral idea of the Symphony is clear, it is almost entirely devoid of literary programmatic content or word image, such as is found in the Fifth and the Seventh symphonies. The slow movements of the Symphony create the impression of deep ideological meaning. Here the composer's indi-viduality, his philosophical lyricism, and his inner restraint are revealed through psychological integration. These movements are also marked by profound romantic contemplation which rises dramatically to a powerful climax. The Eighth Symphony is optimistic and life-asserting. At the same time it does not culminate in a traditional grandiose ending. Shostakovitch brings the Symphony to a close in translucent pianissimo, with colorful harmonies suggesting youthful dreams infused with beauty. In keeping with the composer's wishes, the first performance of the Eighth Symphony will take place under the leadership of Eugene Mravinsky, one of the outstanding Soviet conductors."

When Shostakovitch played the piano score of the Symphony at a meeting of Soviet composers in Moscow, Nicolai Miaskovsky, who is no novice in symphonic composition—he is now working on his twenty-fourth symphony—exclaimed: "In the Eighth Symphony, Shostakovitch achieves full power of his creative genius!"

Between the Seventh and the Eighth Symphonies, Shostakovitch wrote several works of lesser dimensions, a second Piano Sonata, op. 64, and six songs to the texts by Shakespeare, Walter Raleigh, and Robert

Burns, in the Russian translations by Marshak (a well-known author of children's verse) and Pasternak. It is difficult to tell whether Shostakovitch's selection of English poetry for the texts of his songs was an intentional tribute to the English-speaking Allies of the Soviet Union. Shostakovitch did make a fine gesture towards American music in contributing an orchestral piece to the program of American music given in Moscow on July 4, 1943. The piece was named in the Russian text of the program "Return of the Hero," and the hero was no other than Johnny from "When Johnny Comes Marching Home," which song was arranged by Shostakovitch for orchestra specially for the occasion. It is interesting to note that the opening number on the American program was Roy Harris's Overture based on the same song.

It should be remarked in passing that the so-called "Song of the United Nations" is not a new composition by Shostakovitch, but an adaptation, made by a New York arranger, of a theme from Shostakovitch's incidental music to a film, *Counterplan*, produced in 1932. The reappearance of the tune as the "Song of the United Nations" was a surprise to the composer, who heard about it only after the fact.

A few words about the new Piano Sonata. It was written in memory of Leonid Nikolaev, Professor of the Leningrad Conservatory, who was Shostakovitch's piano teacher and who died on October 11, 1942, in Tashkent, Central Asia, where he went after the outbreak of the war. Shostakovitch played the Sonata on the Moscow radio on April 10, 1943. It has three movements: the first movement is a lively Allegretto; the second a Largo; and the third, a theme with variations, in a Russian folk style. The music of the Sonata has been described by a Soviet music critic as "ascetically economical," and likened to a graphic design rather than to a water color.

Despite his tremendous productivity, Shostakovitch feels that he has not done enough. In a message sent to the American Russian War Relief Committee on the second anniversary of the Soviet-German war, June 22, 1943, Shostakovitch said:

On more than one occasion I have asked myself: How did I help my motherland in her days of grave trials? I think every musician, just as any other citizen, is bound to do his duty. I must write good music to the best of my strength and ability. Now I ask: how during the two years of the great Patriotic War did I assist in developing Soviet music? What did

I do? What must be done in the future? I shall list my works. In 1941, after the outbreak of the war, I wrote the Seventh Symphony. In 1942 I wrote six songs to the words of Walter Raleigh, Robert Burns and William Shakespeare and also music for the Song and Dance Ensemble of the Red Army. In 1943 I wrote a Piano Sonata, and now I intend to start working on a ballet "The Golden Key" after a fairy tale by Alexei Tolstoy. In addition to my activities as composer, I appear frequently at concerts, playing my own compositions in Moscow, Kuibyshev, Novosibirsk, and Ufa. Besides, I take part in the public activities of our musical organizations. I am a member of the Presidium of the Organizational Committee of the Union of Soviet Composers, and I have begun to work as a professor at the Moscow Conservatory. . . . During these two years of war I have done something, but unfortunately not enough. I must work more and better. The cruel and perfidious enemy is not defeated as yet, and we shall have to exert great efforts to strike him a final blow.

Part III

AFTER THE
REVOLUTION

15. DEVELOPMENT OF SOVIET MUSIC

Soviet music is the continuation of Russian music. Yet it has acquired traits that are definitely distinguishable from all Russian music, in fact from *all* old music. These traits are connected with the general characteristic of a victorious revolution, for a revolution must be optimistic, or else it will not survive, and Soviet music is optimistic. This is to be understood figuratively as well as literally. Even a Soviet threnody, or mourning ode, has elements of faith in the future and very often concludes in a major key. Revolutionary music must also, to a certain extent, be programmatic, for it is related to the events of each successive year. To paraphrase Stalin's dictum of a national art with socialist content, Soviet music is national Russian music with socialist, i.e., constructive, looking to the future, content. But the word Russian is also to be understood in an enlarged sense. Russian composers have always been partial to the music of national minorities, but never before were national minorities of the former Russian empire so active in the domain of art, and never before has there been a greater opportunity to cultivate their national art. To sum up in a formula, Soviet music is a music of all nations composing the Soviet Union, guided and inspired by the great music of the past and programmatically related to socialist industry.

Historically speaking, Soviet music has passed through three clearly demarcated periods. During the time of War Communism, immediately following the October Revolution of 1917, the musical radicals held sway. A Commissar of Music was appointed under the Commissariat of Education in July, 1918. The first man to occupy this position was Arthur

Ch. 15: originally published in *Research Bulletin on the Soviet Union*, a monthly publication of The American Russian Institute for Cultural Relations with the Soviet Union, New York, NY, April 30, 1937.

Lourie, a musician of great culture, but totally lacking in integrity of purpose. His present transformation into a neo-Catholic in Paris throws light in retrospect on the type of "revolutionary" musical leadership of that period. Using technical expressions, it could be said that the prevalent tendencies of the first period of Soviet music, from War Communism up to the advent of the New Economic Policy, were urbanism, constructivism, and, to a certain extent, expressionism. In this, early Soviet music closely followed similar developments in the domain of theatrical art and painting. Perhaps the most incongruous feature of the period was the Scriabin influence which almost all Soviet composers acknowledged in their works. That Scriabin, who was essentially a mystic and whose greatness is revealed in individualistic subjective art, profoundly egocentric, should have been the inspiration of composers of the Revolution is a significant phenomenon, typical of the period of transition.

After the introduction of the NEP and the beginning of economic reconstruction, free from the chaos of war, Soviet music entered its second phase and began to evolve along sounder lines, influenced to a certain extent by the post-war western music. The works of the French Six,° the music of Stravinsky, the new possibilities opened by Schoenberg's twelve-tone system, the urbanist operas of Ernst Krenek and the expressionist opera of Alban Berg reached Russia and introduced to the Soviet composers a new field of musical expression. In January, 1926, a circle for new music was formed in Leningrad and gave in the course of the five years of its activities concert performances of western operas: Alban Berg's *Wozzeck*, Busoni's *Doktor Faust*, Darius Milhaud's *Les Malheurs d'Orphée*, Prokofiev's *Love for Three Oranges*, Ravel's *L'Enfant et les Sortileges*, and Stravinsky's *Mavra*. Of symphonic and chamber works, compositions by Schoenberg, Casella, Honegger, Satie, Anton von Webern and many others were performed. The compositions of Soviet composers written in the same period, particularly those of Josef Schillinger, Nicholas Roslavets and George Popov, showed the influence of the western technique. Dissonant counterpoint, metrical diversity, special instrumental effects, flight from tonality, or accumulation of conflicting tonalities within the same chord,

---

° Darius Milhaud, Louis Durey, Georges Auric, Arthur Honegger, Francis Poulenc, and Germaine Tailleferre, so named by Henri Collet in his article in the Parisian daily *Comoedia*, January 16, 1920.

culminating in polytonality, all these typical complications of early post-war music are present in Soviet music of the middle twenties. Statistical methods of musical analysis were applied in the Leningrad Music Institute. Theremin introduced the first electrical instrument capable of producing any pitch and any timbre with mathematical accuracy. In keeping with the general tendency towards dehumanization of music, a conductorless orchestra, *Persymfans* (First Symphonic Ensemble), was formed in Moscow and gave its inaugural concert in Moscow on February 13, 1922. The Institute of Musical Science was formed in Moscow on September 25, 1921, and a special Division of Musical History was founded at the Institute of the History of Arts in Leningrad on February 19, 1920. A society especially devoted to the study of quarter-tone music was founded in Leningrad on May 5, 1923, by George Rimsky-Korsakov, grandson of the composer.

The visits of Darius Milhaud, Alfredo Casella, Arthur Honegger and Bela Bartok brought fresh influences from the West. In the summer of 1929, Henry Cowell, the ultra-modernist from the United States, went to the Soviet Union and acquainted Soviet musicians with the achievements of American modern composers. He also gave private demonstrations in Moscow and Leningrad of his new piano technique—"tone clusters"— played with the forearm and the fist, pizzicato and glissando, played directly on the piano strings, etc.

But simultaneously an opposing tide was growing. The Russian Association of Proletarian Musicians was formed in 1924 and in 1929 published an elaborate profession of faith, which condemned western influences as petty-bourgeois, expressionism as harmful to the spirit of collectivism, musical inventions and tricks as cerebral and inaccessible to the masses. In search of a model, Moussorgsky and Beethoven were selected as true revolutionary spirits, building within an organized system and yet sufficiently daring to advance their respective epochs to a new evolutionary stage. The Russian Association of Proletarian Musicians, better known under its abbreviated title, RAPM, was a branch of a national organization affecting literature and the fine arts. It was aggressively communistic, carried on militant propaganda for a new proletarian music. Its declaration is a remarkable document of intellectual and artistic Marxism driven to a point of anti-Marxian absurdity. RAPM acquired a power which was not backed by the general policy of the state, but which impressed musicians with an assumed authority. The situation gradually grew intolerable for all creative elements in the Soviet Union until, to the surprise and the relief of everyone, RAPM was dis-

solved by decree of the Central Committee on April 23, 1932. Here are the
impressions of a Soviet composer upon the publication of the decree:

> Seven o'clock in the evening. In the hall of the Collegium of the People's
> Commissariat of Education there is an atmosphere of excitement—all the
> composers and musical workers of Moscow and Leningrad are gathered
> there. All ages and all wings of creative musical craft of Soviet culture are
> represented, from Ippolitov-Ivanov to the leaders of the RAPM. . . . Those
> assembled are grouped according to trends and tendencies. There is
> restrained talk. On the serious faces, a question: What is going to happen? It
> is apparent that something unusual is in the air. Possibly a decisive battle . . .
> Comrade Bubnov opens the discussion of problems of construction in Soviet
> musical culture, points out some breaks in this field. He asks all to talk frankly
> to the bitter end. . . . Those present take the floor one after another, and
> attack the RAPM with extraordinary vehemence. Its theoretical, creative,
> tactical attitudes are under fire. In many speeches there is rancor; theoreti-
> cal contentions give way to echoes of recent squabbles. Feelings run high. .
> . . It is clear that the RAPM rule, which limits the sphere of creative work,
> causes unhealthy conditions for the development of Soviet music. . . . On
> April 24, the Moscow papers published the decree of the Central
> Committee announcing the dissolution of proletarian art associations.

This memorable date marks the end of the second period of Soviet
music, the period of strife and contention between the two opposing
forces—westernizing liberalism and fanatical pseudo-Marxism in music.
But it would be a mistake to think that with the disappearance of the RAPM
western influences held the upper hand and the music of the masses
received a setback. Rather, the true cause of mass music had won a victory.
Composers received their charter of liberty and went to meet the masses
without being urged and goaded by an isolated group of theoreticians.

Naturally, Soviet music could not show immediate results from its liberation from the RAPM. Only naive people can believe that liberty to write
as one sees fit is a sufficient prerequisite for the creation of a great work,
although several statements of Soviet composers appeared on the first
anniversary of the dissolution of the RAPM, "declaring" their works of the
elapsed year to be a proof of improvement in quality. With all reservations,
it should be stated, however, that the period since April 23, 1932, has been
the most flourishing period of Soviet music. The opposing tendencies have

found some sort of synthesis. Soviet music, while following the national mode of Russian nineteenth-century music, has enriched itself by the contributions of the hitherto unknown musical periphery of Russia. The vitalizing influence of the national folk songs of all the united republics of the Soviet Union has given a new life to these old forms. At the same time the western influences have not, in the least, been "liquidated." Only extreme usages of western musicians, such as the stripped neo-classicism of Stravinsky or the relentlessly logical writing of Arnold Schoenberg, have remained outside the musical experience of the Soviet Union. In this respect the Soviet Union shares the experience of the entire musical world, for great as is the authority and the significance of Arnold Schoenberg in the historical progress of musical science, the amount of his music that reaches the listening masses is exceedingly small.

It is during this third period of Soviet music that the star of Dmitri Shostakovich began to rise. Shostakovitch is above all an amazingly gifted melodist, and his power of invention equals his melodic power. Born September 25, 1906, he studied under Miaskovsky. His progress has been dazzling, and the critics inside and outside of the Soviet Union early recognized him as the white hope of Soviet music. His first opera, *The Nose*, influenced by the urbanist caricature of contemporary European stage music, attracted great interest among musicians but hardly penetrated beyond a limited circle. But his *Lady Macbeth of Mtsensk* seemed to combine the two necessary ingredients of all great art—fine melodic invention and originality of purely musical invention. As such, it was heralded as a major achievement of Soviet music, and foreign visitors were invariably treated to the spectacle at Soviet festivals. The performance of the opera in New York City was a major occasion, too, and performances of the opera were given in several capitals of Europe. Great was the shock when on January 28, 1936, an article in *Pravda* administered a devastating criticism to the opera as a product of petty-bourgeois formalism and insincere and unnecessary trickery. The stark realism of the opera was here denounced as coarse naturalism. The criticism in itself would not have had such repercussions had it been just the expression of a personal opinion. But it was of the greatest importance as an expression of policy. The article read in part, as follows:

Confusion instead of Music

With the cultural development in our country there has been increasing demand for good music. . . . Several theatres present the opera *Lady*

Macbeth of Mtsensk by Shostakovich as a novelty to this new Soviet public. Officious music critics exalt this opera to the high heavens and spread its fame far and wide. The young composer listens to enthusiastic compliments instead of serious business-like discussion which might help him in his future work. The listener is from the very first bewildered by a stream of deliberately discordant sounds. Fragments of melody, beginning of a musical phrase are drowned then emerge again, and disappear in the roar, screeching and squealing. To follow this "music" is difficult, to remember impossible. . . .

All this is not because the composer has no talent, not because of his inability to express simple and strong feeling in music. This music was deliberately turned inside out, so that nothing would recall classical operatic music, nothing would be commensurate with symphonic sonorities, with plain musical speech, accessible to all. This music which is based on the principle of negation of opera, similar to that governing the leftist art which denies simplicity in the theatre, denies realism, understandable imagery, natural sound of speech. It is the extension of Meyerhold's most objectionable traits into the domain of music in a highly enlarged form. It is leftist confusion instead of natural human music. The capacity of good music to stir the masses is sacrificed in favor of petty-bourgeois formalist attempts to create originality by means of cheap clowning. It is a game which may end very badly.

Many former RAPMists were ready to interpret this criticism as a return to their ideals. They were quickly shown this error. The criticism leveled against Shostakovich opened the most recent period of Soviet music which is marked by a campaign against formalism in art. The difficulty of defining formalist as a general tendency is a formidable obstacle in the way of a new synthesis. That it does not mean simplification of art was made plain to the doubters by a second blow which followed a week after the publication of the first article criticizing Shostakovich's "leftist" music. When Shostakovich's ballet *The Limpid Stream*, supposedly reflecting life on a collective farm, and certainly free from all "leftist monstrosities," was performed for the first time in Moscow, he was criticized for stylization and vulgarization. For Shostakovich himself this criticism was undoubtedly the greatest calamity that could befall him. But this criticism did not constitute an administrative decree, putting a stop to his musical career, as many observers hastily concluded. He is now composing a ballet and his fourth Symphony. The character of these new works will show whether he could recover from the blow. On March 25, 1936, Ivan Dzerzhinsky's opera *Quiet Flows the Don*, based on Sholokhov's novel, was produced in Moscow. In contrast to Shostakovich, Dzerzhinsky is distinguished for the extreme accessibility of his musical idiom, which at the same time, does not fall into vulgarization and oversimplification. The talk that Stalin had with the young composer at the time of production of his opera was interpreted as an indication of policy, but it is too early to judge the influence of these events on the future course of Soviet music.

Two other outstanding figures in Soviet composition should be mentioned in this brief survey of Soviet music. An important contribution to Soviet music was the change of residence of Serge Prokofiev, who moved to Moscow and became a full-fledged Soviet citizen in 1935. He first visited the Soviet Union in 1927, after ten years' absence from his native country. His music was "consonant" with the spirit of socialist realism as understood in the Soviet Union. Major modes, square rhythms, clear-cut musical sentences, straightforward melodies, free from all rhetoric, and yet having a lyric note of human emotion, found an instant echo among the musical masses of the Soviet Union. But he, too, was criticized for his occasional lapse into European subjectivism. His opus No. 72, an *Overture on Russian Themes*, is characteristic of his new style, one might say, national with socialist content, addressed directly to the masses and at the same time maintained on a high level of musical craftsmanship.

Serge Prokofiev is the product of the St. Petersburg–Petrograd–Leningrad tradition, rhythmical, dynamic, unprogrammatic. His antithesis is Miaskovsky, the product of Moscovite philosophic introspection, although he is, as is Prokofiev, a graduate of the Leningrad Conservatory. Miaskovsky is the only living composer who has written seventeen symphonies. This is a world record, all the more amazing since each symphony represents an inerasable chapter in Miaskovsky's musical biography. In No. 6, 1936, of the Soviet publication *Sovetskaia Muzyka*, Miaskovsky wrote an autobiographical sketch in which he analyzed his evolution from pre-revolutionary introspective individualism to the optimistic Soviet period. The Sixth Symphony is the most typical of his introspective moods, and the Twelfth, *Collective Farm Symphony*, the most typical of the Soviet period of his music.

To summarize the developments in Soviet music, the following table gives a brief statement of the three periods described above.

Evolutionary Chart of Soviet Music

First Period: Post-Scriabinesque enlargement of the tonal frame,
From the Revolution   heavily programmatic titles, nihilistic and anarchistic
to the NEP   decimation of musical form, interest in scientific and
November 7, 1917–   pseudo-scientific possibilities in music, early attempts
August 9, 1921   at the music of the masses, mostly in the loud
                               proclamatory odes and asymmetric marches.

Second Period: Penetration into the USSR of post-war western
From the NEP to the   European music, including jazz. Emergence of
dissolution of   expressionist drama, opera-bouffe, and satirical opera.
the RAPM   Serious study of atonality and polytonality. Machine
August 9, 1921–   music in both senses—music imitating the sound of the
April 23, 1932   machines, and music produced by the new machinery,
                               incorporated in the orchestral score. Construction of
                               electrical instruments. Ultra-chromatic music (quarter-
                               tones). Struggle between the tendency towards "music
                               for musicians only" and music for the masses. The rise of
                               the Russian Association of Proletarian Musicians (RAPM).

Third Period: Undirected musical activities after the dissolution of
From the dissolution   the RAPM. The rise of Shostakovitch. The acceptance
of RAPM to the   in the Soviet Union of jazz as a sui generis music of
present   the masses. The synthesis of the extreme westernizing
                               trend towards pure musical science and increasingly
                               dissonant texture on the one hand, and the extreme
                               tendency towards ultimate simplification. Return to
                               tonality, in a stylized form. The appearance of
                               Sovietskaia Musyka, an important monthly devoted to
                               the problems of musical policy and musical science.
                               Participation of Soviet composers in the festivals of the
                               International Society for Contemporary Music.
                               Evolution of the music of the masses in a folk style,
                               including national minorities. Gradual materialization
                               of socialist realism in music, increasingly national in
                               form. The sharp criticism of Shostakovitch at the begin-
                               ning of 1936, marking a new phase of Soviet music.

16. THE SOVIET OPERA

During a revolution, the theater reflects changing trends more rapidly than any other form of art. It is rather difficult to write a symphony that will express revolutionary ideas as such, but it is quite easy, by an appropriate selection of the subject, to create a revolutionary opera. To be sure, such an opera will be revolutionary only in subject matter, and the musical essence of it may be no different from any similar product.

The absurdity of adapting essentially old music to a revolutionary idea is illustrated by the attempts, made during the first years of the revolution, to write a new libretto, *The Decembrists*, to Meyerbeer's opera *The Huguenots*. Similar attempts were made to adjust Glinka's *Life for the Tsar*, but they were wisely abandoned. At the present time, a revival of this opera under the original title given to it by Glinka, *Ivan Sussanin*, is scheduled for production in November 1938 in Moscow.

The simple alternative to writing old-fashioned opera music under revolutionary titles, was writing futuristic music designed to break all ties with the traditional music of the pre-revolutionary times. This tendency, however, was never strong in Soviet Russia. In fact, urban music of this type was much more in vogue in the West, and Soviet musicians never accepted it as true music-of-the-revolution.

The natural course for Soviet opera to pursue was to use both revolutionary and historical subjects, and keep the musical idiom between the Scylla of Futurism and the Charybdis of over-simplification. Soviet opera has fluctuated between these two extremes to a considerable extent, until

---

Ch. 16: originally published in *Bulletin on the Soviet Union*, June 15, 1938.

it has found an approximate mean, somewhere in the vicinity of young Ivan Dzerzhinsky's operas, written to the novels of Sholokhov: *Quiet Flows the Don*, produced on October 22, 1935, in Leningrad, and on January 8, 1936, in Moscow, and *Soil Upturned*, produced on October 23, 1937, in Moscow. The criticism leveled against Shostakovich's opera *Lady Macbeth of Mtsensk* condemned its formalistic traits, and this condemnation swung the pendulum again towards over-simplification, although this tendency was soon checked.

Caricature is always a natural outlet during the times when an esthetic style is not yet settled. Early Soviet opera abounded in caricature against the Tsarist past. But the new musical masses craved positive entertainment, without extravaganza, and Verdi and Chaikovsky remained favorites while Soviet composers sought the true type of Soviet opera. So far, according to the admissions of Soviet music critics, no Soviet composer has written an opera comparable in popular appeal with *Eugene Onegin* or *Pique Dame*.

In film music and in mass songs, the composer Ivan Dunaevsky has achieved extraordinary success. His songs and marches are as popular in Soviet Russia as the greatest jazz hits are here. Among opera composers, perhaps only the "Sailor's Dance" from Glière's opera *Red Poppy* has attained such popularity.

The flourishing development of the opera among the national minorities of the Soviet Union has been a very interesting phenomenon. The Azerbaidzhan festival of music and dance, held in Moscow in recent months, showed what is done in music in the constituent republics. The highlight of the festival was the production of the opera *Ker-Ogly* ("A Blindman's Son"), by the Azerbaidzhan composer Uzeir Gadzhibekov. This had first been produced in Baku on January 13, 1937. At the end of the festival Gadzhibekov was awarded the title of People's Artist in recognition of his work.

Another recent production which aroused considerable interest was the opera of the Ukrainian composer Oles Chisko, *The Dreadnaught Potemkin*, based on the story of the rebellion in the Black Sea Fleet in 1905. This was produced in Leningrad on June 21, 1937, and in Moscow on January 5, 1938.

The opera *The Decembrists* by Yuri Shaporin has been completed, and its production is anticipated with great interest by Soviet musicians. Shaporin has a particular talent for vocal writing, and his musical style is deeply rooted in the finest traditions of Russian music. The scenario is written by the leading Soviet writer, Aleksei Tolstoi, which greatly enhances the value of the opera.

17. SOVIET COMPOSERS IN WAR AND REVOLUTION

Hitler's attack on the Soviet Union has stirred Soviet musicians to a new effort. On July 6, 1941, Reinhold Glière addressed a moving appeal to American musicians, in which he said:

> In this portentous hour, when savage Fascist bands have attacked my native land, I should like to greet all my colleagues beyond the ocean who are supporting the Soviet people in its struggle for humanity. We, Soviet composers, together with the people, are employing the medium of our art to help the Red Army wage its struggle against the brutal enemy. Together with the whole country, we have put ourselves on a war footing.
>
> I have written a marching song, *Hitler's End Will Come*. The composers Muradelli, Jatchaturyan, Miaskovsky and Shaporin have written similar songs. When we write these songs we are forging weapons for the front, weapons that will make it easier for the Red Army to fight and win . . . Until now we have been helping the Red Army with our art. But, at the call of our Government, we are ready at any moment to take a gun, and fight alongside the Red Army.

Glière is sixty-six years old. But Shostakovitch, who is only thirty-four, has volunteered, too, in the civilians' army. In his message he said: "I am ready to take up arms or sharpen my pen, and give all for the defense of our great fatherland, and for the destruction of Fascism."

The coming of the inevitable struggle was foreshadowed in Soviet music ever since the emergence of Hitler as a world menace. During the Spanish civil war, Soviet composers took part in the anti-Fascist struggle on the cultural front. Boris Mokroussov wrote a work for large orchestra, chorus and military band, entitled *Anti-Fascist Symphony*, which was produced in Moscow on August 1, 1937. Even children were aware of the political importance of the Spanish civil war, as a prelude to the general conflagration, and to the Fascist attack on the Soviet Union itself. In the interesting collection of compositions by Soviet children, compiled by Professor Alexander Goldenweiser of the Moscow Conservatory, and published in 1938, there is a march, "No pasarán," written by the thirteen-year-old Dima Tasin, and dedicated to the "heroic combatants of Republican Spain."

At the Moscow Festival of November 1939, the compositions that enjoyed the greatest success were Cantatas by Prokofieff, Shaporin and Koval. Prokofieff's Cantata was entitled *Alexander Nevsky*, and was expanded from the music to the film of the same name. Alexander Nevsky was the Russian prince who administered a tremendous defeat to the Teutonic Knights on the frozen surface of Lake Peipus, near Pskov, on April 5, 1242. Prokefieff completed the composition of the Cantata on February 7, 1939, and conducted it for the first time in Moscow on May 17, 1939. The dates are important: the film *Alexander Nevsky* and the cantata drawn from the music to the film were produced before the conclusion of the German-Soviet pact. But three months after the pact, on November 20, 1939, the Cantata was again produced in Moscow during the course of the Festival of Soviet music, as a gentle reminder to Hitler that, should he change his mind concerning the non-aggression pact, the rout suffered by the Teutonic invaders in 1242 might well be repeated seven centuries later, and in the same geographical position.

The second Cantata was *On the Field Kulikov* by the fifty-year-old Youri Shaporin. This Cantata glorified the Russian victory over the Mongol Chief Mamay in 1380. The theme of successful defense against the invader from whatever point of the compass he might come was forcefully demonstrated in these two Cantatas. The third Cantata was *Emelian Pugatchov*, by Marian Koval, a composer of the Ural extraction, born in 1907. This Cantata was of revolutionary rather than purely national significance, and it glorified the peasant rebel, Pugatchov, executed by Catherine the Great for impersonating her late husband, Peter III.

The three Cantatas were greatly praised by the Soviet press. A cartoon in the monthly *Soviet Music* represented Prokofieff, Shaporin, and Koval as the three legendary giants of the well-known painting by Vasnetzov, watching on the border of the Russian earth. The Seventh Symphony by Lev Knipper, played at the same Festival in Moscow, was significantly described as signalizing "the readiness of the Soviet people to answer, blow by blow, the agitation of warmongers."

Themes of social and national significance are the chief subjects of Soviet opera. Ivan Dzerzhinsky has been particularly successful as composer of operas on Soviet themes. His two operas, written to the epic novels by the Soviet writer Sholohov, *The Quiet Don River*, produced in Leningrad on October 23, 1935, and *Soil Uprooted*, produced in Moscow on October 23, 1937, enjoyed hundreds of performances in the Soviet Union. The musical idiom of Dzerzhinsky's operas is typically national, ultimately derived from Borodin and Moussorgsky, but the composing technique is modern including such devices as consecutive triads, polytonal scales, and free chromatic alterations of tonal chords.

Tijon Jrennikov is another important name in Soviet opera. Like Dzerzhinsky, he is a native of the Tambov district, where he was born in 1913 (Dzerzhinsky was born in 1909). Jrennikov's opera, *During the Storm*, produced in Moscow on October 28, 1939, is based on a story of the civil war, and Lenin appears on the stage in the second act. Like Dzerzhinsky's operas Jrennikov's opera is built according to the Italian model of separate arias, choruses, and orchestral interludes, rather than the Wagnerian principle of operatic continuity.

Not all Soviet works with a social program possess the musical contents corresponding to such a social program. One of the most interesting cases of self-adaptation to the new conditions is presented by Nicolas Miaskovsky, the sixty-year-old composer of twenty-one symphonies, all of which have been performed and published—a world record no doubt in modern times. In his autobiographical notes published in the Moscow monthly, *Soviet Music*, of June, 1936, he relates how painful was the process of his inner "switching over" to the Soviet themes. Miaskovsky is the product of the Moscow school before the World War, when pessimism and individualism were the chief factors in Russian literature, art, and music. In his Twelfth Symphony dedicated to the fifteenth anniversary of the Revolution, Miaskovsky tried to portray collectivization of the farms, but he acknowledged his failure in this attempt.

Dmitri Shostakovitch, who is acknowledged as the greatest talent produced by Soviet music, has from the very first proclaimed his dependence on social themes, but he has had difficulty in creating a work that would fittingly reflect the positive achievements of the Revolution. The sharp criticism of his satirical opera *Lady Macbeth of the District of*

Mzensk, voiced in the now famous article "Confusion instead of Music," published in *Pravda* on January 28, 1938, nearly wrecked his career. The blow was repeated in another article in *Pravda* condemning Shostakovitch for his frivolous treatment of the theme of the collective farm in his ballet *The Lucid Stream*. But Shostakovitch recovered successfully, and in his Fifth Symphony, first performed in Leningrad on November 21, 1937, he has created a work of epic dimensions, which aroused wide-spread admiration in the Soviet Union and abroad. Not only music critics, but Soviet writers, among them Alexei Tolstoy, and the aviator Gromov, who flew to California over the North Pole in 1937, came out with articles praising the new work. But it is interesting to note that Shostakovitch's most successful symphonies, the First and the Fifth, bear no program, while his Second Symphony, "October," dedicated to the tenth anniversary of the Revolution, and the Third Symphony, subtitled "May First," have completely faded from the repertoire after the initial performances. The Fourth Symphony was put in rehearsal by the Leningrad Philharmonic Orchestra in 1936, but was withdrawn from performance by Shostakovitch himself. After the pronounced success of the Fifth Symphony, Shostakovitch announced the composition of a new Symphony which was to be called *Lenin*, with a choral finale to the text by a Caucasian popular poet. But he apparently felt inadequate to the task, for when the Sixth Symphony was performed at the Moscow Festival on December 3, 1939, it contained only three movements without the Leninist program. But it is announced that the Seventh Symphony in which Shostakovitch is now engaged will definitely be a Lenin Symphony.

18. SOVIET MUSIC AT QUARTER-CENTURY MARK

In November, 1942, Soviet music celebrated its twenty-fifth anniversary amid the din of battle. But Soviet musicians, in the army, or on the artistic front, continue to serve their country. I have just received a letter from Gregory Schneerson, an eminent Moscow musicologist. He writes: "After a year in the army, I returned to Moscow. I can tell you that musical life here is flourishing; our composers are extremely active, and so are our musicologists. Our spirits are high, and our faith in victory is unshakable."

In the same mail I received from Moscow two volumes of a monumental *History of Music Culture* by Gruber. According to the printer's colophon, this edition was set in type in October 1941, at the time the Nazis were on the approaches to Moscow!

Leningrad was under siege for seventeen months until it was broken in January 1943, and the people of the city suffered untold privations, but there was always music in the city. Leningrad's great Philharmonic Orchestra was evacuated to Novosibirsk, but another orchestra was formed, and a special broadcast performance was given in August 1942 of the famous 'Leningrad' Symphony by its native son Dmitri Shostakovitch.

This Symphony of Shostakovitch has overshadowed all other music coming from Russia. The romance and the drama of its composer, serving as a fire warden at the Conservatory in a city under air attack; its illustrative power in pitching the Russian Freedom theme against the motive of the Nazi machine; the Victory sweep of the Finale: all this has made Shostakovitch's work pre-eminently a War Symphony. It has thundered all

---

Ch. 18: originally published in *Musical America*, February 10, 1943.

over the free world, and it has earned for Shostakovitch a place in history books.

Shostakovitch's Symphony is not the only example of Russia's continued activity in the domain of the arts. Even more astonishing is the productiveness of Nicolai Miaskovsky who, at the age of sixty-one, is the author of twenty-three symphonies, of which twenty-one have been already published and performed. Miaskovsky wrote his Twenty-second Symphony in a Moscow bomb-shelter, during Nazi air-raids. The Twenty-third Symphony was composed in Nalchik, a Caucasian town, later taken by the Nazis, but recaptured by the Russians during their winter offensive. Miaskovsky's Twenty-first Symphony has been heard in America; it is a deeply-felt, very Russian lyrical work, and it promises to be Miaskovsky's most enduring composition. Miaskovsky writes: "My music reflects but one thought; our heroes' blood has not been spilled in vain. We have saved the country! The Victory will be ours!"

The name of Prokofieff stands high in the annals of modern music. After fifteen years abroad, he went back to Russia in 1933. Since then, he has identified himself with the cause of Soviet music. His most popular work, the symphonic fairy-tale, *Peter and the Wolf*, was written in April 1936 for the Children's Theater in Moscow; its immediate object was to teach orchestral instruments to children: Peter was characterized by the strings, the bird by the flute, the duck by the oboe, the cat by the clarinet, the grandfather by the bassoon, the wolf by three French horns. But there was a political prophesy behind these fairy-tale characters: Peter, the Soviet partisan, in union with his friendly allies, captures the wolf-Hitler by exercise of wit and coordinated action.

After the "wolf" attack on Russia, Prokofieff joined other musicians in the task of writing war music. He wrote a symphonic suite in three movements entitled *1941* and a cantata, *Ballad of the Unknown Boy*. His recently completed opera, *War and Peace*, after Tolstoy's great novel, bears a significant parallel to the present war. Prokofieff has also written music to the film *Partisans of the Ukraine*, glorifying the heroes of the people's fight against the German occupants in 1918.

In his cantata *Alexander Nevsky*, produced at the Moscow Festival in November 1939, Prokofieff chose a historic subject, related to the present conflict, the rout of the Teutonic Knights, administered seven centuries ago (on April 5, 1242, to be exact) by the Russians to Hitler's arrogant forebears. Another cantata was presented at the same Festival: *On the Field Kulikov*, by Youri Shaporin, a composer of Prokofieff's own generation (he was born in 1889, Prokofieff in 1891). Its theme was the repulse of the Mongol chieftain Mamay in the year 1380. These "defense" cantatas were enthusiastically received in the Russian press. A cartoon, published in the monthly *Sovietskaya Musica*, pictures Prokofieff, Shaporin, and Marian Koval, the author of the cantata *Emelian Pugatchoff*, as three giants, on the lookout for the enemy, after the well-known painting by Vasnetzoff.

Russian composers of the old generation, Reinhold Glière, Alexander Goedicke, and Sergei Vassilenko, now in their late sixties, have joined in the common effort to build the "musical front." Immediately after Hitler's assault on Russia in the summer of 1941, Glière addressed a message to American musicians, in which he said: "We, Soviet composers, are employing the medium of our art, to help the Red Army wage its struggle against the brutal enemy." Glière himself wrote a marching song, 'Hitler's End Will Come.'

Even before the outbreak of the present war, Russian musicians fought Fascism through the medium of music. Thus, Boris Mokroussoff wrote a work for large orchestra, chorus, and military band, entitled *Anti-Fascist Symphony*. It was produced in Moscow on August 1, 1937. Even children contributed to the common effort. In an interesting collection of pieces written by Soviet children between the ages of eleven and fifteen, and published in 1938, there is a march, 'No pasarán,' written by the thirteen-year-old Dima Tasin, and dedicated to the "heroic fighters of Republican Spain."

Soviet music comprises manifold tendencies: lyrical and gay; conservative and advanced in idiom and technique; distinctly Russian, or reflective of Caucasian, Turkmenian, or Kirghiz folklore. The Soviet Union is a federation of republics of many races; Soviet music absorbs these racial elements and re-creates them in an art product. Often, a Russian composer is delegated to gather melodic materials in another part of the Soviet Union. Thus, Glière wrote an opera based on the folklore of Azerbeidzhan; Mossoloff, the author of the famous realistic piece *Iron Foundry*, with a steel sheet in the orchestration, went to Turkestan in quest of native songs, which he later transcribed in an artistic form; Maximilian Steinberg, Rimsky-Korsakoff's son-in-law, pictures the Turkestan-Siberian railroad in his symphony *Turksib*. Michael Gnessin and Alexander Krein cultivate Jewish musical lore. Aram Khatchaturian, the rising star of Soviet music, writes in the tradition of Armenian melos.

Up to the outbreak of the present war, festivals devoted to the folk arts of the federated republics of the Soviet Union were given annually in Moscow, and were attended by large audiences, including Government officials. A ten-day Festival of Buriat-Mongol Art was given in Moscow in October 1940, and presented a Mongol musical drama, *Bair*. Festivals of indigenous theatrical and musical arts of Azerbeidzhan, Turkestan, Kirghizia, and Soviet Armenia were staged in previous years. These Festivals revealed a hitherto unknown source of folk art, and gave an impetus to a serious study of new national treasures.

Symphony and opera dominate the creative field of Soviet composers. As shown by the example of Shostakovitch, a Soviet composer can achieve popular success by symphonies and chamber music quite as much as by songs and marches. On the debit side of Shostakovitch's balance sheet, as far as public and official recognition is concerned, stand his operas and ballets. Shostakovitch's fall from grace after the Moscow production of his opera *Lady Macbeth of the District of Mzensk* and the ballet *The Sparkling Brook* is a matter of Soviet history. And Shostakovitch's earliest theatrical work, *The Nose*, written after Gogol's story of a nose detached from the face of a petty Government official to live a life of independence, was never revived after an experimental production in 1930. Curiously enough, it was Shostakovitch's "absolute" music, the First and Fifth Symphonies, and the Quintet, which were most successful, not the programmatic 'October' or 'May First Symphony.' And we must not forget that, though his celebrated Seventh is often referred to as the 'Leningrad' Symphony, no such subtitle appears on the score, which bears the opus number 60, and nothing else.

The most successful opera composer in Soviet Russia is Ivan Dzerzhinsky, a young man, born in Tambov on April 8, 1909. For the librettos of his operas he selected the famous novels by Sholohoff, dealing with the civil war in the Cossack region. After the Moscow production of Dzerzhinsky's first opera, *Quiet Flows the Don*, in 1936, he received the commendation of Stalin himself, who came to hear it. This commendation was particularly significant for it followed shortly after a rebuke to Shostakovitch for *Lady Macbeth*. The second opera by Dzerzhinsky, *Soil Uprooted*, produced in Moscow on Oct. 23, 1937, enjoyed a similarly favorable reception from the public and the critics. During the present war Dzerzhinsky wrote a one-act opera, *The Blood of the People*, for a broadcast performance. Dzerzhinsky's music follows the characteristically Russian

operatic tradition, particularly in lusciously harmonious choruses and melodious arias. But he treats these elements with terse diatonic dissonance.

A composer whose name is closely associated with Dzerzhinsky's is
Tikhon Khrennikoff. He was born on June 10, 1913, in Eletz, in the same
province as Dzerzhinsky (a Soviet cartoon presents him with Dzerzhinsky
as two partisans playing the accordion). Khrennikoff's opera *During the
Storm*, was produced in Moscow on October 28, 1939. His Symphony, a
very successful work, has been heard in the United States.

It is interesting to note that many operas by Soviet composers are
written on the subjects of the Revolution and the War. In Russia, the
immediacy of events does not prevent the presentation of these events on
the stage with familiar characters from the news columns appearing as
actors and singers. Incidentally, the established usage of Soviet opera is to
characterize the enemy musically by the whole-tone scale, and augmented triads. Is it a coincidence that the same progressions are also used
in the incidental music in Hollywood's moving pictures, whenever a sinis-
ter personage appears on the screen?

The name of Aram Khatchaturian is beginning to acquire more and
more significance on the Soviet scene. He was born in Tiflis on June 6,
1903, a son of an Armenian bookbinder, went to Moscow at the age of
nineteen, and only then began to study music. In 1934 he wrote a symphony. Its melodic structure suggests the scales of the East.
Khatchaturian has also written a concerto for piano and orchestra, and a
violin concerto, both remarkable by the freshness and brilliance of
melodic and instrumental treatment. He is now at work on an oratorio,
Heroic Moscow. Shostakovitch writes this about Khatchaturian's symphonic *Poem about Stalin* ("Sovietskoye Iskusstvo," December 2, 1938):
"The most interesting among new Soviet orchestral works is undoubtedly
Khatchaturian's 'Poem about Stalin.' The composer has embodied in a
musical form the people's thoughts of the great leader. The poem amazes
by its ideological depth, by the power of its inspiration, and the brilliance
of its technique."

Dmitri Kabalevsky (born in Leningrad on Dec. 30, 1904) is the
author of three symphonies in a sonorous Russian manner. He is now at
work on an opera, *At the Approaches to Moscow*. Another Soviet symphonist, whose music has not as yet reached America, is Leo Knipper
(born in Tiflis on Dec. 16, 1898). He has composed seven symphonies, of
which the last was characterized at its performance at the Moscow

Festival in 1939, as a "solemn warning to warmongers of Russia's readiness to beat back the enemy."

Soviet music has its neo-classicist in the person of Michael Starokadomsky (born on June 13, 1901, in Brest-Litovsk), who writes in modern counterpoint while preserving the form of the eighteenth-century classics. But his opera and oratorio are written on Soviet themes.

To these names should be added Marian Koval (born in Moscow, Aug. 17, 1907), author of the cantata *Emelian Pugatchoff*; Vissarion Shebalin, a romantic symphonist (born on June 11, 1902, in Omsk); Alexander Veprik, a symphonic and choral composer (born on July 23, 1899, in Balta); Vassili Shirinsky (born in Ekaterinoslav, on Jan. 17, 1901), a modernist composer of chamber music; Boris Shekhter (born in Odessa on Jan, 20, 1900), who has specialized in the music of Soviet Turkmenia; Valery Zhelobinsky (born at Tambov, on March 12, 1912), whose piano Preludes are widely played; Vano Muradelli (born at Gori, in the Caucasus, on April 6, 1908), a Georgian composer, author of a symphony; Victor Belyi (born in Berditchev, on Jan. 14, 1904), who is now writing a choral symphony entitled *The Red Square, Nov. 7, 1941*; Anatol Alexandroff (born in Moscow, on May 25, 1888), author of numerous piano pieces; Samuel Feinberg (born in Odessa, on May 26, 1890), a composer-pianist; Boris Liatoshinsky (born in Kiev, on Jan. 4, 1895), a Ukrainian opera composer; Leonid Polovinkin (born in Kurgan, on Aug. 13, 1894), composer of brilliant piano pieces; Gabriel Popov (born in Novotcherkassk, on Sept. 12, 1904), a Soviet modernist; and the Krein family of musicians: Alexander Krein (born in Gorki, on Oct. 20, 1883), known chiefly by his symphonic poem *Lenin*; his elder brother, Gregory Krein (born in Gorki, on April 15, 1880), who has written music on Hebrew themes, and Gregory's son, Julian (born in Moscow, on March 5, 1913), a precocious romantic talent, who began to compose at the age of eleven. Boris Asafiev (born in Leningrad, on July 29, 1884) is a prolific composer of ballet music, who is also known as an astute critic, writing under the nom de plume, Igor Glebov.

Michael Gnessin (born in Rostov, on January 23, 1883) writes dramatic music based on Jewish folklore. Maximilian Steinberg (born in Vilna, on July 4, 1883) is the teacher of a generation of Soviet composers, as well as a symphonist in his own right.

Nina Makarova (born at Yourin, on Aug. 12, 1908) represents Russia's musical womanhood. She excels in impressionist piano pieces, but has also written a symphony.

In the field of popular music, the best known name is that of Isaac Dunaevsky (born in Lokhvitza, on Jan. 30, 1900), whose vigorous marches and sentimental songs enjoy great success in Russia. That popular music is not unappreciated in the Soviet Union, is demonstrated by the award to Dunaevsky of the highest Soviet decoration, the Order of Lenin.

The Red Army is marching on to the music of Soviet composers, and it sings the heartwarming songs created by Russia's melodic genius. In war, in peace, in constructive work, Russian music plays a great, tangible part.

19. THE CHANGING STYLE OF SOVIET MUSIC

The study of Soviet music presents a unique problem. For the first time in history, the aesthetics of an art has been conditioned by the political and national ideology of a secular power. The academic matters of harmony and tonality have been subjected to administrative rulings, and all-powerful leaders of the state have become involved in technical discussions of a politically desirable style of composition.[1]

Schematically, the evolution of Soviet music may be divided into three phases: (1) 1917–1927, when radical Russian musicians attempted to create a new revolutionary art on the ruins of the old; (2) 1927–1936, signalized by the emergence of so-called proletarian music; (3) 1936–1950,

---

1. An interesting precedent was the administrative pressure on Russian musicians by the Czarist government in the wake of the abortive Revolution of 1905. *The Musical Courier* ran this editorial in 1906 commenting on the Russian situation in music: "Moscow and St. Petersburg are very far from New York, and it is seldom that musical happenings travel over the Russian border far enough to be caught up in the maelstrom which sweeps all such matters toward this office. *The Musical Courier* has tried several times, experimentally, to establish a correspondent in Russia, but his letters were censored so severely that they were of no use to us. Conservatories, orchestras, teachers, composers—nearly everything musical in Russia is in some way connected with the Government, and is therefore protected from criticism outside of Russia, and even from comment. The article which we print in this issue will surprise the Russians, for it contains the details of a row of which only the merest echoes had previously been allowed to penetrate into the pagan press of Europe and America. We are sending a marked copy of this issue of *The Musical Courier* to His Majesty the Czar, with a subscription blank and our advertising rates enclosed. Is *knout* that a good idea?"

Ch. 19: this paper was delivered in New York on December 27, 1949 at the fifteenth annual meeting of the American Musicological Society and published in its fall 1950 *Journal*.

when cosmopolitan modernism and proletarian sectarianism were abandoned, and the ideal of Socialist Realism, "an art national in form and socialist in content," in Stalin's phrase, became the approved slogan.

It is natural that in the first flush of the Revolution extreme tendencies should have prevailed in the arts as well as in politics. In 1920 the Russian musicologist, Arseny Avraamov, wrote a letter to the Department of Education, proposing the confiscation and destruction of all pianos as a step towards the abolition of tempered pitch. Others urged the junking of stringed instruments as well. New revolutionary music, they argued, could not be created by "scraping dried cows' guts with horsetail hair."

In the early period of the Revolution, Russian composers were urged to glorify in their music the noises of the factory and the hubbub of the city streets. It was to be the music of the machines, the music of the working proletariat. Realistic imitation of industrial noises was applied by Alexander Mossolov in his ballet, *Zavod* (1927), which included in the orchestration a sheet of steel, producing overpowering clatter. In the "October" Symphony of Shostakovitch, there is a part for a factory whistle. To imitate the sound of a steam engine, Julius Meitus, a Ukrainian composer, includes in the score of his ballet, *Dnieprostroy*, a contraption consisting of three tin cans tied to a stick, and filled with dried peas.

The musical ideology of the Russian modernists in the early years of the Revolution is illustrated by this statement in the pamphlet, *October and New Music*, published by the Leningrad Association of Contemporary Music in 1927:

> What is closer to the proletariat, the pessimism of Tchaikovsky and the false heroics of Beethoven, a century out of date, or the precise rhythms and excitement of Deshevov's *Rails*?

Rails by Deshevov

During the playing of Beethoven, the workers were utterly bored, and patiently, with polite endurance, waited for the music to end. But contemporary Soviet compositions aroused contagious emotion among the audience. Proletarian masses, for whom machine oil is mother's milk, have a right to demand music consonant with our epoch, not the music of the bourgeois salon which belongs in the era of the horse and buggy and of Stephenson's early locomotive.

The urge towards musical innovation in Soviet Russia produced at least one invention of major importance. In August 1922, Leon Theremin (b. 1896), a Russian scientist and amateur violoncellist, gave the first demonstration, at the Technological Institute of Moscow, of his electronic instrument, later named Thereminovox, in which sound is produced by the movement of the hand towards and away from a metal rod thus generating varying electromagnetic waves translated into sound vibrations. Theremin worked in America from 1928 to 1938, and then went back to Russia. He was never heard of again, and articles on electronic musical instruments published since in the Soviet press studiously avoid the mention of his name, although the undoubted priority of his invention compared with similar instruments produced in other countries ought to be a source of pride to Russian science.

The revolutionary drive for emancipation from all "bosses," in economy as well as in art, led to the formation of a conductorless orchestra, the *Persymphans* (abbreviation of the words First Symphonic Ensemble), established at Moscow in 1922. It flourished for five seasons, during which classical and modern works were presented. Then, with the dimming of the early ardor for collective music making, the *Persymphans* was disbanded, and the conventional conducted performances were restored.

The sociological significance of conductorless orchestras was pointed out by a representative of the Soviet Government in a speech made during the first *Persymphans* season:

The First Symphonic Ensemble has dispensed with the conductor, and thus demonstrated that even in such a complex undertaking as the interpretation of a musical work, individual knowledge contributed by the leader can be replaced by a collective interpretation. It is particularly dear to Soviet listeners, because it confirms the power of collectivism as a guiding principle in the revolutionary transformation of the social and economic system.

Theoretical work in music emphasized the scientific aspect of the art. An Institute of Musical Science was organized in Moscow on September 25, 1921. In Leningrad, George Rimsky-Korsakov, grandson of the composer, established a Society of Quarter-Tone Music, which was inaugurated on May 5, 1923. Characteristic of the prevalent modern tendencies was the formation in the 1920s of a music publishing house *Tritone*, so named after the interval of the augmented fourth, fundamental in atonal composition.

The pro-modern trend in Soviet music was bitterly opposed by the Production Collective of Composers (PROCOLL) which was founded in Moscow on April 1, 1925. Even more violently anti-modern was the position of the Russian Association of Proletarian Musicians (RAPM), organized in 1924. In its declaration of aims, the RAPM stated:

> The brilliant development of musical culture of the ruling classes was made possible by their possession of material and technical tools of musical production. As a ruling class, the *bourgeoisie* exerts great influence upon all strata of the population, systematically poisoning the worker's mind. In the field of music, this process follows the lines of religious and petty-bourgeois aesthetics, and recently, the erotic dance music of contemporary capitalist cities (fox trot, jazz, etc.).

American jazz was denounced in the RAPM publication, *Za Proletarskuyu Musiku* (For Proletarian Music), in its issue of March 1930:

> The new American dance music comes to us from a country where slavery was, and still is, widely practiced, with all the physical and spiritual demoralization that goes with it. Negro slaves once were private property of the feudal plantation owner. Now Negro slavery is nominally abolished, but in actual life it continues to exist. But America has slaves among the whites as well. A vast number of unemployed workers is concentrated in America's industrial cities. A considerable portion of these men includes former small businessmen gone bankrupt, declassed members of the aristocracy, and even intelligentsia. . . . Here, among these slaves of America, was born the new American dance music. It expresses the most loathsome characteristics of slavery, the mockery at one's own subhuman standard of living, at one's own degradation. American dance music is cultivated in the interests of capitalism. Its aim is to make workers weak and submissive, to

divert them from the task of rising and seizing the factories. The revolutionary spirit of the masses is dulled by American dance music.

Jazz was later accepted in Soviet Russia as a type of city folklore. There was even an attempt made to create Soviet jazz, of which "Song about Love" by Dunayevsky is a fair example.

Soviet Jazz: *Song About Love* by Dunayevsky

With the advent of the musical cold war in 1946 and 1947, jazz was once more relegated to the realm of forbidden art. In the July 1948 issue of the leading Soviet music periodical, *Sovietskaya Musica*, Gregory Schneerson, formerly a cautious friend of Western music, let go a terrific blast at American jazz. Describing a broadcast of the Voice of America, he writes:

> Heart-rending animal cry of trumpets and trombones in the highest register fills the air. It is the cry of a baboon, the roaring of a wild boar. It is the sound of the jungle which has nothing in common with human speech. . . . There is no sign of melody, not a single living song inflection. It is a rhythmically organized chaos of deliberately ugly neuropathological sounds. . . . Thus every night, propagandists of the Voice of America regale us with samples of American music, apparently convinced that such musical seasoning of the verbal propaganda of "Americanism" will attract the greatest number of listeners.

The RAPM attacked also the domestic manifestation of the bourgeois spirit in music. In an interesting brochure, *Protiv Nepmanskoy Musiky* (Against Nepmen's Music, Nep being the abbreviation of New Economic Policy of the 1920s), published in Moscow in 1930, the author castigates gypsy songs once so popular in Russia, calling them "propaganda of prostitution." Quoting a line from a popular song, "You ask me for kisses, but

I am so tired of love," he scornfully asks: "What type of woman would regard love as work causing fatigue?"

In another pamphlet published by the RAPM in 1931, entitled *Nevinnaya Propaganda Imperialisma* (Innocent Propaganda of Imperialism, with the word "innocent" put in ironic quotation marks), the author, one G. Krasnukha, exposes the imperialistic design implicit in the ballet suite, *In a Persian Market* by the English composer Albert Ketelbey. He writes:

> The music of Ketelbey's suite is reduced to a common fox trot tempo, in the manner of pseudo-Negro dance music born in the American cocktail lounge. It is clear that this music has nothing in common with the Persian people, but is the manifestation of the degraded primitive psyche of the *bourgeoisie*.... In fact, the suite *In a Persian Market* had its "immaculate conception" in imperialistic colonial England. The composer's intention is to convince the listener that all's well in the colonies where beautiful women and exotic fruits mature together, where beggars and rulers are friends, where there are no imperialists, no restive proletarians.

The musical ideology of the RAPM demanded simple harmonic writing and symmetric rhythm. Among classical composers, the RAPM accepted Beethoven and Moussorgsky and the Russian National School. It rejected Wagner and the entire modern school, Russian and Western. The RAPM urged Soviet composers to write mass songs and cultivate ensembles of folk instruments.

It had seemed that the RAPM was going to assume absolute power of style dictation over Soviet music. Then, without warning, on April 23, 1932, it was dissolved by a decree of the Soviet government, along with the similarly "proletarian" organizations in the fields of literature and art. To Soviet composers it was a day of liberation from an oppressive dogma. One composer gleefully exclaimed: "Now I can write music in three-four time," in allusion to the insistence of the RAPM theorists that march-time, as a natural rhythm of the masses should be exclusively cultivated in proletarian society.

A new slogan was launched to replace the discredited concept of proletarian music. It was Socialist Realism. The ingredient of Socialism in this formula emphasized the musical representation of Soviet life. The concept of Realism opposed the individualistically romantic and religiously mystical music, while rejecting literal musical representation,

which was defined, derogatorily, as Naturalism. The failure to meet these
definitions by Dmitri Shostakovitch, in his opera *Lady Macbeth of the
District of Mzensk*, brought on his head a stormy rebuke in an unsigned,
and therefore all the more authoritative article, entitled "Sumbur Vmesto
Musiky" (Bedlam Instead of Music), which appeared in *Pravda* on
January 28, 1936. The article said in part:

> Our music critics swear by the name of Socialist Realism. In Shostakovitch's
> opera, we are served the grossest kind of naturalism. The predatory mer-
> chant's wife, coming into possession of wealth and power through murder,
> is portrayed as a victim of the old regime. . . . The music quacks, grunts,
> growls, and chokes in its attempt to represent the amatory episodes as nat-
> uralistically as possible. "Love" is smeared all over the place in the most vul-
> gar manner. The merchant's double bed occupies the center of the stage,
> and on it all so-called problems are solved. . . . Shostakovitch's opera enjoys
> great success with the bourgeois audiences abroad. Is it because its fidgety,
> shrieking, neurotic music tickles the depraved tastes of the *bourgeoisie*?

Shostakovitch had hardly recovered from the shock of this assault
when a new article appeared in *Pravda* of February 6, 1936. Under the
title "Baletnaya Falsh" (False Ballet), it attacked Shostakovitch's ballet
Svetlyi Ruchei (The Limpid Brook), this time for the frivolous treatment
of a peculiarly Soviet theme, since the ballet represented the life of a fic-
tional *Kolkhoz* (collective farm). Thus Shostakovitch stood condemned
for failing on both the "socialist" and the "realist" counts.

After this rebuke Shostakovitch abandoned the composition of operas
and ballets and turned to symphonic works. His vindication came in 1937
with the Fifth Symphony, which was hailed as a great achievement, not
only by professional critics but by non-musicians as well. "Glory be to our
people which produces such talents as Shostakovitch!" exclaimed Alexei
Tolstoy. The aviator Gromov, hero of the non-stop flight to America over
the North Pole, wrote that Shostakovitch's Fifth Symphony is "conceived
in the true spirit of Russian symphonism," and that "it holds the audience
in a state of joyful tension."

After an indifferent reception of Shostakovitch's Sixth Symphony
came the sensational success of his Seventh, often referred to as the
"Leningrad" Symphony, because it was composed partly during the siege
of Leningrad in September 1941. Its first movement depicts, in sonata

form, the struggle against the Germans who are represented by the second subject, a puny march-like tune. The first subject, a broad Russian theme, drowns out the German march until nothing is left of it but a muted trumpet accompanied by a military drum.

The musical biography of Shostakovitch is a perfect mirror of the changing policies in Soviet music. Shostakovitch is the product of Soviet life; at the time of the Revolution he was only eleven years old. His talent was precocious. He wrote his first symphony at the age of 18. Early in his career, Shostakovitch expressed the belief that satire and humor are the natural forms of expression for a Soviet composer. In this style he wrote his first opera, *The Nose*, to the story by Gogol, dealing with a Czarist army major whose nose vanished from the surface of his face when he fell asleep in a barber's chair. The opera opens with a gigantic orchestral sneeze in major sevenths. It contains some fanciful orchestration (the strokes of the razor are imitated by high harmonics in the double basses), and some extraordinary canonic constructions. In one scene, eight janitors sing eight different advertisements in inverted canon at the minor second.

Opening Sneeze in *The Nose* by Shostakovitch

In another work, *The Golden Age*, a ballet portraying life in capitalist society, Shostakovitch uses the tool of musical satire to poke fun at the Geneva Disarmament Conference in a sharply dissonant "Polka."

The musical language of Shostakovitch in his early works is the quintessence of Soviet modernism. It cannot be said that Shostakovitch created this new musical idiom. The seeds of Russian modernism were planted long before the Revolution in the chromaticism of Scriabin, in the sophisticated vulgarity of young Prokofiev, and in the atonal music of such composers as Nicolai Roslavetz. When the Soviet government assumed power in November 1917, Russian music was characterized by the following usages, which remained also characteristic of Soviet music during the first decade of the Revolution:

Harmony: ninth and eleventh chords, with alterations resulting in quasi-polytonal combinations; protracted pedal-points; a pronounced tendency towards the flatting of the secondary degrees in major scales, leading to the formation of a curious major-minor tonality.

Counterpoint: extremely meager in polyphonic substance, and reduced mostly to free imitation.

Melody: conditioned by harmonic progressions, tending towards the minor mode, and abounding in suspensions and appoggiaturas, mostly falling a semitone down.

Instrumentation: full and rich, with frequent doubling of instruments; universal predilection for full orchestra rather than chamber combinations.

Form: cyclic construction, with a more or less complete return of the original statement at the end of a work.

One of the most important formative factors in Soviet music was the influence exercised on young Soviet musicians by Serge Prokofiev (b. 1891). Politically, his position was peculiar. He left Russia in 1918, traveled widely in Europe and America, and associated himself with the Russian ballets of Diaghilev in Paris. In 1933 he decided to return to Russia, where he was acclaimed as a truly Soviet talent. Prokofiev's natural preference for vigorous march-time rhythms fitted well into the pattern of Soviet musical life. His melodic lyricism, touched with irony, suited the mood of sophisticated neo-romanticism which replaced Russian rhapsodic sentimentalism of the pre-Revolutionary years. His harmonic devices and melodic clichés were unconsciously adopted by many Soviet composers. A particularly interesting device is the use of displaced tonality, wherein a sudden cadence shifts the key chromatically a semitone up or down. Thus, in Prokofiev's *Peter and the Wolf*, "a symphonic fairy tale" written in 1936 for the Children's Theater in Moscow, an ascending C major scale shifts to C-sharp minor by equating the tonic C to B-sharp. Then the C-sharp minor scale is led back to C major by a similar procedure. Another example of such displaced tonality is the sudden modulation from B-flat major to A major in the main subject of Prokofiev's March for band, Opus 99.

Displaced Tonality: *Peter and the Wolf* by Prokofiev

Displaced Tonality: *March for Band*, Opus 99 by Prokofiev

Displaced Tonality: *Lady Macbeth from the District of Mzensk* (Act II, scene 4) by Shostakovitch

The technique of displaced tonality is effectively used by Prokofiev by alternating two keys whose tonics are at the distance of a semitone from each other. An example of this usage is the "March to the Zoo" from *Peter and the Wolf*, in which D-flat major is alternated with the second inversion of the C major chord serving as a functional dominant.

Alternating Chords: *Peter and the Wolf* by Prokofiev

Prokofiev's cultivation of plagal cadences, with their implicit melodic progression of a falling fourth, imparts a Russian flavor to his music. But Prokofiev's Russianism is stylized, and he never resorts to actual quotation of Russian folk songs. Meeting the demands of growing nationalism, Prokofiev increased the amount of Russian-inspired melodic elements in his later works. Concomitantly, his harmonic style mellowed considerably, the tonal elements coming to the fore and the contrapuntal scheme being reduced to a basic two-part construction. His rhythmic style, with its characteristic percussiveness, has remained his permanently distinctive trait.

Parallel triadic progressions, and parallel seventh chords along the diatonic degrees of the scale, are widely used by Soviet composers. This usage, adopted in Western music as soon as the academic taboos against consecutive fifths were lifted, is not a specific Soviet development. But it suited the diatonic language of Russian music better than ultra-chromatic Western idioms, and was easily assimilated by Soviet composers.

Parallel Triad Harmonies: Overture from *Podniataya Tselina* (Ploughed-up Fallowland) by Dzerzhinsky

Parallel Seventh-Chord Harmonies: *Sonatina for Piano* by Kabalevsky

The problem of bringing Soviet music up to date while keeping its idiom understandable to the masses gave the greatest concern to Russian musicians. Composers of the older generation solved it by "switching over to Soviet thematics," to use the catch phrase of the time. They adopted revolutionary subject matter in their operas and symphonies while retaining the old-fashioned harmonic style of their music. Thus Reinhold Glière (b. 1875) wrote the ballet *Red Poppy* to the story of Soviet sailors' visit in revolutionary China. Sergei Vasilenko (b. 1872) composed a *Red Army Rhapsody*. Maximilian Steinberg (1883–1946), pupil and son-in-law of Rimsky-Korsakov, contributed the *Turkish Symphony*, depicting the building of a new railroad connecting Turkestan and Siberia.

Nikolai Miaskovsky (1881–1950), the composer of 26 symphonies—a record number for any composer since Haydn's time—tells of the difficulty of adjusting his style in his revealing "Autobiographical Notes," published in *Sovietskaya Musica* of June 1936:

When the first news of the plan of collectivization of rural agriculture reached me, I decided to write a symphony that would reflect the struggle for the new social order in the villages. But my Symphony did not come off as I had planned. It was schematic. I failed to find an adequate form for the last movement, which expressed my basic idea in a merely external manner, without inner conviction. . . . It was not the language I was seeking, not the language of a contemporary artist. What that language should be, I do not know, and have no formula for it. Neither Russian folk music nor our city songs can provide the material for the musical idiom of Socialist Realism.

In their desire to modernize and Sovietize the old operas, Soviet producers hit on the simple device of repainting the librettos in red. Meyerbeer's *Huguenots*, a constant favorite in Russia, became *The Decembrists*, with the action switched to the unsuccessful palace revolution of December 1825 in St. Petersburg. The action of Puccini's opera *La Tosca* was transferred to the time of the Paris Commune. In the Soviet version, the heroine became a Communarde who kills General Gallifet, the leader of the anti-Communard forces. It mattered little to the writers of the new libretto that the real General Gallifet survived the Commune by nearly 40 years, dying of natural causes in 1909.

The most spectacular changes were attempted in the libretto of Gounod's *Faust*, with Mephistopheles presented as a positive character fighting against the moral prudery of organized religion. He saves Marguerite from perdition by explaining to her the essential biological equality of legitimate and illegitimate children. Both Faust and Marguerite then return to useful work, Faust to teaching, and Marguerite to spinning, while their child is taken care of by the state.

In the meantime, new operas on revolutionary subjects were written and produced in rapid succession. Realism, whether Socialist or not, was the keynote of these new operas. It reaches its extreme point in the opera *Battleship Potemkin* by Oles Tchishko, in the episode of the mutiny when the sailors refuse to eat borsht with rotten meat. "We won't eat borsht with worms," cry the sailors in a chorus, with the harmony chromatically modulating from B-flat minor to C major, via the diminished seventh chord.

We   won't   eat   wor-my   borsht!

Chorus from *Battleship Potemkin* by Tchishko

Operatic journalism in Soviet librettos is further exemplified by a scene in the *Podniataya Tselina* (Ploughed-up Fallowland) by Ivan Dzerzhinsky, in which a member of a collective farm reads aloud Stalin's article in *Pravda*. Dzerzhinsky, who belongs entirely to the Soviet generation (he was only eight years old at the time of the Revolution) came closest to the official ideal of socialist realism in Soviet opera. When his opera *Tikhii Don* (The Quiet Don River) was produced in 1936, Stalin, who attended the performance, publicly commended Dzerzhinsky for his treatment of a Soviet subject. This episode occurred only a few days before the publication in *Pravda* of the article denouncing Shostakovitch. Ironically enough, the score of Dzerzhinsky's opera was dedicated to Shostakovitch. Dzerzhinsky declared in an article published in the *Leningradskaya Pravda* of January 24, 1936: "Comrade Stalin said that the time was ripe for the creation of a classical Soviet opera. He pointed out that such an opera should be emotionally inspiring, and that melodic inflections of folk music should be widely utilized. The music ought to make use of all the latest devices of the musical technique, but its idiom must be close to the masses, clear and approachable."

Dzerzhinsky's harmonic style is characterized by triadic parallelism, with modulatory shifts along the degrees of the diatonic scale. His melodies are broadly Russian in their inflection, and his rhythmic formula often cuts the phrasal period short, resulting in momentary metric changes. This method, a compromise between the academism of Russian music of the turn of the century and incipient modernism, was independently arrived at in the works of several other Soviet composers of the younger generation. Among them Tikhon Khrennikov (b. 1913) was successful in approximating this desirable formula in songs, symphonies and operas, so much so that he later emerged as a commanding influence in shaping the political destinies of Soviet composers.

Among other names prominent in Soviet music to be mentioned are Leo Knipper (b. 1898), composer of nine symphonies in a stylized Russian manner; Vissarion Shebalin (1902), a symphonic composer of advanced ideas; Dmitri Kabalevsky (b. 1904), who has written some effective piano music; Gabriel Popov (b. 1904), one of the early Soviet modernists; and Michael Starokadomsky (b. 1901), the only Soviet composer who adopted a neo-classical style. One of the strongest talents among Soviet composers is Aram Khatchaturian (b. 1903). The principal distinction of his music is its colorful melo-rhythmic complex, tinged with the oriental character of his native Armenia. Among women composers the most alluring is Nina Makarova, whose musical miniatures have an impressionistic touch. She the wife of Khatchaturian.

By 1936, the problem of a desirable musical style in Russia was clearly outlined, even though the semantics of the various catch phrases and slogans were too elastic for Soviet composers to follow. Summarizing the state of music during the period of Soviet music which saw the demise of militant proletarianism and the denunciation of operatic naturalism and modernism of all kinds, we find the following conditions:

Harmony: emphasis on tonality; cadential forms of displaced tonality wherein the final tonic is a semitone higher or lower than the key of the beginning; parallel triadic progressions along the diatonic scale as a means of instant modulation; employment of dissonances of considerable harshness, mostly as a result of chromatic voice leading in divergent motion; non-tonal diatonic passing notes in scale passages producing the effect of mild atonality within the essential tonal framework.

Counterpoint: scant development of formal polyphony; continued absence of fugal writing.

Melody: considerably chromatic in instrumental writing, and broadly diatonic and folk-song-like in the vocal line.

Instrumentation: return to the orthodox orchestration of old Russian symphonic music, with a considerable role given to the lowest and the highest registers, such as the bass tuba and the piccolo.

Form: persistence of cyclic constructions, with elaborate codas in larger forms; preludes and sonatas (without formal development) preferred in instrumental works; revival of program music, often with political connotations.

Early Soviet music was essentially Russian music. With the spread of musical education in the Soviet Union, the minority republics began to cultivate music of their own, largely derived from folk songs. In order to stimulate artistic development in these republics, the Union of Soviet Composers assigned their members to write operas and symphonic works based on native folklore. The Ukrainian composer, Boris Liatoshinsky, wrote an opera *Shchors* named after and based on the life of a Ukrainian revolutionary commander. Glière wrote the opera *Shakh-Senem* on Caucasian themes; Brusilovsky composed *Kyz-Zhybek*, derived from the folklore of Kazakhstan; Shekhter wrote *Yusup and Akhmet* on Turkmenian motives; Tchemberdzhi contributed the opera *Karlugas* on

Bashkyrian folklore; Kozlovsky wrote *Ulugbek* (Tamerlane's grandson) on
Uzbek melodies; Balasanian wrote a Tadzhik opera, *The Song of Wrath*;
Frolov composed a Buriat-Mongol opera, *Enke Bular Bator*; Paliashvili is
the composer of the Georgian opera *Abessalom and Eteri*.

The harmonic idiom of these operas is in the tradition of Russian orientalism, with extensive pedal points and chromatic leads in the inner
voices. Native instruments are used in many of these productions. Visits
of native artists in performances of native music at festive occasions in
Moscow have further enhanced cultural exchange between Russia proper
and the peripheral republics. Shostakovitch spoke of these developments
in his address as a delegate at the Cultural and Scientific Conference for
World Peace in New York on March 27, 1949:

> Today, in the five capitals of the five Soviet Republics in Middle Asia,
> there are five first-rate theaters of opera and ballet. . . . The national art
> works performed on the stages of these theaters are eloquent testimony
> to the fact . . . that new, peculiarly national branches of international
> musico-dramatic arts have been created. The Uzbek operas *Buran* and
> *Leyli and Medjnun* provide the greatest pleasure to a listener of any
> nationality. . . . I could also bring similar illustrations from the musical
> life of other united and autonomous Soviet Republics—as remote as
> Buriat-Mongolia.

The evolution of the melodic, rhythmic, and harmonic language of
Soviet songs in the popular vein reveals changes that are spontaneous,
non-intellectual, and free from ideological compulsions. The writers of
Russian popular songs are, with few exceptions, amateur musicians possessing an innate melodic gift. The exceptions are Leo Knipper, whose
song "Meadowland" was originally the choral ending of his fourth symphony, and Ivan Dzerzhinsky, whose operatic arias have attained great
popularity in Russia. But Shostakovitch, Prokofiev, Miaskovsky, and
Khatchaturian never succeeded in producing such popular songs, a cir-
cumstance that was reproachfully pointed out to them by Soviet critics
who saw in this a lack of spiritual contact between the most prominent
among Soviet composers and the people. Needless to say, this separation
of cultured music from popular songs is not confined to Soviet Russia, but
is a universal phenomenon. Popular songs everywhere are written mostly
by musicians lacking formal education while the greatest composers of

the classical past rarely if ever produced songs that people sing.

Soviet popular music follows the harmonic scheme of Russian folk songs with their characteristic melodic phrases in a broad diatonic style. But whereas Russian folk songs never go beyond the implied harmony of the three principal triads and in melody are confined to the hexachord, new Soviet songs of popular appeal are wider in melodic range, and their harmonic scheme includes modulatory shifts in parallel triads. Knipper's song "Poliushko Pole" (Meadowland) is built on melodic groups of triads in parallel construction. Blanter's song "Katiusha," which became extremely popular during the war, is close in its metrical, rhythmic, melodic, and harmonic structure to Russian sentimental romances of the 19th century, with just a touch of syncopation quickening its pace.

Choral Finale from *Fourth Symphony* by Knipper

Korobeiniki (Hucksters)

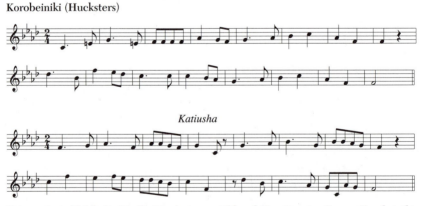

Katiusha

Harmonic and Melodic Similarities between Old and New Russian Songs: *Korobeiniki* (Hucksters), c. 1900 [top] and *Katiusha* by Blanter, c. 1935 [bottom]

Another popular Soviet song, "Taking Her Home" by Zakharov, maintains a modal character and metrical freedom typical of the oldest folk songs of Russia.

Taking Her Home by Zakharov, c. 1930

When during the war the Soviet government decided to establish a new national anthem to replace the *Internationale*, the choice fell on the *Hymn of the Bolshevik Party* by Alexander Alexandrov (1883–1946).

Hymn of the Bolshevik Party, Soviet National Anthem since 1944

A new set of words was adapted to the music, with an emphasis on the national rather than the party sentiment. *Literatura I Iskusstyo* (Literature and Art), in its issue of January 1, 1944, gives a description of the idiom of the song which may be taken also as an authoritative statement of what Soviet mass music ought to be:

> A song which for a number of years has served as a Hymn of the Bolshevik Party best suited to express the socialist essence of the Soviet State. It is a mighty and majestic song. Its stately and flowing melody is imbued with power, and is national to the core. Its coloring is stern as befits a fighting nation, a nation that has in countless battles won its freedom and independence. In its melodic and harmonic texture, in its rhythmic structure, the music of the new National Anthem follows the great tradition of Russian musical classicism.

The recession of artistic internationalism in the 1930s and the rising tide of Russian musical nationalism accelerated the process of absorption of the so-called national heritage of Russian classical music. To be sure, great Russian composers were never rejected outright except by the extremists of the modernist movement of the 1920s. Casuistic reasons were offered by some musical Marxists from the RAPM to explain away the popularity of such works as Tchaikovsky's *Pathétique* among Soviet audiences, namely that this symphony is a superb requiem of Tchaikovsky's own class of dying nobility. What is more natural than the thorough enjoyment of this splendid funeral service of the *bourgeoisie* delivered with such supreme eloquence? But serious Soviet historians realistically accepted the fact that Glinka, Balakirev, Rimsky-Korsakov, Borodin, Moussorgsky, Tchaikovsky, and others were no revolutionaries. They argued that their music, as the soil of Russia itself, rightfully belonged to the Soviet heirs of Russian culture. There were some difficulties regarding performances of such works as Glinka's opera *A Life for the Czar* or Tchaikovsky's *1812 Overture* (which features the Czarist hymn symbolically defeating the *Marseillaise*). Glinka's opera was reinstated in the repertoire 22 years after the Revolution, under Glinka's original title, *Ivan Susanin*, the name of the Russian peasant who led astray in an impenetrable forest a group of Polish agents sent to assassinate the first Czar of the Romanov dynasty. With some revisions in the libretto, eliminating references to the Czar, the opera was produced in Moscow on February 27, 1939, as a patriotic spectacle at the time of sharp antagonism between Poland and Russia. Tchaikovsky's *1812 Overture* had to wait even a longer time for its Sovietization; it was performed in Leningrad under siege, on December 9, 1941.

Paradoxically, the music of Rachmaninov, an outspoken enemy of the Soviet regime, who left Russia immediately after the Revolution, has remained extremely popular in Russia. With singular reverence, Soviet musicologists unearthed student works of Rachmaninov, and the production of these in Moscow was acclaimed as a major event. When Rachmaninov died in 1943 his passing was regretted in the Soviet press as a great loss to Russian culture.

During the period of international tension before the outbreak of World War II, Soviet composers were urged to write music on patriotic themes from the Russian past. Two patriotic works were featured at the Soviet music festival in Moscow in December 1939: the cantata, *Alexander Nevsky* by Prokofiev, which glorified the rout of the Teutonic Knights on Lake Peipus on April 5, 1242, and *On Kulikovo Field* by Yuri Shaporin, commemorating the victory over the Tartar chieftain Mamai in

1380. Other works were dedicated to revolutionary figures in Russian history, such as *Emelian Pugachov* by Marian Koval, on the life of the 18th-
century rebel who was hanged by Catherine the Great.

Relatively few works by Soviet composers have dealt directly with the
figures of Lenin and Stalin. Alexander Krein wrote an *Ode to Lenin*
shortly after Lenin's death. Shostakovitch had announced on several occasions his intention to write a Lenin symphony with a choral ending but
never carried out this plan. Several composers, among them Prokofiev
and Miaskovsky, have written jubilee overtures on Stalin's 60th birthday.
Prokofiev also wrote a cantata to words from the writings of Marx, Engels,
Lenin, and Stalin. None of these works had more than a polite reception
after a single performance. More durable was the *Poem about Stalin* by
Khatchaturian, composed in 1937. Written in the monodic style of
Caucasian folk music (Khatchaturian comes from the same region as
Stalin, although he is an Armenian and Stalin is a Georgian), it ends with
a choral glorification of Stalin, "our friend, teacher, leader, our priceless
Stalin." The harmonic idiom of this choral ending is fairly complicated,
abounding in dissonant chromatics, but clearing up in the final plagal
cadence.

Choral Ending of *Poem about Stalin* by Khatchaturian

If Soviet musicians have failed to create a distinctive style corresponding to the dialectic formula of Socialist Realism, they have succeeded in
reflecting the turmoil of the events on the national and international
scene. When the German war came, Soviet composers mobilized themselves into a propaganda unit to help fight the war on the cultural front.
Many composers of the younger generation, including Shostakovitch, volunteered to go on the fighting front, but their services as soldiers were
declined in order to let them use their creative powers to build up the
morale of the nation. Their role in the war effort is not to be underestimated *ex post facto*. The first performance of Shostakovitch's "Leningrad"
Symphony on March, 1942, in the temporary Soviet capital at Kuibishev

on the Volga, when the German army was at the approaches to Moscow, was marked by a tremendous moral uplift. The finale of this symphony, jubilant with the anticipation of the as yet uncertain victory, must have stirred the audience of Red Army officers and government officials, as well as diplomats and reporters of the allied nations, to a pitch of excitement that could almost be measured in military terms.

The promptness of the fulfillment of "defense tasks" by Soviet musicians in writing not only fighting songs for the army, but also large symphonic works, ballets, and even operas, was remarkable. Prokofiev wrote a symphonic suite entitled *1941*. Khatchaturian's ballet, *Gayane*, performed in the town of Molotov on December 9, 1942, featured in its final scene the military events of but a year before. This ballet extolled the patriotic spirit of the Caucasian girl Gayane, who exposed the anti-Soviet machinations of her husband, and after his liquidation married the liquidator. The Sword Dance from this ballet, rich in quasi-oriental chromatics and vibrant with rhythmic energy, has since become extremely popular.

In 1944, Yuri Shaporin wrote a cantata, *Tale of the Battle for the Russian Land*, in a series of episodes from the story of the then current war. Khrennikov composed a full-fledged opera, *The Blood of the People*, descriptive of the war events. In 1945, Prokofiev wrote an *Ode on the End of the War*, scored for an interesting combination of four pianos, eight harps, sixteen double basses, brass, and percussion.

The problem of an ideologically correct style of Soviet music, which during the war was confined to proper selection of subject matter, came once more under discussion after the end of the war. The stylistic status of Soviet music had changed little in the years after the denunciation of modernism in 1936. Soviet composers continued to write music that was harmonically far beyond the ideals of 19th-century Russian music that they professed to follow. Shostakovitch's declaration that in his creative work he was inspired by Tchaikovsky was a verbal act of allegiance to the greatness of the Russian past. On the basis of impartial analysis, Soviet music at the end of the war was undeniably a 20th century product, marked by a complete freedom of the modulatory idiom in basically tonal harmonies, and an acceptance of dissonant combinations, particularly in chromatic progressions, which could not be undone by any ideological proddings. It was certainly not the spirit of defiance that animated Soviet composers when they persisted in writing music that failed to conform to official aesthetics. Among Soviet composers of sound craftsmanship, Shaporin alone came close to writing music in the great tradition of the Russian national school, with but a few individual innovations that distinguished his harmony from that of Borodin and Balakirev. Other composers who tried to reduce their musical language to a harmonic minimum were accused of "oversimplification," the opposite extreme of formalism, more venial, but nonetheless objectionable.

The contradiction between the ideologically desirable style of musical composition and the living language of Soviet composers culminated in a major eruption when, on February 10, 1948, the Central Committee of the All-Union Communist Party issued a resolution condemning Soviet composers for their persistence in modernistic practices and their failure to create music expressive of Soviet reality.

The immediate pretext for this official condemnation was the production of the opera *Great Friendship* by the Georgian composer Vano Muradeli, which took place in Moscow on November 7, 1947. The opera, written on the subject of the revolutionary events in the Caucasus, was denounced as a "defective, antiartistic work, with not a single memorable melody." Its music was described as "confusing and discordant, full of continuous dissonances and earsplitting combinations of sounds." The resolution went on: "The fiasco of Muradeli's opera is not an isolated event. It is closely related to a precarious situation of Soviet music in general, and to the spread of formalistic practices among Soviet composers."

Shostakovitch, Prokofiev, Khatchaturian, Shebalin, Popov, and Miaskovsky were specifically named as proponents of formalism described as "the cultivation of atonality, dissonances and disharmony . . . infatuation with the confused neurasthenic sonorities transforming music into cacophony." These Soviet composers were further accused of aping the practices of "modernistic bourgeois culture."[2]

---

2. In Soviet semantics, formalism stands for *formulism*, that is, adherence to formulas, particularly formulas of modern music. Linear counterpoint, dissonant harmony, syncopated rhythm, tricky orchestration, special instrumental effects, atonality and the twelve-tone technique were the specific formulas condemned as formalistic. The desirable opposite of formalism was "realist music," that is, music rooted in national folklore, and characterized by harmonic euphony, classical orchestration in the manner of the Russian academic school, spacious diatonicism, and steady non-syncopated rhythm. Realist music was also described as optimistic music, and formalism as pessimistic.

The resolution attacked both the Committee of Fine Arts and the Union of Soviet Composers for their failure to direct Soviet music along the path towards Socialist Realism and Russian classicism. The Committee of Fine Arts was especially reprimanded for announcing Muradeli's opera for production in Leningrad, Sverdlovsk, and Riga even before the rehearsals began, and also for spending 600,000 rubles for the Moscow production, demonstrating "the irresponsibility of the Committee in inducing the State to give out large sums of money without justification."

The Soviet composers whose names were mentioned in the February 1948 resolution as formalists responded in a characteristic fashion. The chief culprit, Vano Muradeli, declared: "Although I have been a convinced exponent of composition inspired by folk songs, I was unable to pursue this realistic path. Instead, attracted by false innovations, I have accepted the formalistic techniques of musical modernism." Shostakovitch made a similar statement: "I deviated in the direction of formalism, and began to speak a language incomprehensible to the people. Now when the Party and our entire nation condemned this tendency in my music, I know that the Party is right; I know that the Party shows its solicitude for Soviet music and for me as a Soviet composer." Prokofiev, in a letter addressed to Khrennikov as General Secretary of the Union of Soviet Composers, while admitting that he "indulged in atonality" and that "elements of formalism" were present in his music, "apparently through infection from contact with western ideas," protested that he "never questioned the importance of melody."

Perhaps the most curious of these declarations was a letter by Aram Khatchaturian published in the February 28, 1948 issue of the *Information Bulletin* of the Russian Embassy in Washington. In this letter he objected to a favorable review of his *Symphonie-Poème* which previously appeared in the *Bulletin*. He wrote:

> Instead of developing the realistic trend in my music, and upholding the tradition of Russian music, which is of a popular nature and combines high content, clearness, and truth with artistic perfection of musical form, in my most recent composition, the *Symphonie-Poème*, I followed a formalistic path alien to the Soviet artist.
>
> I have seen an article entitled *Aram Khatchaturian, Soviet Composer*, by G. Lvov, which recently appeared in the Bulletin published by the Soviet Embassy in Washington. This article, which

expressed the personal tastes and impressions of the journalist Lvov, contained statements about my compositions with which I cannot agree. When the article was written, Lvov had not heard—he could not have heard—the performance of my latest work, the *Symphonie-Poème*, as it was not yet finished. I cannot agree with the over-enthusiastic dithyrambic tone of Lvov's article. Praise of this kind, bestowed by certain critics on many works by our composers, has failed to stimulate the development of soviet music, and has led to contrary results. This is sufficiently, clearly, and justly pointed out in the decision of the Central Committee of the Communist Party of the Soviet Union.

I know that there are some abroad who are attempting to present this decision as a document evidencing a species of "purge" among the composers of the Union of Soviet Socialist Republics. Such an assertion could come only from those who do not wish or who are unable to understand what is going on in the Soviet Union.

How can there be any question of "purging" when the Central Committee, while pointing out very justly the errors into which a number of Soviet composers have fallen, indicates the path which should lead Soviet musical culture to the creation of work of really high quality and finish, such as may be comprehensible to all people, and also offers full opportunity to the composers named in the decision to participate in this work?

All the statements by composers accused of formalism contained a promise to create works conforming to the new dicta. A collective letter was dispatched to Stalin promising to apply every effort in order to produce "vivid realistic music that reflects the life and the struggles of the Soviet people."

This pledge now waited on fulfillment. Miaskovsky wrote a symphony on Russian themes. Shostakovitch wrote a score to the film, *The Young Guard* (the story of a heroic resistance group during the German occupation), and later a *Forest Cantata*, dealing with the Soviet afforestation program. Muradeli and Popov composed melodious choruses. Shebalin wrote a string quartet in a simplified instrumental manner. Khatchaturian composed a symphonic dithyramb in memory of Lenin. All these works were accepted by the Union of Soviet Composers as fulfilling the 1948 directives. In contrast, Prokofiev's new opera, *The Tale of a Real Man*, dealing with a Soviet flyer hero who remained in service after the loss of both legs, was condemned in violent terms in an editorial of *Sovietskaya Musica* of December 1948:

Prokofiev's opera demonstrates that formalism still lives in the conscious-ness of some musicians. In his new opera, Prokofiev goes back to all the neg-ative and repulsive usages present in his operas of the period of reckless infatuation with modernistic trickery. Chaos, coarse naturalism, complete absence of melody, preposterous inclusion of songs written in an inappro-priate style, harmonic muddiness, bad taste, and lack of any lofty ideas, such are the characteristics of this radically vicious work. Commercialized treat-ment of the subject results in a decline of his compositional technique in this work. The members of the administration of the theater that produced the opera were so politically near-sighted, so wrapped up in their chummy personal relations with the formalists, that they failed to see through the nature of this outrageous and repulsive product.

The 1948 musical policy in the Union of Soviet Composers was out-lined by its new general secretary, Tikhon Khrennikov. His views, anti-Western and anti-modern, were summarized in a brochure, *The Paths of Evolution of Soviet Music*, issued by the Musicological Committee of the Union of Soviet Composers in 1948. It stated among other things:

> In his interview with the first delegation of American workers, Stalin pointed out that communism creates conditions for a full flowering of the arts. In communist society, art will become a part of human life; it will enter the consciousness of every citizen to an extent undreamed of by the most progressive artists of the past. Hence the imperative necessity to activate in every way the artistic and musical education of the masses during the period of gradual transition to communism. Hence the task of merciless exposure and eradication of alien bourgeois influences in the arts. Guarding our art against the infiltration of elements of decadent dissolution, securing the ide-ologically purposeful, broadly organized aesthetic education of the masses, the Party blazes the trail towards the unprecedented flowering of the arts which will be attained in the period of communism.

In a curious semantic switch-over, modern music was declared to be the product of reaction; conversely, Russian romantic music of the 19th-century brand was extolled as a progressive art. David Zaslavsky, the polit-ical writer of *Pravda*, entering the fray, glibly referred to "the reactionary composers Hindemith and Schoenberg." Zhdanov, speaking at the meet-ing of Soviet composers shortly after the issuance of the February 1948 resolution, said: "The neglect of program music is a departure from pro-gressive traditions. It is well known that Russian classical music was, as a rule, program music." By an obvious inference, Zhdanov thus identifies progress with a return to old traditions. This new nomenclature confused Hanns Eisler, the German left-wing musician, who tried to reconcile new Soviet policy in music with his own progressive ideas. "The musician's task today," he said, "is to push music a little back, from the individual to the social. In the society of free men, in which exploitation of man by man is eliminated, music may again acquire a more joyful character, overcoming the effort, the torment, and revulsion against itself." He was chided for his dialectic misapprehension by Gregory Schneerson, who commented in the pages of *Sovietskaya Musica*:

> Can it be that Eisler, who went through the hard school of anti-fascist struggle, does not understand that the movement from the individual to the collective is a movement forward, not backward? In these words of Eisler there are reflected the influences of a backward and reactionary phraseology of bourgeois individualism, inimical to progressive art.

Ironically, Schneerson's former attitude towards modern music put him in the wrong with the new spokesmen of musical policy. In a brief note published in the selfsame *Sovietskaya Musica*, he was reported as pleading "political illiteracy" to explain his own deviations from the cor-rect line, a plea that was found "unconvincing" by the reporter.

In the wake of these discussions, a fresh assault was made on western European and American music. Any yielding to foreign influences, no matter how picayune, and no matter how remote in the past, was now recalled with sneering emphasis. In an article in *Sovietskaya Musica* of December 1948, I. Nestiev wrote:

> In the early editions of Popov's works, even his Russian name Gavril Popov is changed to the effective foreign Gabriel Popoff, and the early dedications clearly demonstrate his undeviating tastes and predilections. Thus, his opus I, *Expressions*, is dedicated to Arnold Schoenberg.

American jazz, which was for a time admitted in Russia as a legitimate rhythmic technique, was again declared unfit for Soviet composers. Isaac Dunayevsky, a popular composer who had dabbled in Soviet jazz, now came forward with a public apology for his lapse into the ideologically impermissible.

Simultaneously with the denunciation of formalism and foreignism, an attack was launched in the Soviet musical press against all speculative music theory. Theoreticians who investigated the possibilities of new harmonic systems were now ridiculed and ostracized. Thus, Alexei Ogolevetz, the author of a voluminous work on scales and modes, was lampooned in *Sovietskaya Musica*, in a cartoon representing him as a stone idol, with an abstruse quotation from his writings placed on the pedestal. A perplexed Soviet musician and a boy with a violin were shown standing before the statue, and saying: "I wonder what he means by all this?"

Novel theories promulgated abroad bore a double stigma in the eyes of Soviet conformists. Before his demotion, Gregory Schneerson published a violent article in *Sovietskaya Musica* of March 1948, under the heading "American Musical Engineering," attacking the Schillinger system of composition. Schillinger was one of the leaders of the Leningrad Association of Contemporary Music in the 1920's, where he evolved his mechanistic concepts of musical composition. He settled in New York in 1926, and died there in 1943.

"In the United States of America," writes Schneerson, "this classical country of soulless technicism, Schillinger found favorable environment for his methods of ready-made musical composition. . . . The Schillinger system, like similar systems of other musical speculators, was engendered by the reality of American musical life. To attract more customers, such is the secret motto of these business men of music who are willing to trade in any kind of merchandise provided they can get attention and dollars."

A footnote to the article takes a jab at still another book published in America:

We have received a book by Nicolas Slonimsky, *Thesaurus of Scales and Melodic Patterns*, which is a meticulously systematized handbook for manufacturing melodies. . . . The Schillinger system, Slonimsky's manual of melody, and numerous other works of the same type designed for the manufacture of popular jazz music by conveyor belt methods, illustrate the established creative methods of American musical life. . . . Observing such phenomena typical of the degenerate art of the capitalist world, one cannot help recalling the wise words of the Resolution of the Central Committee of the All-Union Communist Party (Bolsheviks) of February 10, 1948, warning Soviet composers against treading the deadly path of contemporary modernistic bourgeois music of Europe and America which reflects the dissolution of bourgeois culture.

Neo-classicism, as a compromise solution between the modernistic present and the venerated past, was rejected in an authoritative article by Marian Koval, a right-wing Soviet composer, who, together with Khrennikov, assumed a leading influence in the Union of Soviet Composers. The article, published in the May 1948 issue of *Sovietskaya Musica*, and dealing specifically with Shostakovitch, stated:

> Neo-classicism is in its substance a parasitic phenomenon. This is not a return to the past for the sake of developing progressive traditions of classical music. . . . The neo-classical school is consistent in only one respect: it distorts both the past and the present. For modernistic surrealism, devoid of all musical feeling, neo-classicism is a safety belt, to give the listener a respite from the urbanistic racket of modern music.

As an example of objectionable neoclassicism, Koval quotes the fugue from Shostakovitch's Fourth Symphony. (This was a symphony withdrawn from performance by Shostakovitch in 1936, after a preliminary rehearsal by the Leningrad Philharmonic.) Koval comments:

> With sadistic persistence, strictly following the "classical" form, the composer releases his fourth formalistic serpent [the fourth entry of the subject], and all the four serpents, in monstrous entanglement, assail the human ear and human nerves. Great Bach himself must turn in his grave from this torture, wondering: Can it be that this shameless formalistic orgy has its source in my music?

The conflict between traditionalism and modernism in Soviet music has temporarily been resolved in favor of the old. The parallelogram of dynamic forces now has its resultant diagonal biased in the direction of a simplified musical language. In a larger sense, this conflict is but part of a universal struggle between progressive and retarding tendencies in world music. And the final solution must also come on a world basis.

20. A NEW TUNE IN SOVIET MUSIC

After six long years of squirming under the oppressive esthetic decrees for-
mulated by the late Andrei Zhdanov, Soviet composers are beginning to
show signs of real independence. Zhdanov's notorious *obiter dicta* were
embodied in a Resolution of the Central Committee of the All-Union
Communist Party, dated February 10, 1948, and for a long time they effectively influenced all musical composition in the USSR. Recently, however,
Soviet musicians have dared to question the Zhdanov esthetics. Now
comes the most forthright declaration of independence to date in the form
of a direct attack on the Zhdanov policies by Aram Khachaturian, in his
article "On Creative Boldness and Inspiration," conspicuously featured in
the November 1953 issue of *Sovietskaya Musica.*

Khachaturian was one of the Soviet composers named in the 1948
Resolution as an adherent to a "formalistic and anti-national movement"
which practised "atonality, dissonance, disharmony, and neuropathologi-
cal conglomerations of sound which transform music into cacophony."
Furthermore, Khachaturian was specifically accused of negligence as
head of the Steering Committee of the Union of Soviet Composers.

In his article, Khachaturian is careful to avoid an appearance of retro-
spective self-justification. He loyally quotes Zhdanov's words: "The new
must be better than the old, or else it has no meaning." And he seemingly
reiterates his faith in the correctness of the musical policy of the 1948 decree. The fire of his article is concentrated on the two hapless institutions
that were entrusted with carrying out the Zhdanov policies: the Union of
Soviet Composers and the Committee of Fine Arts. To the functionaries

---

Ch. 20: originally published in *The Saturday Review*, January 30, 1954.

of these organizations Khachaturian throws his challenge: "J'accuse!" The charges are administrative bureaucracy, obsequiousness, timidity, mediocrity, and lack of imagination.

Khachaturian's solution of the problem is simple: let composers write music as they please. This, of course, effectively cancels all ideological controls established over Soviet music by Zhdanov. Ostensibly attacking the executive branch, Khachaturian defies the central idea that composers must be "told" what to compose and how to compose. Considering the atmosphere of Soviet music since 1948, this is a revolutionary proposal. Like all revolutions, big and little, political and artistic, the musical revolt in Moscow did not arrive all of a sudden. The notion that Stalin's death released liberal ideas in Soviet music (as it may have done in other arts) is not supported by a careful reading of the Soviet musical press. In fact, every point raised by Khachaturian, had been anticipated in editorials, or special articles published in the same journal, *Sovietskaya Musica*, before Stalin's death in March 1953.

In the article "On Musical Mastery" (March 1952), Kabalevsky warned the Union of Soviet Composers not to confuse solid technique of composition with formalism and not to tolerate the lowering of technical requirements under the pretext of fighting formalistic tendencies. In a statement published in the November 1952 issue of the magazine, Shostakovich questioned the absolute prohibition of dissonances: "Life constantly brings on new problems and demands creative innovation from Soviet musicians . . . If the subject of a certain work requires a strong dissonance at a given moment, the listener will accept it as just."

In three consecutive editorials (January, February, and March 1953), *Sovietskaya Musica* attacked the growing bureaucracy of the post-1948 musical organizations. In the first of these it stated: "We can no longer ignore the fact that many musical works produced during the last few years are stillborn. The complacent leadership of the Union of Soviet Composers and those among our music scholars who are willing to condone the poor artistic quality of these works because of the 'actuality' of their subject matter and the 'good intentions' of the composer render a bear's service to Soviet music." (A bear's service is an act of officious stupidity, from Krylov's fable in which the bear, guarding his owner's sleep, drops a huge rock on his forehead to kill an annoying fly.)

From the February 1953 issue: "Unfortunately, the Committee of Fine Arts and the Union of Soviet Composers have not yet overcome the bureaucratic methods of creative guidance. Noisy sessions with plenty of commotion on petty subjects create an illusion of feverish activity . . . For a year the opera committee of the Union of Soviet Composers has been compiling and discussing with wearisome monotony a long list of some sixty titles of Soviet operas. Yet the members of the opera committee, headed by the secretary of the Union of Soviet Composers, Dmitri Kabalevsky, know only too well that most of these operas are non-existent and are used only for accounting purposes."

In October 1953 *Sovietskaya Musica* published a cartoon representing a Soviet composer typing out his music on a rubber-stamp machine. A poem accompanied the drawing:

> He's a composer, and his inspiration
> Had brought him universal admiration
> And won some prizes from the grateful nation.
>
> But now he's left sonatas to the dead
> And writes his notes with rubber-stamps instead,
> Indexed and filed in blue and green and red.
>
> His present musical preoccupation
> Is simply bureaucratic compilation.

Khatchaturian's article, which appeared in the next issue of *Sovietskaya Musica*, was a dialectical summation of the cartoon and the poem ridiculing the new figure of "composer-bureaucrat." Clearly, it was not published as a personal expression. When such debatable views are aired in the Soviet press the editors usually protect themselves by inserting a meaningful footnote: "This article is published in the order of discussion." No such footnote accompanies the Khachaturian article. It is therefore to be assumed that the article is a policy-making one.

Like most Soviet musicians, Khachaturian writes fluently and easily. But Soviet prose in general is marked by repetitiousness, superabundance of cliches, and various redundancies that make the reading pretty turgid in the original, and stultifying in complete translation. The Khachaturian article possesses all these qualities, of which the following paragraph, in a fairly literal translation, is a sample:

TO SATISFY IN EVERY WAY THE CONSTANTLY INCREASING
SPIRITUAL DEMANDS OF THE PEOPLE—This lofty objective,
which constitutes an integral part of the basic law of Socialism, is erro-
neously interpreted at times by some musical personalities, acting from
the position of thoughtless "adaptationism." Not a few works have been
produced here, calculated to satisfy some "arithmetical mean" of public
taste, works in which the composer, having lost his creative individuality,
camouflages himself behind gray, shopworn musical phraseology . . . But
the people reject second-hand merchandise. They demand from us an
art that is new, fresh, beautiful, attractive, and inspired.

"Adaptationism" is the nearest possible translation of the Russian
word *Prisposoblentchestvo*, the suffix *tchestvo* representing "ism" in many
Russian neologisms. The meaning of the word is "an obsequious and
insincere effort to adjust oneself to the prevalent opinions of important
people." In Soviet criticism this word appears quite often.

Khatchaturian then reports the fact well-known not only to Soviet
composers but to any reader of the Soviet press, namely that mediocre
musicians have secured important positions for themselves and had their
works performed by the simple stratagem of writing music on patriotic
Soviet themes:

How many times have we heard "monumental" works requiring a huge
body of performers and presenting a grandiloquent musical vacuum,
with an important "realistic" theme expressed in the programmatic subtitle! How often were we willing to overlook the obvious faults of such a
work only because it was marked on the jacket with a great stirring
theme of the love for the motherland, struggle for peace, and friendship
among the nations!

Zhdanov called Soviet composers back to the Russian classics;
Khachaturian reminds that the classics themselves were the modernists of
their time:

Bach, Beethoven, Glinka, Mussorgsky, Tchaikovsky—they all were innovators in art. They blazed new trails in the service of the people,
responding to the demands of living reality, obedient to lofty Inspiration.

Such is the thesis of Khachaturian's article. Good dialectician as he is, he follows his exposition by an antithesis:

Some musical personalities misunderstand the nature of innovation, so important in the development of progressive art. They confuse innovation with the chase after "original novelty" peculiar to the creative straining of foreign composers-formalists. Such "innovation" is profoundly repugnant to us, and we are prepared to fight such formalistic music-making with unrelenting energy.

By way of digression, Khachaturian takes up a vigorous defense of Prokofiev and Shostakovich as true Soviet artists and genuine innovators:

The significant works by Prokofiev and Shostakovich reflect with great artistic power the images of our intense reality saturated with revolutionary energy. I here refer not only to the thematic content of individual works, not only to programmatic descriptions of the stirring pages of our history and events of our time, but to the very sense of the rhythm of contemporary life, the "tuning" of the spiritual world of Soviet Man. . . . I feel the pulse of our revolutionary reality even in such works as Prokofiev's cantata "Alexander Nevsky," which goes back to the remote past of the Russian people. . . . Service to his people, service to progressive humanity, these were the guiding principles of Prokofiev, Soviet composer-patriot, in the best works of the last two decades of his life.

Khachaturian ends his eulogy of Prokofiev with an appeal to young composers to emulate Prokofiev in the uncompromising and bold pursuit of his ideals. He draws an unflattering parallel with some new Soviet composers, the "adaptationists," devoid of creative daring such as Prokofiev had:

One cannot produce a work of revolutionary romanticism, inspired by an ardent love for the motherland, and for the people of our Socialist reality without creative elan, with a cautious glance over the shoulder just to make sure that nothing untoward would happen. There are works produced here in which everything seems to be all right on the surface; the program is fine, the themes are national in character, the harmony is well arranged, the orchestration is competent, and yet the artistic result is almost nil, for the music is devoid of creative boldness and inspiration.

The climactic part of Khachaturian's long disquisition comes with a direct accusation against the bungling musical bureaus and an appeal for liberation:

> It seems to me that the time has come to re-examine the established system of institutional guardianship over our composers. I will say more: we must resolutely abandon the vicious practice of interfering with the composer's creative process on the part of members of our musical bureaus. A creative problem cannot be solved by administrative and bureaucratic methods. . . . Trust the artist more, and he will approach the creative problems of our life with greater freedom and greater sense of responsibility.

Khachaturian gives us a glimpse of what is actually happening in the bureaucratic musical institutions in Moscow and elsewhere in Soviet Russia:

> Under the existing system of "guardianship" the composer is relieved of all responsibility. When he brings a song to a musical organization, every functionary deems it his duty to offer "advice," to suggest an "improvement" in melody or in rhythm, or to correct his harmony. In short, he receives "guiding directives" for a complete refitting of his song. Strange as it may seem, there are composers who agree to all these alterations. They surrender their most cherished ideas, over which they worked so painfully, and dress up their creation like a hairdresser's dummy.

Then Khachaturian repeats his appeal:

> There is no need of guardianship! Let us take a risk and entrust the writing of operas and other musical works to our best composers. . . . Our musical institutions must cease their petty surveillance. . . . The Union of Soviet Composers has no right to assume the function of an infallible appraiser in the service of our musical bureaus. Within the Union of Composers, discussion of new works should be in the nature of free exchange of opinions. . . . I can even imagine that some works rejected by the Union of composers should none the less be published and performed. Life itself will correct the original evaluation should it prove erroneous or biased.

There is something in Khachaturian's article reminiscent of April 1932, when Soviet composers rebelled against the Association of Proletarian Musicians, which had held unofficial power for several years. At that time the Soviet Government simply disbanded the self-styled proletarian group, and the Soviet composers were given their freedom to compose as they pleased, and not only in march-time, as the proletarian musicians wanted them to do. The pendulum swung once more in 1936 when Shostakovich was assailed in a famous article in *Pravda*. Three years later Shostakovich was returned to the fold. But the *Pravda* article was recalled by Zhdanov in the 1948 decree and confirmed as a correct expression of musical policy.

From this recurrence of attacks a theory of cycles may be evolved. The controls over the Soviet musical mind seem about to fall. Then the composers will once more write as they please. For how long? The theory of cycles would give the period of grace of about four years. Or else the reactionary forces in Soviet esthetics may finally give up the fight and allow Russian musical art to flourish unhampered.

21. SCHOENBERG IN THE SOVIET MIRROR

The Soviet attitude towards Schoenberg is anomalous. The orthodox theoreticians in the USSR reject Schoenberg's method of composition as ideologically unacceptable and completely incompatible with the basic tenets of Soviet music, a sort of musical populism, classical in technique and contemporary in programmatic application, a style which is officially called Socialist Realism.

In the early years of Soviet music there was a great interest among composers and performers for the new music of the West; after all, the Soviet Union was the greatest revolutionary nation, and it was therefore expected to foster the most revolutionary systems of musical composition. The syllogism did not work, however, and very soon the timid growth of Soviet musical modernity was brutally squelched in the name of the people, who preferred nice tuneful music to the strange atonal sounds of the West. Yet, a modest little monograph on Schoenberg by Ivan Sollertinsky was published in Leningrad in 1934, and there were some performances of Schoenberg's music; Alban Berg also received a Soviet accolade in those early times; there were concerts of contemporary music given in Leningrad, a city much more musically progressive than staid Moscow. But Nikita Khrushchev finished off Schoenberg and Schoenbergianism with peasant bluntness, but not without rough humor: "They call it *dodecafonia*, but to us it's plain *cacofonia*" (the words rhyme in Russian).

The troublesome part in the Soviet rejection of Schoenberg, Anton Webern, Berg *e tutti quanti* was that Western modernists were militant

---

Ch. 21: originally published in the *Journal of the Arnold Schoenberg Institute*, February 1978.

anti-Fascists, several of them direct victims of the Nazi barbarism. Luigi Nono, a resistance fighter in Italy and a member in good standing of the Italian Communist Party, was received with great honors when he visited Russia in 1963, but only as a political associate, not as composer of dodecaphonic music and son-in-law of Arnold Schoenberg. Nono's music is still rarely if ever performed in the USSR. Even more of an ideological paradox was presented by the case of Hanns Eisler, composer of numerous mass songs widely sung in the Socialist Block and author of the official national anthem of East Germany. He was a loyal disciple of Schoenberg who declined to make an act of contrition that would have cleansed him of the dodecaphonic taint. His collected works now being published in East Germany include pieces written in the twelve-tone technique.

The final blow to the Khrushchev equation, dodecafonia = cacofonia, was administered by, of all people, Shostakovich, who made use of explicit twelve-tone rows in his Thirteenth String Quartet and Fourteenth Symphony. Younger Soviet composers, such as my nephew Sergei Slonimsky, make no bones about using Schoenbergian procedures.

As a person, Schoenberg was always respectfully regarded by official Soviet music critics. The adjective "honest" was most often applied to him, as if to say that he was honestly misled into a bourgeois decadent path. Among Soviet musicians, particularly young musicians, Schoenberg was a Bethlehem star, remote, mystical, but divine in its epiphany. When I revisited Russia in 1962 I found a curious notation in the "book of requests" in the largest music store in Moscow, signed by some desperate soul; it said: "Can't we at last be given a chance to examine the music of Schoenberg which is not allowed to be published in our country? Do we have to be fed only stuff that passed for new music here?"

In 1972 Professor Mikhail Druskin, an erudite Soviet musicologist, published in Moscow a monograph entitled *On Western European Music of the 20th Century*, which contained a lengthy chapter on Schoenberg and one on Anton Webern. He had an opportunity to study all of Schoenberg's and Webern's scores and peruse all available materials on the Second Vienna School in German, French, and English. The result was an exemplary and highly sympathetic study of Schoenberg's musical legacy. But—and this is most revealing—the book was prefaced by a statement from the publishers, sounding a caveat to the reader: "M. S. Druskin endeavors to trace the formulation of the aesthetics of

Schoenberg. But he gave more attention to the personality of Schoenberg and of his closest disciple Anton von Webern than to their creative method which is based on the false premises of dodecaphony. Only when we examine the entire complex of contradictions, creative aberrations, and ideological failures of the composers of the New Vienna School, will we be able to understand why the avant-garde trends derived from Schoenbergianism and post-Webernism can lead only to the corruption and dissolution of the art of music in the West."

A most interesting and quite unusual paper dealing with Schoenberg was published in the Soviet Union in 1973. Its author is F. Gershkovich, who was born in Bessarabia when it was part of the Russian Empire under the Czars, and who went to live in Moscow after World War II. Entitled "Tonal Sources of Schoenbergian Dodecaphony," the essay appeared in a volume, *The Works on Sign Systems*, a scientific publication of the State University of Estonia. It is frankly an apologia of Schoenberg, but the point of view is taken so as to demonstrate that Schoenberg, far from being a monster sent by a satanic anti-musician to corrupt and destroy the art of music, as the Soviet publishers plainly put it in their caveat in Druskin's book on new Western music, was a man of genius who opened new paths for old music suffering from harmonic and melodic anemia. The concluding paragraph of Gershkovich's paper expresses this notion with poetic ingenuity: "Schoenberg, this Columbus of music of our time, having discovered America, in reality found a new route to dear old India."[1]

Let us quote a few salient statements from Gershkovich's paper: "According to Schoenberg, consonances and dissonances are not separated by a deep chasm. The same interval, or a chord, is perceived differently by different generations. Today's consonance is but yesterday's dissonance, just as today's dissonance may be tomorrow's consonance. . . . In other words, a consonance represents a rehabilitated dissonance. . . . The motive force in the evolution of the tonal system was the spread of the hegemony of the tonic to all twelve chromatic tones. If formerly the appearance of a chromatic note in harmony was regarded as a deviation from tonality, now, sixty years after Schoenberg's definition of three basic

---

1. Gershkovich's phrase seems to play upon a sentence in Schoenberg's unfinished text, *Der musikalische Gedanke* . . . : "If one sets out with the intention of getting to India, one can at worst discover America." See Alexander Goehr, "Schoenberg's *Gedanke* Manuscript," *Journal of the Arnold Schoenberg Institute* 2:23. ED.

concepts, the secondary dominant, the minor subdominant, and transitional chords, we must accept the chromatic tone not as a centrifugal phenomenon in relation to the tonic, but quite to the contrary as the effect of the gravitational force of the tonic which attracts the chromatic tones into the sphere of its hegemony. This diametrical difference between the illusion and the truth is a parallel to the ancient illusion of the revolution of the sun around the earth."

Gershkovich then continues his parallel between the gravitational force of the tonic and the centrifugal force of the tonal "planets." By creating the concept of a secondary dominant, Gershkovich maintains, Schoenberg establishes an equality, a democracy of all twelve tones of the tempered scale; and he states the Schoenbergian axiom with ultimate clarity: "dodecaphony does not recognize the hegemony of the tonic, because there is no tonic."

There are many other interesting insights in this unusual tract. The author speaks of the "allergic repugnance of atonal dodecaphony towards the repetition of a tone," and particularly against an octave duplication, whether horizontal or vertical. Since the tonic is ruled out, an octave is perceived by the ear as an "antidissonance" which is false in a total tonal democracy. Somehow this description evoked in me a distant memory. When I conducted Schoenberg's *Begleitungsmusik zu einer Lichtspielszene* at the Hollywood Bowl in 1933 (it was the first performance of this piece of imaginary film music in the film capital), I found to my dismay that both the first and the second trumpet in a certain bar had C, in an octave relationship. I could not immediately locate the dodecaphonic thread which would correct the obvious error, but I changed the note in the second trumpet to C-sharp by guesswork. Seven years later, after Schoenberg was in Los Angeles, I asked him about it. He looked at the score, and said, with considerable astonishment, "Das ist falsch!" Yes, I said, but what should be the right note? "Ich erinnere mich nicht mehr," Schoenberg replied somewhat wistfully. Another few years elapsed, but the "false octave" still bothered me, and I mentioned it to Roger Sessions who was visiting Boston where I lived at the time. We sat together at the piano, and Sessions soon located the dodecaphonic thread: it was C-sharp! My intuition was right. I wonder whether the error has been corrected in the engraved score; in 1933 I used a music copyist's score.

To return to Gershkovich's paper: he argues that dodecaphony and tonality are not incompatible; dodecaphony does not imply cacophony, to use Chairman Khrushchev's memorable parallelism. Therefore, Schoenberg's method of composition with twelve tones related only to one another is really a system of tonal dodecaphony! Once more, the neurons and synapses in my cerebral cortex were triggered into electric activity: the twelve chromatic tones can be arranged in four mutually exclusive triads, two major and two minor (e.g., C major, F-sharp major, D minor, G-sharp minor), which happens to be my favorite "discovery." The intellectual interest of Gershkovich's paper consists in this triggering of various spin-offs of Schoenberg's method. Gershkovich seems to have succeeded in demonstrating that Schoenberg's method was not a destructive force but a unifying, constructive idea, in which the entire series of twelve different tones is in reality an entity of a higher exponential power, and that consequently Schoenberg should be hailed as a great builder of new values, not as the destroyer of the old time-honored values. In other words, Schoenberg was an organizer, not a mindless revolutionary of the Bakunin type, for it was Bakunin who said, "Die Lust der Zerstörung ist eine schaffende Lust." To quote from the memorable letter Schoenberg wrote me from Hollywood on 3 June 1937: "I personally hate to be called a revolutionist, which I am not. What I did was neither revolution nor anarchy. I possessed from my very first start a thoroughly developed sense of form and a strong aversion for exaggeration. There is no falling into order, because there was never disorder. There is no falling at all, but on the contrary, there is an ascending to higher and better order."[2]

---

2. Nicolas Slonimsky, *Music since* 1900, 4th ed. (New York: Charles Scribner's Sons, 1971), p. 1316.

Part IV

PERSONAL EXPERIENCES

22. RUSSIA REVISITED

When, after an interval of some twenty years, I sailed forth to visit the country of my birth it was, apart from sentimental reasons, with a double purpose: to collect first-hand information about Soviet music from Soviet composers themselves, and to arrange for performances of American music in the U.S.S.R. I was more or less conversant with the chief problems of Soviet music, had followed the rise and the downfall of the RAPM (an organization of self-styled proletarian composers, dissolved by Government decree on April 23, 1932, along with similar organizations in literature and art), had read the Soviet music periodicals, *Proletarian Musicians*, *Music and Revolution*, *Contemporary Music*—all now extinct—and *Sovietskaya Musika*, the most long-lived of the Soviet music magazines. I had acquired some perspective. For instance, I knew that Mossolov's exercises in machine music are considered less important within the bounds of the U.S.S.R. than they are abroad. On the other hand, the importance of the old Russian school in Soviet Russia was greater than had been imagined. (As a supreme compliment to Shostakovitch's *Lady Macbeth*, an important critic compared it to Tchaikovsky's *Pique-Dame.*)

All this I had read, but I could not form a living picture from the mosaic. For myself, I indulged in some statistics. Russian music is notoriously "sad," pessimistic; it is fashioned on the minor modes. There are more symphonies, sonatas, quartets in minor keys than in major. But in Soviet music, successor to Russian music, I was to find the opposite mood. The prevalence of major tonality is striking, and determines the very spirit of Soviet music. And rhythmically, march time is greatly favored, with the eight-bar period as a symmetric unit. At the time of the RAPM's hegemony, 4/4 time and major tonality were almost *de rigueur.*

After the dissolution of the RAPM an encouraged composer, in a state-ment given to *Sovietskaya Musika*, declared: "Now I can learn how to write in 3/4 time again!"

However the RAPM only emphasized to the degree of absurdity a tendency that was natural. Russian music could stand a lot of majorization and squaring of time. The great popularity of Prokofieff's music, particu-larly his first visit in the U.S.S.R. in 1927, was due to the fact that Prokofieff fitted into the times; he was "consonant" with the epoch, as the current saying has it. And in Prokofieff's music, until recently, square time and major tonality were dominating outward features.

The shining star of Soviet music is, of course, young Shostakovitch. (He accents his name on the third syllable). So it was not without frank curiosity that I went to see him at his apartment on Dmitrovsky Pereulok in Leningrad. I momentarily forgot whether it was house number 5, apartment number 3, or the other way around; but it was a warm September day and the windows were opened; someone was playing the piano so energetically, and the music was so unmistakable in style, that I knew at once this could be only Shostakovitch. I directed my steps towards the sounds; the door bell rang inharmoniously and the music stopped. So this is Shostakovitch, at last! Young, dynamic, bespectacled, he looks like his pictures—a rare phenomenon in the musical world. We went into the studio and plunged right off into a discussion of his music. I flung questions at him. Does he believe in utilizing vulgar music (gal-lops, sentimental street-songs, military band marches) without submitting it to musical distillation? How does he regard his work *The Nose*, which was driven out of the opera house by the then powerful RAPM? Why did he depart from the modern uses of this opera's music? Is he interested in the twelve-tone system? Shostakovitch was eager to answer. He does not repudiate the music of *The Nose*, and he would show me the full score, as soon as it was returned from the theatre, where it still remained despite the cessation of performances. Yes, he was interested in the twelve-tone system, he knows Schönberg, and still better does he know Berg, but he finds he cannot do anything with the Vienna idiom. He tried, though, and some of his progressions reflect the schooling of Schönberg. I told him that Stravinsky was present at the performance of *Lady Macbeth* in New York and commented favorably on the music. Shostakovitch admires Stravinsky and produced an arrangement for piano in four hands which he had made from the score of the *Symphony of Psalms* in order to absorb the musical substance of that work by frequent hearing and playing. I was frankly amazed at his patience and industry, and this in the midst of composition of his own fourth symphony, which he feels is going to be his most important work. It was my turn to give information. Among other things, I told him of the orchestra of percussion that Varese uses in *Ionization*. To my surprise Shostakovitch had heard of the work and even had the score, which was given to him by a friend. He seemed to be well informed about music abroad. During his recent trip to Turkey he got hold of Stokowski's recording of his own First Symphony and brought the disc to Leningrad.

In the meantime tea was served, and I met Shostakovitch's mother and his wife. We started a vague conversation about Shostakovitch's coming to America. He is shy about his pianistic powers, although he graduated from the piano section of the Leningrad Conservatory as early as 1923. But he is going to compose a special concerto for America—next year, perhaps. The present Piano Concerto is scored for a string orchestra and a trumpet only, and it has already been played in America.

On to Moscow, to look over the archives of Tchaikovsky's House-Museum at Klin. In the suburban train I made musical observations; a group of youngsters singing songs modelled after the familiar Russian patterns, but infused with new strength. There is nothing lackadaisical about them. Hanns Eisler, along with Soviet composers, writes many of them. These songs are not anonymous, and yet they possess the flavor of "naturals." Needless to add, they are all in the optimistic major tonalities, some in the Mixolydian mode so well suited to rapid dance tunes. The youngsters got off at a station, and, as though specially for the purpose of demonstration and comparison, a woman with a child took a seat in my car and started an "individualistic" song in a very, very minor mode.

At Klin I proceeded to the Tchaikovsky museum and arranged to see the manuscripts. While absorbed in the original of *Pique Dame*, I met a stocky, bald man, Youri Shaporin, a symphonist now making his mark, who also was staying in Klin, working at his opera *The Decembrists*. With a professional lack of dignity I attacked him, and he willingly played for me and discussed his own music and familiar technical matters. His Symphony, very Russian, built on a large scale, has been heard in London, and his name is often mentioned with Shostakovitch's. But what a contrast! Shaporin is no experimenter in new music. He writes solidly and believes in the virtue of unshakable tonality. Had there not been an evolution in our own conception of modern music, Shaporin could hardly be classified as a modern. There is nothing in his symphony or in his opera that could not have been written fifty years ago. . . . It is characteristic, however, that in his earlier works, in the two piano sonatas, in the incidental music to Zamiatin's *The Flea* there is a modicum of modernity. The score of *The Flea* is particularly interesting because of the orchestration, which calls for sixteen *Domras* (an old Russian string instrument, ancestor of the balalaika) and three *bayans* (accordions, called bayans by their trade name just as our gramophones are called victrolas, even when they are not Victrolas).

Lest someone should imagine that Soviet music is conservatively regimented, I hasten to introduce a Soviet modernist, a Moscow conservatory professor, Heinrich Litinsky. My first acquaintance with him was through a caustic article in *Sovietskaya Musica*, which showed him to be a master of his metier, but evidently a promoter of meaningless art. However there was so much meaning and musical sense in the musical examples that I forgot the critic and made it a point to get hold of his music. I was not disappointed. I do not know of many works in the literature for solo instruments equalling in inventive craft Litinsky's Sonata for Violin Alone, and a Sonata for Viola. What is particularly attractive in these works is the sober realization of rich potentialities of new scales without the octave terminal. He has also written five quartets, all of them fine pieces of effective composition. Litinsky says his entire musical outlook has been created by the spirit of the proletarian, and his declaration has a political import. If the Revolution can give a place to Litinsky and to Shaporin, both admirable workers in their disparate fields, then a wide range of professional activity may be considered as definitely assured in the U.S.S.R.

Moscow days proved as feverish as those in Leningrad. Julian Krein paid a call. After several years in Paris, he had come back to Moscow, where he started ten years ago as a musical prodigy of thirteen. At twenty-three he still remains a prodigy. He has produced an enormous bulk of work, astonishingly mature. Where is he to be placed in our parliament of composers? His idiom is "modern" in the 1920 sense, too modern for 1935. There is no question as to his talent. He has found his style, too, and even in our backward times he can go on being modern without retreating to some safe antiquity.

On a second trip to Leningrad I called on Rimsky-Korsakov's son, Andrey, to get copies of those Hartmann exhibition pictures which inspired Moussorgsky to compose his famous suite; there I met Gniessin. His music is not new to the world; his formative years were well rounded before the Revolution. But it was interesting to see his newest scores, the *Symphonic Monument*, a sort of musical panorama of the inter-revolutionary years, 1905–1917, and also his incidental music to a play about a village Jew, liberated and exalted by the revolutionary upheaval.

The wife of Andrey Rimsky-Korsakov is Julia Weissberg, a composer well-known from the Balaieff days. She played her *Negro Lullaby*, which seemed to contain a little too much Moussorgsky for a Negro piece. I like much more the Wagnerian breadth of her orchestral ballads and fairytales.

The last day was spent with Maximilian Steinberg, now Director of the Leningrad Conservatory. His latest symphonic work, the *Turk-Sib*, is written to glorify the famous railway. With a fine sense of humor he warned me that there was nothing militantly modern in the score, but I feel I can enjoy Steinberg's orchestral writing even without compulsory dissonances.

Leaving Russia, in the railway cars in Poland you can, for the price of one zloty, have the use of a pair of ear-phones to listen in on the radio. I heard Moscow and, while listening to the music, summarized my impressions. Soviet music is not Russian music, it is larger, for it includes the music of all the other peoples of the U.S.S.R., and this music, Turkmenian, Bashkirian, Georgian, Armenian, begins to exercise its influence on Russian music in a manner different from the days of the National School when Moussorgsky and Balakirev used Oriental motives for the sake of local color. The *Turk-Sib* has really done something to music—composers as different from each other as Steinberg, Mossolov and Litinsky have utilized "Turkmenian music," with excellent effect. Now, with gramophone recordings and scientific ethnological expeditions in search of songs, authenticity of material seems to be secure.

Parallel to the revival of regional music, the art of mass song fortifies the waning spirit of Russian folk-music. An international revolution, by some paradox of dialectics, has reinforced the national stream and has created new national tributaries. In the process, "leftist" music may have suffered a setback. But then the conceptions of "right" and "left" in art have become so confused during the last fifteen years that we no longer know whether we are radicals or reactionaries in defending "modern" music as our own esoteric creed.

23. STIMULATING TALKS REVEAL EXTRAORDINARY PARADOXES

If conclusive evidence of a cultural thaw in the relations between America and Russia was required, it was amply furnished by the outpouring of radiant energy in the direction of five Soviet composers and one musicologist who have just completed their Sputniklike trajectory in the United States.

The composers were, in the Russian alphabetical order: Fikret Amirov, Konstantin Dankevich, Dmitri Kabalevsky, Tikhon Khrennikov, and Dmitri Shostakovitch. The musicologist was Boris Yarustovsky.

From the moment of their arrival, they became the objects of admiration, friendship, and good-will. Their appearances at musical gatherings were rated as social events of the highest interest; their visits were eagerly sought by institutions of musical learning.

The language barrier was formidable; only Kabalevsky speaks tolerable English; Shostakovitch can form English sentences but, according to his own admission, gets lost when a stream of English words, sounding totally different from their appearance in print, is directed at him. Amirov, Dankevich, and Khrennikov speak only Russian. Yarustovsky can get along in rudimentary German and French. There was no lack of translators, however, and communication became feasible.

But it was the international language of music that served to establish an intimate understanding between Americans and their Soviet guests. American symphony orchestras changed their planned programs to find room for Soviet music. And seldom were the ovations more thunderous, the welcomes more spontaneous.

Ch. 23: originally published in *The Christian Science Monitor*, November 21, 1959.

There were also professional discussions, on television, on the radio, and in private meetings of American and Soviet musicians. I served as a moderator and translator on some of these occasions, and experienced that peculiar thrill of intellectual collision, clarification and ultimate understanding, that are the prerequisites of progress in ideas.

A Russian proverb says: "Talk, but don't argue; and if you have to argue, don't start a quarrel." There was plenty of argument between American and Soviet composers, but never a quarrel. The Americans questioned the Soviet uniformity of musical style; the Soviet guests denied the imputation: "Is the style of Shostakovitch the same as that of Amirov, who cultivates the folk manner of his native Azerbaijan? Did Prokofiev write in the same style as Miaskovsky?"

To some Soviet listeners, all American compositions sound alike. Does it mean that there is no diversity in American music? As another Russian proverb says: "You can't play well on someone else's pipe."

Shostakovitch asked me: "Why is dodecaphonic and electronic music so successful in America?" I reassured him that performances of dodecaphonic music in America are few and far between, and that even the works of Schoenberg, the creator of dodecaphonic music, are rarely heard. As for electronic music, produced on the magnetic tape by record-ing natural and artificial noises and tones, works of this type are heard once in a blue moon, at special gatherings, in modernistic exhibitions, and in California.

Naturally, there was a discussion of jazz. Many Soviet composers have written jazz pieces, and jazz techniques attract great interest in Russia. But, Soviet composers agreed, jazz must be artistic, such as Gershwin presented in his best works, in order to achieve respectability.

The musicologist Yarustovsky pointed out, in a television program, that American folk tunes are greatly loved in Russia. He mentioned specifically "Mississippi," which he said was a favorite of his small son. To their embarrassment, none of the Americans present could readily iden-tify the title until Yarustovsky hummed the tune, which turned out to be "Ol' Man River" from Jerome Kern's *Showboat*.

The ability of the Soviet guests to present their views articulately and develop them consistently and logically impressed everyone. And there were paradoxes. Tikhon Khrennikov, supposedly a representative of a materialistic society, insisted on the primacy of spiritual values in music, as against the purely technical endeavors. Shostakovitch's statement of ideals was particularly absorbing. He emphasized that music should have not only an esthetic, but an ethical goal, that it should glorify goodness, love, beauty, and morality, as against evil, hate, ugliness, and vice.

The Americans were, of course, in perfect agreement with their Soviet guests regarding these laudable aims, but the question was raised: "Why not experiment in the new resources? What was regarded as ugly yesterday is beautiful today. Wasn't Beethoven's music regarded as strange in his time?" To this Kabalevsky responded with ardor and passion: "Beethoven wrote his music for humanity, but the present-day modernists compose only for themselves, their relatives, and their friends." And he exclaimed: "Take your dodecaphonic, electronic, cacophonic, serial, and concrete music! We have no use for it!"

The discussion grew so animated that, in my capacity of a two-way translator, I was overwhelmed by the polytonality of American and Russian voices begging to be heard and understood. As the Russian proverb says: "I hear the bell ringing, but don't know where it comes from." Yet somehow the hosts and the guests began to penetrate the meaning, even without immediate translation, through the common Greek and Latin roots of modern musical terminology. The discussion was resumed at a more deliberate pace.

As another Russian proverb says: "Gently go, farther get!"

24. MOSCOW: MUSICAL INTERLUDE

This was to be my last day in Moscow, but the airport at my next destination, Warsaw, was, in the technical phrase of airmen, "not accepting" on account of ground fog. I already had said my fond farewells to my professional colleagues and personal friends among Soviet composers and musicologists. We had even gone through the traditional ritual of sitting down for a few minutes before a final send-off, an allegorical bon voyage concluding with wishes of Godspeed, which sounds even more emphatically religious in Russian: "With God!"

My reappearance in Moscow after I had to return from the airport was therefore greeted with embarrassing inquiries as to what had happened, followed by second and somewhat anticlimactic farewells. But to that ground fog in Warsaw I owe a most interesting afternoon at the home of Aram Khatchaturian, renowned Armenian-born Soviet composer.

I was taking a leisurely walk in the ancient quarter of Moscow, in the neighborhood of the Conservatory, when I almost collided with him on a narrow sidewalk. He, too, asked me if I was still in Moscow, which I obviously was. Then he asked me to drop in "for a quarter of an hour" at his place nearby.

He was carrying a bulky score under his arm, which, he explained to me, was his latest work, a piece for violin and orchestra originally entitled *Rhapsody*, but renamed *Rhapsody-Concerto*.

"A concerto is music played with the chandeliers ablaze" he explained, "but in a rhapsody the lights are dimmed. The violin part in my piece is written in brilliant lights, so it has to be a concerto."

Ch. 24: originally published in *The Christian Science Monitor*, August 21, 1963.

Khatchaturian's apartment was in a street recently named after a famous Russian soprano, Nezhdanova (musical streets are abundant in Russia; the American Embassy is situated on Tchaikovsky Street). Construction and urban renewal were in full swing, and wooden planks were laid out for pedestrians to cross uprooted intersections.

Khatchaturian led me with assurance over these makeshift pathways. We entered his house and took an operative elevator to apartment No. 19, where he lived. He opened the door and called his wife from an inner room. I heard her pleasantly resonant Russian voice inquiring, "Nikolay Leonidovitch Slonimsky?" and soon she entered the living room to greet me.

I apologized for my unheralded visit, but with a characteristic Russian knack of making an unexpected guest feel immediately welcome, she said, why of course she knew my name, and wasn't I the first to write about her in the American press? Indeed, Mrs. Aram Khatchaturian, under her maiden name Nina Makarova, is a distinguished composer in her own right, possibly the most original woman composer of the Soviet Union.

An atmosphere of free and animated exchange was established at once. Khatchaturian said he wished there were more food in the house— it was about 4 o'clock in the afternoon—but I assured him that I came principally for intellectual and artistic food.

Still, we sat down at the table. Caviar and other hors d'oeuvres appeared as if by magic. I expressed my appreciation of these Russian delicacies and was about to rise from the table in anticipation of leaving when a middle-aged Russian niania, the unchangeable image of a Russian nurse, came in carrying a large soup tureen.

The dish was marvelously prepared. I complimented everyone concerned, when the niania brought in a plate of sturgeon. So this was a regular dinner, and I asked Khatchaturian what he meant by saying there was no food in the house.

By way of reply, he told an anecdote about a hostess who had to go out and left a note for her house guests: "In case there is nothing to eat in the house, take a ham, porridge, and eggs from the ice box and serve with strawberry jam."

The joke came true when niania reappeared with a roast chicken. Was there anything else that was in the category of "nothing to eat"?

No, really nothing, except of course blancmange, pastry and other sweets.

My fifteen minutes stretched to nearly three hours. We adjourned to Khatchaturian's piano study and plunged into a discussion of the validity of modern music. What is wrong with dodecaphonic composition, I wanted to know, that makes this formidable word a term of opprobrium in the Soviet press? Peaceful coexistence between dodecaphonic, or twelve-note music, and tonality is entirely possible.

Khatchaturian sat at the piano and ran over some polytonal arpeggios from one of his symphonies. I suggested that, by completing the cycle of four triads, all twelve different notes of the chromatic scale could be used and yet the music would remain clearly tonal.

Khatchaturian became interested and asked me, with a chuckle, if he could borrow my quadritonal combination (F-sharp major, E major, D minor, C minor) for his next composition.

We bandied some more ideas, and I was impressed by Khatchaturian's grasp of different musical problems. Yet his musical knowledge was never ostentatious, and he preserves the popular touch that is the secret of the immense success of his music. I told him that his "Saber Dance" was still playing on juke boxes everywhere in the United States.

But why was his ballet *Spartacus* so violently attacked in the New York press?

I could offer no explanation, for I had never heard the music. It was one of my greatest disappointments that I could not attend a performance of *Spartacus* in Erivan, capital of the Armenian Soviet Republic. It was put on especially to enable me to hear it, but I missed the event because of another incidence of ground fog in my air journey through the vast expanses of the Soviet Union.

"Well, here is *Spartacus*," Khatchaturian said, and he pulled out a freshly printed score of the ballet. He inscribed it to me in his florid but intelligible handwriting. Any other scores? I rattled off a list of desirable items, and Khatchaturian handed them to me one by one.

But wouldn't it be too heavy to carry them with me by air?

I would manage, I replied, eager not to let go of the precious scores. As a matter of fact, the very next day I mailed the music to myself from Moscow to Boston. A most commendable and convenient service exists in Russian post offices. For 15 kopecks, the clerk will wrap up your package, address it at your dictation, place some pretty stamps on the cover, and ship it off.

But when I handed the score of *Spartacus* to the girl clerk at the postal desk of the Sovietskaya Hotel where I was staying, she tarried a moment, then asked: "What is your sincere opinion of *Spartacus*? Do you regard it as really superior to *Gayane*?" (*Gayane* is a ballet Khatchaturian wrote 20 years ago, and it contains the famous "Saber Dance.") I must admit that this simple question coming from a postal clerk astounded me, both as a testimony to Khatchaturian's popularity and to the incredibly high level of artistic interests in all strata of Russian society.

Khatchaturian's secretary came in to take some dictation. He has an enormous amount of correspondence from all over the world. On the occasion of his recent 60th birthday he had to resort to newspaper columns for acknowledgment of numerous messages he had received. Once more it seemed a propitious and even compulsory moment to take my leave of the Khatchaturians, but Nina Makarova took me to her piano study and played some of her pieces for me, intricate but harmonious, masterly in technique and yet somehow feminine in expression. Then she played and sang arias from her opera, *Zaya*, named after the heroic Russian girl who was a guerrilla fighter during the war.

How Russian this music sounded! What round harmonies, what wavy melodies! It was totally different from Khatchaturian's, which derives its substance from the orientalistic melos of the Caucasus and is infused with elemental rhythmic animation. Musically, Mr. and Mrs. Khatchaturian do not influence each other; they retain their separate artistic individualities.

Now I was definitely leaving. My musical baggage was supplemented by several pieces from Nina Makarova, some of them the last copies in her possession. I was reluctant to take these. Music in Russia sells out so rapidly that composers themselves have trouble getting extra copies but she was in a generous mood, and I was in a receptive frame of mind.

I was already on the way out when Khatchaturian said he wanted to have a word with me, so once more I went to his study.

"Can you help me to go to America?" he asked without preliminaries. I was amazed at this request.

"But all you have to do is to ask," I said. "You are a famous man. Any musical organization will be glad to sponsor your appearance in America."

Yes, Khatchaturian said, he did have an offer for an American tour, but it was unacceptable. He was to conduct a couple of concerts on the Pacific Coast, then rush to the East for some engagements in Washington without an opportunity to stay more than a day or two in each city.

"I want to *see* America," he protested. "Everybody goes to America," he said. He named several Soviet composers who had been recent visitors in the United States.

He pointed out that he was a competent conductor, and that his concerts always played to full houses wherever he appeared—in England, in Australia, in Iceland, in South America—so there was some assurance of satisfactory returns.

"Besides," he added, "In Boston there is a large Armenian colony, which will support my concerts."

Would he authorize my making his wish known to American readers? Yes, he would. "I *like* American," he said, "I *love* the American people."

25. CULTURAL EXPLOSION IN THE U.S.S.R.

I was the sole passenger in the Aeroflot plane flying from London to Moscow. Three Soviet officials occupied a forward compartment. One of them asked me, in article-less English (there are no articles, definite or indefinite, in the Russian language), whether I needed anything. I replied in my native and still instinctively fluent Russian that I had no particular wishes except to borrow the latest issue of *Pravda* invitingly spread on his chair. He handed the paper to me. There were no screaming headlines: *Pravda* never screams at readers, but rather declares and expounds, in restrained 24-point type. The typographical sobriety of its communiqués dealing with threats to the "Island of Liberty" by "imperialist pirates" made the substance all the more ominous. For I was winging my way to Russia at the height of the Cuban crisis. Understandably, no other tourists boarded the Soviet plane.

But I was on a mission, sent by the State Department, as an American Specialist under the Educational and Cultural Exchange Program. Concurrently, I was invited by the Union of Soviet Composers, who were to take care of all my expenses within the Soviet Union. My guide sheet from the State Department said that "American Specialists go abroad for the purpose of rendering a specific service for the United States" and that their task was to "develop good will, understanding and respect for the United States, its policies and institutions." To miss such an opportunity would have been an act of unjustifiable cowardice, and I have never lacked passive courage.

For stimulating reading matter, I took along a copy of *Fail-Safe*, the notorious novel which ends in an atomic obliteration of Moscow and self-immolation of New York City. It was favorably reviewed in *Pravda* as confirming the Soviet notion that nuclear war can erupt by accident, and so I was sure I could pass it through the Soviet customs.

New York had its share of jitters in real life. A woman acquaintance called up my daughter to announce that she was leaving the city, the prime target of the Soviet nuclear attack. "Lots of people are going away," my daughter commented, "my father among them." "Where is he going?" "To Moscow!" The effect was electric.

We were flying east, and the darkness came on at an accelerated pace. Moscow was a sprawling sea of intermittent lights as we came in to land. Moscow—MOCKBA! I remembered the Pushkin lines I learned in school:

> Oh Moscow! What is in this sound
> That makes a Russian heart resound?

But I was born in St. Petersburg—a city that changed its name twice since then, to Petrograd to Leningrad—and my Russian heart became thoroughly Americanized in the interim. I was beset by pragmatic rather than literary thoughts at my first contact after decades with the land of my birth. Would anyone meet me at the airport? Would I be welcome as a guest of the Union of Soviet Composers? I looked anxiously for signs of recognition at a group of people gathered in front of the plane. Yes, this was my reception committee—a cultural attaché from the American Embassy and two eminent Soviet music critics, Yuri Keldysh (brother of the President of the Soviet Academy of Sciences) and Ivan Martynov, both of whom I had met at a musicological congress in New York a year before. There was with them also a tall young man. Keldysh introduced him to me: "This is your nephew, Sergey Slonimsky, a talented Soviet composer. Seriozha, meet your uncle!"

There were definite family characteristics in his cast of countenance, but this unexpected realization was to me more than an emotional call of the blood. It was proof positive that there was no longer any danger for a Soviet citizen to welcome close relatives from abroad. True, my nephew was a member of the Union of Soviet Composers delegated to meet an invited guest, but consanguinity must have played a part in his selection. We became friends. In Leningrad I spent many an uninhibited evening at the home of his father, my brother Mikhail Slonimsky, a novelist of considerable stature. In 1948, during the Stalinist purification campaign he was sharply rebuked for the incorrect line he took in one of his books, but was subsequently restored in favor and was awarded the Order of the Red Banner. My other Russian brother, Alexander, is a literary critic as well as a novelist; he, too, suffered a temporary setback for having expressed an unorthodox opinion of the essence of Gogol's humor, but was soon vindicated. His wife is a translator of American literature. At their home in Moscow I received unstinted hospitality.

But I had a duty to perform. In my task of radiating good will I was formidably helped by the United States Information Agency. Acceding to my ambitious request, the Agency airlifted to me, care of the American Embassy in Moscow, at unimaginable cost in air freight, thousands of published works by American composers, many of them in duplicate and triplicate, and hundreds of recording albums of American music, from jazz to dodecaphonic symphonies. I worked arduously in the consular section of the American Embassy housed in an old mansion on Tchaikovsky Street, often staying after the official closing hour, sorting out these musical treasures to decide who should get what. The lion's share went to the Union of Soviet Composers in Moscow. As a result, it now has the largest library of American music in Europe.

The Leningrad composers showed interest for American music of the avant-garde and for jazz. Accordingly, I gave most of such material to them. The Ukrainian musicians in Kiev had a predilection for music based on folk songs, and so I sent them a lot of music in this category. The most modern-minded of all Soviet composers are the Georgians, in the Caucasus, and they received a lot of music by American dodecaphonic composers.

I made complete lists of what music went where, with a view to arranging performances. Since there is no copyright agreement for publication or performance, the modus operandi is very simple: the Russians copy orchestral parts and perform the work without bothering about the complexities of the right of performance. When Samuel Barber visited the Soviet Union in March 1962, he was presented with a copy of the Soviet edition of his piano sonata. It was a pleasant surprise to him for he had no idea that this work was republished by the Soviet Music Publishing Company in Moscow.

In order to expedite delivery, I carried batches of American music and the rather heavy recording albums manually, from the American Embassy to the Union of Soviet Composers by taxi. The Soviet chauffeur of the American Embassy was not supposed to do any physical cartage and I was my own porter from the mail room down a few steps to the ground floor and through the gate to the street. Two Soviet militiamen were stationed at the entrance to the Embassy, but I was never challenged by them when I hauled packages out of the building. I was therefore taken aback when on a later visit one of them asked me in a curiously oblique form of inquiry: "You are not mistaken?" I replied I was an American citizen going about my business with the Embassy. The sentinel gave me a salute and let me through without asking for documents. I realized afterwards that the reason for this was my wearing a luxuriant karakul hat I had purchased the day before, and which gave me a very Russian look.

The interest that American music aroused among serious Soviet musicians can be demonstrated from the following episode. On December 1, 1962, I gave a collection of eighteen recording albums to a representative of the Composers' Union of the Soviet Republic of Georgia in the Caucasus, among them such advanced works as *Three Places in New England* by Ives, Second String Quartet by Elliott Carter, Third String Quartet by William Schuman, String Quartets by Irving Fine and Leon Kirchner, and Jazz Abstractions by Gunther Schuller. The batch also included seven works by Aaron Copland, eight symphonic compositions by Samuel Barber, several pieces of chamber music by Roy Harris, suites by Virgil Thomson, and some Negro spirituals. Before taking these record albums to Tbilisi, the Georgian representative let a Moscow violinist re-record the music on the magnetophone, or tape recorder. They spent fourteen hours in a single day to finish the job. I should guess that these and other American records were re-recorded many times afterwards. It is my educated guess that each record album which I imported into the Soviet Union procreated a dozen magnetophone tapes.

The Foreign Commission of the Soviet Composers' Union in Moscow prepared a multigraphed two-page schedule of my activities during my stay in the Soviet Union. It was a well-balanced plan, which included travel, sight-seeing, theaters, museums, visits to conservatories and music schools, meetings with composers and musicologists, excursions, etc. In addition to travel tickets and prepaid hotel rooms and meals, I was handed a goodly sum in rubles for incidental expenses.

Most of my time was spent in Moscow and Leningrad, but I also made extended visits to Kiev, the capital of the Ukrainian Soviet Republic,

Tbilisi in Georgia, Erevan in Armenia, and as far as the oil city of Baku in Azerbaijan on the Caspian Sea. I had no difficulty in language, for Russian is spoken everywhere in the Soviet Union. The Ukrainian language is a dialect quite easy to understand, but the national language of Georgia and Armenia, and the Tatar language of Azerbaijan belong to totally different linguistic groups, with non-Cyrillic alphabets.

In Moscow, in Leningrad, in Kiev, in Tbilisi, in Erevan and in Baku, I was invited to give talks to local composers and musicologists on the subject of modern music, and specifically American music. This was the first time, I believe, that an American was given the opportunity of addressing his colleagues in the Soviet Union in public lectures completely free and without a scintilla of implied censorship. Since the hottest subject in the musical life of the Soviet Union is dodecaphony, or 12-tone composition, I allowed myself to announce the subject of my talks with a somewhat flippant subtitle "Peaceful Coexistence Between Dodecaphony and Tonality."

For many years Soviet cultural spokesmen have inveighed against dodecaphony as if it were an abomination, a monster created by the misanthropic theoreticians of the decadent West. Shostakovich once asked me: "Show me a piece of dodecaphonic music that is harmonious, that sounds well, and I will concede that twelve-tone compositions have merit." What I proposed to demonstrate in my lectures in the Soviet Union was the possibility of writing tonal dodecaphonic music, using major and minor keys, by dividing the twelve notes of the chromatic scale into four mutually exclusive triads, two major and two minor, as, for example, C major, F-sharp major, D minor and G-sharp minor. I could further demonstrate that this succession of triads was used by Debussy and Strauss, even though they were not aware that there was such a thing as dodecaphony.

It is amazing to reflect that the method of composition excogitated by an Austrian musician, Arnold Schoenberg, should become the bone of contention between the as yet cautious avant-garde and the mighty Soviet government itself. For Premier Khrushchev himself took note of the penetration of dodecaphony into Soviet music. In his speech at the meeting between Communist Party leaders, Soviet government officials and writers, artists and musicians which took place in Moscow on March 8, 1963, Khrushchev assailed new fashions in music with a force of invective much more vivid than the language employed by some American antimodernist critics. Khrushchev even made an entirely acceptable pun when he said that dodecaphony was the same as cacophony. What other head of government has ever ventured into the field of musical techniques and used esoteric terminology with such accuracy? Khrushchev's remarks on dodecaphony are worth quoting:

> It seems that there are young men and women among our musicians who try hard to prove that melody has lost its right to exist and that it is being supplanted by some kind of new music, dodecaphony, the music of noises. A normal person has difficulty in understanding what is hidden behind the word dodecaphony, but according to all probability, it must be the same as cacophony. Well, we are determined to make a clean sweep of this cacophony in music. Our people cannot accept this rubbish into its artistic arsenal. (Voices: Right!) (Applause)

At my lectures I reassured my audiences that I was not a fanatical adherent of dodecaphony, but that I felt that progress in music requires experimentation. I also spoke on new American rhythms. I am a pianist of sorts, and I played some Gershwin, Ives, Barber, Roy Harris and, to conclude, Henry Cowell's tone clusters, performed with the aid of fists, forearms and elbows.

My audiences consisted of members of local composers' unions, graduate conservatory students, musicologists and university professors. I held forth on the average of two and a half hours at each one of these lectures, but few people left the hall, and none, as far as I could observe, succumbed to narcolepsy, which is the occupational disorder of listeners to technical talks on music. In Baku I started at 3 o'clock and it was 6:30 when our session, which included a question period, finally came to an end. Almost as long was the talk I gave in Leningrad. It was a musicologist's Utopia. When I was asked after my talk in Tbilisi if I had any particular wishes to express, I replied that my most heartfelt wish was to import my audience to my hometown, Boston.

In Moscow, Leningrad and Kiev I also gave talks on musical lexicography, which attracted a galaxy of Soviet musicologists whose books and articles I have read for years. I met Gregory Schneerson with whom I had conducted a long correspondence and who had been my chief purveyor of accurate information about Soviet music. During the musical cold war our correspondence waned, and Schneerson took a few jabs at me in print. In his book *Music Living and Dead* my name appears in Part II together with other dwellers in outer darkness. I twitted him during the question period about his effort to bury me, but he said it was all a mistake, a by-product of a regrettable period. He is preparing a new edition of *Music Living and Dead* in which I will hopefully be taken out of Part II and into Part I. I had a wonderful evening with Schneerson and his family in his apartment, drinking Russian tea with Russian jam and listening to the Soviet news broadcast on the Moscow Radio. It was difficult for me to reconcile the impression of this mild-mannered, amazingly well informed Jewish-Russian intellectual, a musician and a linguist fluent in several languages, with the fire-breathing publicist leading an assault with the fanaticism of a musical Savonarola against the unspeakable vices of dodecaphonic perversion and the diabolical wiles of the Musique Concrète.

But dodecaphony refuses to lie down and die under all these attacks. I heard a dodecaphonic violin sonata by a professor of the Leningrad Conservatory, performed by a laureate of the Tchaikovsky Competition; several other composers use modified forms of twelve-tone composition in their works. The names of Schoenberg and Alban Berg and Webern are universally known among Soviet musicians, and the few scores by these composers that are found in conservatories and music libraries are eagerly studied. Anticipating this interest, I took along with me as many scores by Schoenberg, Berg and Webern as I conveniently could, as well as recordings of their works, and made happy several outstanding Soviet composers and musicologists by presenting these scores to them as a gift.

A striking illustration of this interest in western modern music was provided for me in a book of suggestions in the music store Number 41 situated near the Moscow Conservatory. Under the rubric, "What Ought to Be Published", I found the following items:

Stravinsky: Canticum, Agon, Violin Concerto
Webern: Collected Works
Berg: Chamber Concerto

Schoenberg: Violin Concerto, or at least something by Schoenberg. It is impossible to continue to discriminate against this great composer. Recall that he was being published in the 1920's! Follow the practice of your predecessors, of course, not the immediate predecessors of the years 1938–1953.

More of this, also Honegger, Milhaud, Krenek, Bartók, and less opus numbers of the type of [here the name of a fairly well known Soviet composer was cited].

The request concluded with these words: "I am not giving my address—you won't publish anything anyway!!!"

Another request in the same book, from a student of the State Conservatory of Azerbaijan, was for the republication of a theoretical work on music, with a postscript: "Send a few hundred copies to Baku; they will be sold out in two days."

The confident promise by this student from Baku that a theoretical work on music would sell hundreds of copies in a couple of days points at another Utopian aspect of Soviet culture. The incredible sales of books, all kinds of books, books on music, books on literature, translations of foreign authors, Russian classics, anything in book form, except perhaps complete texts of dull treatises by official bureaucrats. A veritable bookstore explosion!

Everything gets published in the Soviet Union, but there are never enough copies to go around. I collected some statistics: there are three brochures on Prokofiev's opera *War and Peace*, 80, 48, and 20 pages each respectively. The smallest brochure was published in 25,000 copies in 1960, and the author had hardly any copies left by 1962. A brochure on an obscure 19th-century Ukrainian singer and composer Semyon Stepanovitch Gulak-Artemovsky has sold 20,000 copies within a couple of years. A Soviet translation of Stokowski's book *Music for All of Us* was announced for publication, but the entire edition of 13,000 copies was sold out to priority holders before any copies reached the music stores. One of my Leningrad friends told me that he intercepted a copy when it went to an unauthorized person, and got it for himself.

Music magazines sell out so quickly that it is virtually impossible to get a back number. I missed the May 1962 issue of *Sovietskaya Musica* because of a lapse in my subscription from America and could not get it even in the editorial office of the magazine a few months later when I arrived in Moscow.

When it was announced in Tbilisi that the collected works of Charles Dickens in a Russian translation were to be made available on subscription on a certain date, a line was formed before the bookstore at midnight on the eve of the day of publication. A rollcall was made every hour on the hour during the night, and those who did not respond lost their turn. A member of the Georgian Composers' Union lost his turn at 6 A.M. when he fell asleep and did not declare his presence.

In Klin a new translation of Jack London's *The Call of the Wild* was put on sale at a local bookstore. A line was formed, in the dead of winter, early in the morning. A man who stood in that line and had a number in the 700s got his book at the cost of frostbite.

Books of information, particularly dictionaries of all types, are sold out almost immediately.

The prices of books are low in comparison with American publications. Volume II of *Theatrical Encyclopedia* containing 1,211 pages, with copious illustrations, published in 1963, is priced at 3 rubles. Its first printing of 43,000 copies was gone at subscription almost immediately upon publication.

The same instantaneous sales are made in music stores. I was very eager to obtain the complete score of the *Pathetic Oratorio* by Yuri Sviridov, which had just been published and performed when I was in Moscow. When I naively asked for a copy in the Conservatory Music Store the sales lady gave me a pitying look. How could I expect to have any copies left? I asked Sviridov himself to give me a copy, but he had none at his disposal. Knowledgeable friends told me that I might have a chance to stumble on a copy in a provincial music store. Eventually I did get one, in Kiev.

The Eighth String Quartet by Shostakovich seems never to have reached the music stores. Even the Union of Soviet Composers could not give me a copy at the time.

An edition of 150 copies of a Sonata for cello solo by an Armenian composer was sold out in six weeks. The composer gave me his own copy. I made this fact known at my lecture in Erevan, and asked a rhetorical question: "Is Armenia populated by Casalses?"

Indeed, the Armenian musical eruption is remarkable. There was hardly any musical development there at the end of the war in 1945, but in 1962, with a total population of 1,800,000 and an area of 27,000 square kilometers, Armenia had 116 symphonic composers, that is, one composer per 233 square kilometers or per 15,517 Armenian men, women or children.

I was determined to discover whether these sales were in any way fictitious, the facades of so many Potemkin villages. I suspected that large quantities of books and musical scores were deposited in some warehouse and never moved to the stores. I voiced these suspicions quite openly to Tikhon Khrennikov, Secretary General of the Union of Soviet Composers. He smiled and tapped sympathetically on my shoulder, as if to say he had wished it were so. But no, the Union of Soviet Composers and the State Music Publishing House simply did not have enough paper to publish more copies. The vocal score of Khrennikov's own opera *During the Storm* has been alloted only 400 copies, not enough for an opera that has had a successful run in the Soviet Union.

To clinch the case, I checked on the sales of books and music of my own relatives. My nephew told me that the original printing of 150 copies of his viola sonata was sold out in six weeks. *The Mastery of Pushkin*, a rather specialized stylistic treatise by my brother Alexander sold 10,000 copies in a few months, and a new printing of 20,000 copies was ordered. A large printing of 100,000 copies of a novel by my brother Michael went in a matter of weeks, so that the author himself missed out on the sale and could not get extra copies that he sorely needed for personal gifts.

Soviet composers and authors occasionally grumble about the slowness in the production of their works, but to me their schedules seem fantastically expeditious. Again to take an example from my own relatives, my nephew's symphony was submitted to the Union of Soviet Composers for a judgment on publication in December of 1962. I was invited to the hearing conducted by a committee of composers and musicologists and was impressed by the earnestness and impartiality of the opinions. The decision was in favor of publishing; the manuscript was sent to the engraver in March 1963, and the symphony was published in August 1963. It comprised 164 pages, and was priced at 2 rubles, 67 kopecks. The first printing was only 150 copies, of which I got one. Last, but not least: My nephew received 1000 rubles for the composition of the symphony, and is expected to receive proportionate benefits from sales of copies and performances.

Financially speaking, composers, and "creative workers" in general, are privileged citizens. They have a fairly definite assurance of publication of their productions, assuming a professional competence. Intellectuals and musicians of eminence get virtually everything published. Nikolai Miaskovsky wrote twenty-seven symphonies, all of which are printed in full score, with a set of orchestral parts for each.

There are no prima donnas among Soviet performers. Conductors of the highest rank are easily accessible to the humblest composer.

Instrumentalists are remarkably democratic in their professional attitude. It is quite common for celebrated artists to appear in performances of new works in a special concert. I heard a laureate of the Tchaikovsky competition play second violin in a performance of Shostakovich's Eighth String Quartet.

The usual question asked when these Utopian statistics are cited is this: All right, Soviet composers are given exceptional opportunities to have their works published and performed, but are they free to compose as they please? Doesn't the Soviet government tell them how and in what style to compose? Aren't they forced to glorify the Soviet Union in their music and to follow a narrowly circumscribed style?

The answer to this controversial problem is provided from close observation of the inner workings of the Union of Soviet Composers, the State Music Publishing House and other organizations in charge of development of Soviet music. The Soviet government does not in any sense control the style and technique of Soviet music. This control is exercised by the Union of Soviet Composers which holds periodic hearings of new music submitted for publication and performance. There are definite limitations as to the techniques employed in such works. Obviously, avant-garde music, such as is widely published in Poland, will not get through the inner councils of the Union of Soviet Composers, because the entire direction of Soviet music is opposed to ultra-modern ways of musical composition. But works of a very advanced nature, complex and dissonant, are often accepted if they have intrinsic merit.

As an invited guest of the Union of Soviet Composers, I have been privileged to obtain a copy of its Charter, an extremely important document published in 500 copies and not generally distributed. The fundamental clause of this Charter sets down the following postulates:

> The Union of Soviet Composers is a voluntary social organization that unites composers and musicologists actively participating in the progress of Soviet music. In attaining full mastery of the Marxist-Leninist theory which equips a creative worker with the capacity of observing the authentic essence of life in all its totality and all its complexity, Soviet composers are guided by the method of Socialist Realism. Socialist Realism demands from the composer a truthful reflection of actuality in its revolutionary development, high mastery in artistic realization of life's images. While opening multilateral opportunities for the

expression of individual traits, Socialist Realism offers a wealth and variety of artistic media and styles, a broad creative initiative in the struggle for Communist ideological content and the ethnic peculiarities of the multinational musical art of the Soviet Union.

There follows the enumeration of eleven tasks of the Union of Soviet Composers. Task No. 4 is "the postulation of Soviet music as a progressive force in world musical culture and irreconcilable struggle against the influences of the bourgeois ideology."

Since the essence of the bourgeois ideology is, according to Soviet music philosophers, Formalism, it is perhaps desirable to quote a definition of this elusive concept from the third edition of the *Brief Music Dictionary* by A. Dolzhansky, published in Leningrad in 1959:

FORMALISM (from Latin, forma, external aspect; in a philosophical sense, detachment of form from content), a bourgeois cosmopolitan tendency opposed to realism in art, thus destroying its ideality, its national autochthony and progressivism, and instead preaching individualism and pessimism, distorting the images of reality and investing them with intentionally contrived, ugly forms.

It must be pointed out that the term progressivism, as used in this definition and elsewhere in Soviet declarations on music, is applied to what outsiders would call national traditionalism. Conversely, advanced types of musical composition, particularly dodecaphonic music, are invariably referred to in the Soviet press as reactionary. In such connection, the word avant-garde is usually put in derisive quotation marks.

Khrushchev's speech of March 8, 1963, may again be quoted: "When I listen to the music of Glinka, tears of joy appear in my eyes. Perhaps it is old-fashioned, but I am no longer a young person, and I like to hear David Oistrakh play the violin, and I like to hear the violin ensemble of the Bolshoi Theater. I cannot pretend that my perception of music should become a norm for everyone. But really we cannot pamper people who serve a cacophony of sounds in a guise of good music, and treat music loved by the people as being out of fashion."

New and striking talents grow and flourish in Russia. In music, an art in which genius reveals itself at an early age, there are prodigies rising in clusters. For some unfathomable reason, violinists, pianists and violoncel-

lists proliferate in the regions of Vilna and Odessa, and they are mostly of
Jewish stock. The names of Oistrakh, Richter, Gilels, Rostropovich are
known to the whole world. There is also a handful of remarkably talented
young Soviet conductors.

For some time before my Russian trip I had been in frequent correspondence with a Ukrainian musician Igor Blazhkov. He revealed an
extraordinary knowledge of modern music, and was remarkably well read
in musical literature in several languages. Naturally I was eager to see him
the moment I arrived in Kiev where he lived, and I was astounded to find
that he was only twenty-six years old and in fact looked even younger. He
told me that there are several young musicians in Kiev whom I would like
to meet, and I expressed my ardent desire to become acquainted with
these fresh sprouts of Soviet music. Blazhkov's wife, a charming young
woman, turned out to be a musicologist in her own right. Together we
went to a friend's apartment, cluttered up with music, books, an ancient
grand piano, and homemade records. One of Blazhkov's young friends
played for me some dodecaphonic piano pieces of the highest distinction,
lyric, and yet structurally compact. There was something inspiring in this
group of young people searching for new ways of self-expression. But
soon I learned there was also trouble.

Blazhkov's wife, writing under her maiden name Galina Mokreyeva,
contributed to the Polish music magazine *Ruch Muzyczny* a report on the
concert life in Kiev, in which she praised the young Ukrainian composers
and made some deprecatory remarks about the musicians of the older
generation. She wrote: "A recent concert of works by young composers of
Kiev has shown that new talents are appearing in the Ukraine, searching
for individual paths and capable of contributing something new in music.
Among a multitude of imitative, lifeless and helpless compositions by
local musicians, a splendid and illuminating flash of light was suddenly
exploded by a group of interesting and audacious creations of our
youngest composers, some of them still Conservatory students."

Mrs. Blazhkov then proceeded with a detailed account of works by
some of these young musicians; in discussing one particular work she said
that in this music there was present something of the spirit of the
"American pioneer of genius Charles Ives."

The article incurred the greatest displeasure on the part of established Ukrainian composers. Who was that girl who dared to dismiss the
achievements of a generation of Ukrainian composers in such a cavalier

fashion? She was charged in several newspaper articles with treachery of her native art in publishing such an article in a foreign magazine. By association, Igor Blazhkov was also attacked as a modernistic cosmopolitan whose interests lie beyond his own country. It was recalled that he insisted on conducting Stravinsky's *Firebird* at the time when Stravinsky was not very acceptable in the Soviet Union—Blazhkov was finally persuaded to take the piece off his program. He was the proud possessor of several personal letters from Stravinsky. He had in his personal library an impressive collection of ultra-modern scores by western composers. He was an avowed modernist.

There was another charge brought out against Blazhkov in a local newspaper: that he abandoned his post as music organizer in a small Ukrainian mining settlement to which he was officially assigned, because, the accusation continued, he believed that his energies were wasted on a small task such as this. He thus failed in his social duty. There were dark hints at false rumors that Blazhkov was a victim of "repression."

I was deeply concerned by these attacks on Blazhkov's integrity as a citizen and musician combined with criticism of his wife's article, and I wondered how he would get out of this double trouble. Curiously enough, the articles in question never specifically stated that Galina Mokreyeva was Mrs. Blazhkov. But then personal connections are rarely mentioned in Soviet journalism. Even in biographical dictionaries of contemporary Soviet figures family history or kinship with another eminent person of the same surname is usually left out.

It was a great relief to me when Blazhkov suddenly appeared in Moscow as conductor at a concert in the course of a festival of Ukrainian music there. I was then back in Moscow from Baku, and I was delighted at the opportunity to hear Blazhkov. I knew that he was competent and extremely knowledgeable, but his showing at the concert was a revelation. He conducted everything from memory, demonstrating his complete mastery of the difficult music, a composition by Leonid Grabovsky, one of the Ukrainian youngsters praised in his wife's article. His precision (I particularly remembered the certainty with which he indicated a minor cue for the suspended cymbal), his rhythmic verve, his imaginative dynamics, his poise and grace (he is six feet tall) were tremendously impressive. "But you are an absolutely first-class conductor!" I told him after the concert. He declined the compliment. "I simply tried to present the music as effectively as possible," he said. Grabovsky's composition carried the first prize at the competition held in connection with this festival, and Blazhkov's superb performance undoubtedly played a role in this award.

I felt a necessity of expressing my admiration for Blazhkov's talent to my Ukrainian friends. I sat down and dashed off a letter to my Kiev host, Konstantin Dankevich, Director of the Kiev Conservatory and President of the Union of Composers of the Soviet Socialist Republic of the Ukraine: "Dear Konstantin Feodorovich, I am writing to you to express my sincere enthusiasm for Igor Blazhkov as a symphonic conductor. I had known him chiefly as a young musicologist of remarkable knowledge and ability, but his genius for conducting was a revelation to me. I am convinced that should he appear with an American orchestra, he would be a sensational success. Glory be to the Ukrainian Soviet Socialist Republic which raises such talents as Igor Blazhkov! Glory be to you personally, my dear Konstantin Feodorovich, for having fostered this talent in your capacity as an eminent Ukrainian music educator!"

As a rule, professional organizations in the Soviet Union attend to the financial and other needs of their members. National unions of Soviet composers maintain special music funds to help their members in various ways. They provide fares to travel to any point in the Soviet Union where a performance of a large-scale work by a member is presented. They organize "creative evenings" presenting works by one composer. They pay for the copying of orchestral and choral parts. Occasionally they give a hundred rubles or so as an "encouragement" to a composer who is, for some reason, discouraged. When an encouraged composer fails to complete a work for which he was given a monetary encouragement, he is cajoled or chided in the public press. Yuri Shaporin worked for nearly twenty years on his opera *The Decembrists*. So eager were his colleagues to see the opera finished and performed that they addressed an open letter to him in the press urging him to complete his work, long awaited by the Bolshoi Theater for performance. He finally did. This spectacle of reluctant or procrastinating composers has something of a morality play quality in it, and there is profound satisfaction in it when virtue triumphs over acedia.

A country place for composers and musicologists is provided at Ruza, a couple of hours' ride by automobile from Moscow. An atmosphere of delightful rusticity is maintained there. My own excursion to Ruza gave me an opportunity to meet a number of interesting musicians all at once, among them the composers, both Jewish, of two popular Russian songs, "Do Russians Want a War?" to a bitterly ironic poem by Yevtushenko, and

"Fourteen Minutes before the Start," originally an Air Corps song, which subsequently was adopted by the Soviet cosmonauts as their unofficial hymn.

In Ruza I unexpectedly met Lina Ivanovna Prokofieva, Prokofiev's first wife. She sounded extremely cheerful despite the trials and tribulations she had undergone in the dark period before 1953. She confirmed the rumor that she spent several years in a labor camp, and was incarcerated in a prison cell for eight months. She also told me that she was never legally divorced from Prokofiev and therefore regarded his second marriage as invalid. This personal history is perhaps not a matter for publication, but it is interesting to note that Soviet citizens seem to feel free to recount such painful episodes.

The more I associated with Soviet musicians, the more admiration I felt for them. The labors of Soviet musicologists in particular aroused my profound respect. The quantity and the quality of publications of original research that they have produced during recent years are without parallel or precedent. They possess a flaming fanaticism which is paramount in such unrewarding tasks. In addition to the inherent difficulties of research, Soviet musicologists work under a disheartening handicap: because of the lack of foreign currency, they are unable to purchase the necessary reference works from abroad, and depend on barter with foreign colleagues to obtain these materials. The few copies of foreign music publications in the major State libraries are in constant demand.

Like everyone visiting the Soviet Union for any length of time, I heard hair-raising tales of surveillance, taciturn men in trench coats casually crossing your path, provocateurs trying to engage a tourist in an illicit deal, and hidden microphones in hotel rooms. A former cultural attaché to the American Embassy in Moscow, now stationed in another country, had an extremely exciting beginning but unfortunately with an anticlimactic ending. It is common knowledge that in Russia men and women are placed indiscriminately in separate compartments in railroad trains. In one of his journeys by train he found himself in his coupé in the company of the most gorgeous brunette he had ever encountered in Russia, according to his own description. Two young Soviet males were with her and he expected that they would remain in the compartment which had four berths. But when the third bell rang, and the train was ready to depart, her friends made a hasty exit. He took an upper berth, and the lady occupied a lower berth. "Do you want to undress first?" she asked, and made a movement to leave. He said yes, undressed, put on his pajamas, and ensconced himself in his berth awaiting further developments. She returned and discreetly undressed herself under the covers. She asked him a few innocent questions, but by that time he was in a state of panic, and these inquiries sounded ominous to him. At any moment, he thought, she would hoist herself to his berth, the two young men would rush in, with cameras and flashbulbs and he would be hooked. "So what happened?!" I asked him. "Nothing, but I couldn't sleep a wink." "Why? Because you regretted your inaction?" "No, it was nothing like that." And he reported the entire incident to his superiors as well as to his wife.

I, too, found myself in a similarly embarrassing situation in the Red Arrow night train from Moscow to Leningrad, but my would-be companion weighed about 200 lbs., and both she and I protested vehemently against being put together. The woman conductor claimed at first that there were no individual coupés, eventually relented and gave me a separate compartment.

I heard an amusing story in Russia which seemed to debunk the melodramatic accounts of Soviet electronic spying. An American businessman in Moscow was determined to ferret out any potential listening devices in his hotel room. His attention was attracted by a suspicious elevation under the carpet which, as often in Russian apartments, covered the entire floor. Laboriously, he turned it up, and to his profound satisfaction, espied a triangle of bronze screws. He unscrewed them, and went to bed gloating over his ingenuity. During the night there was a fearful crash accompanied by the thunder of broken glass. He woke up with a start, and ran downstairs in his pajamas to find out what had happened. He had unscrewed the supporting rods of the chandelier in the room below, and it crashed down from the ceiling barely missing the occupant.

I had a dream-like sensation hearing Russian spoken in the streets, an experience I had not had in years. I was an Outside Insider, understanding everything linguistically, but not always semantically. The new Russian language had undergone curious changes. Its tempo seemed slower than in my Russian days, and the language had acquired a peculiar theatrical quality. I had already noticed this quality in the Soviet movies: a deliberate caesura, a rhetorical cadence, a pause separating the subject from the predicate, but I had thought that it was an affected form of dramatic performance. It was a surprise for me to find that this was the new Soviet speech.

Even more surprising was the poetic diction of Soviet conversational prose. One would logically expect a vulgarization of language after a shattering revolution, but exactly the reverse is true in regard to the Soviet language. I was amazed to hear a customer address a salesgirl in a Russian equivalent of "young maiden." The old form of address was "young lady," but since the word "lady" had feudal connotations it had to be removed from circulation. Another paradoxical change in the manner of speech was the widespread habit of using Russian diminutives, the kind used in old Russia by peasants or mendicants. In *Boris Godunov*, the village idiot laments: "They took my little kopeck from me!" But in Soviet Russia the diminutive for kopeck is used almost universally, the littleness of the kopeck being expressed by a suffix. I could hardly suppress a smile when I heard a Russian Army officer ordering his dinner: "I want some soupee, some chickee, a crustlet of breadie, and a jerkin of little tea with sugarkins." But after a few weeks I found myself saying kopeck in the diminutive.

There were other kinds of new Soviet words. One of my Soviet colleagues, showing me some paperbacks, explained: "We call them *book-leti*." He was genuinely surprised when I told him that a paperback is a booklet in America, too.

The young maiden on the plane was called *stewardessa*, and the plane itself was a *lainer*. Other American-Soviet words titillated my fancy: *kontainer, booldozer, dzheep, trolley-booss*. The airplane was not the aeroplane of my youth, but a self-flyer, a word taken from the Russian fairy tales. Every time I boarded a Soviet self-flyer I felt an impossible association with a flying carpet.

The poetry, the rusticity and the simplicity of the new Soviet language assumed at times self-contradictory usages. Politeness and "cultureness" are constantly preached. The Minister of War, General Malinovsky, issued recently an order forbidding profanity in the Soviet Army, particularly the expressive sexual profanity known as "three-storey" cusswords. In fact, I never heard this familiar form of linguistic indulgence used in the streets, although I observed many drunks and hooligans in action. Incidentally, the word hooligan is heard much more often in Russia than in England from whence it came. A juvenile delinquent is a hooligan. A man who habitually beats his wife is a hooligan. An American cultural attaché arrested for molesting a Russian maiden (a convenient allegation for declaring a foreign diplomat persona non grata prior to deportation) is a hooligan.

I have said that I was an Outside Insider in Russia, but soon I realized that my insideness was effective only as far as language, literature and history were concerned. In a Moscow bakery, where I got some delicious Russian bread, I asked for a paper bag, and received an astounded stare in response. Paper bags are virtually non-existent in Soviet shops. For expensive pastry, cartons are sometimes provided; fish and meat are wrapped in newspapers.

Because of my ignorance of the small facts of Soviet life, cartoons and jokes in the Moscow satirical weekly *Krokodil* were as impenetrable to me as the *Punch* cartoons are to a denizen of the Bronx. But I learned quickly, and soon I was able to make up topical jokes of my own.

Although I was travelling under the auspices of the State Department, an institution daily maligned in the Soviet Press, no Russian ever tried to put me to shame for being an emissary of an evil power. My Russian friends had no compunction in giving me a lift or accompanying me on foot or by street car (tramway) to the American Embassy, and of course I made no secret of my daily visits there. Yet the Cuban affair was still very fresh in everybody's mind. The crudely made placards and boards used during the manifestation against the United States in front of the American Embassy were still lying in a heap in the courtyard, with ungrammatical signs HANDS DOWN WITH CUBA.

A durable and perhaps indelible souvenir was a huge vermilion splotch on the wall near the entrance to the Embassy, the result of an expertly thrown bottle of colored ink.

As a part of the new rusticity I must mention the growing application of the familiar form of address in the second person singular rather than plural, ty instead of vy. I was quite shocked when a woman in a crowded bus addressed me in this fashion.

In peasant talk, as recorded by Tolstoy and Turgenev, there is a lot of this second person singular familiarity, but before the Revolution it was confined exclusively to relatives and close friends. Among members of the intelligentsia (an original Russian word by the way) the respectful form is obligatory. My newly-found nephew insisted on addressing me formally as Nikolai Leonidovitch, even though I called him by his diminutive name Seriozha, and used the second person singular.

Throughout my stay in the Soviet Union I was haunted by a persistent thought. It seemed to me that had I stopped reading newspapers, or listening to news broadcasts, I would have been unable solely from the empiric reality of Soviet life to find out that there had been a revolution. As a Rip Van Winkle, I could notice the new melodiousness of the language and the neologisms. Housing architecture has changed less in Russia than elsewhere in the world, so that a Rip Van Winkle would not have been able to tell the passage of time from the new geometry of buildings.

But it was enough to turn to the newsstand to wake up to political reality. Only one type of publication was available: *Pravda*, *Izvestia*, *L'Humanité*, *Neues Deutschland*, *Unità*. There was also the *Daily Worker* of London, which provided the liveliest reading, including the candid report on the current divorce trial of the Duke of Argyll. It made fantastic reading in the austere surroundings of moralistic Moscow.

But Moscow is not as moralistic as all that. Spicy stories are still much in vogue. The central agency manufacturing such jokes is the mythical Armenian Radio. There is a real Armenian Radio Broadcasting Center, but it is not the one that is credited with the jokes. They say that a Russian-speaking displaced person was caught in the Soviet Union and was accused of spying. He loudly proclaimed his innocence. Then the arresting Soviet officer asked him about the Armenian Radio. He could not answer and was immediately indicted, sentenced and shot.

The legend of the Armenian Radio originated in 1948 when the real Radio Broadcasting System of the Soviet Socialist Republic of Armenia instituted a department of questions and answers. It is asserted that the opening question of the program was: "What is the Renaissance?" and that the answer was: "We do not know."

Some questions have a sharp political sting. Question: "What is the difference between capitalism and socialism?" Answer: "Under capitalism man is exploited by man. Under socialism it is the other way around." Question: "Can a dog have a heart attack?" Answer: "Yes, if a dog is forced to lead a man's life." Question: "What would result from mating a snake with a porcupine?" Answer: "Two meters of barbed wire."

Jewish jokes of the Armenian Radio are direct descendants of sempiternal pre-Revolutionary Russian-Jewish anecdotes, told mostly by Jews themselves. Here are some Armenian samples: Question: "How can we make Petrosian the chess world champion?" Answer: "By organizing a little Jewish pogrom." (Historical note: Petrosian became world champion without a pogrom when he defeated Botvinik, a Jew, in 1963.) Question: "Why did the Armenian Radio interrupt its broadcast?" Answer: "Rabinovich died."

The Armenian Radio also broadcasts sick jokes, some of them very similar to the American prototype. Sample (father to son): "Stop pulling grandmother's ears, or else I'll close the coffin."

But the chief stock-in-trade of the Armenian Radio is indecency, with a particular stress on homosexuality. Question: "Can a man become pregnant?" Answer: "No, but experiments continue." Question: "Is it true that Tchaikovsky was a pederast?" Answer: "Yes, but this is not the only reason why we admire him."

So great is this admiration for Tchaikovsky that all reference to his proved homosexuality has been eliminated from Soviet publications. A huge edition of Tchaikovsky's collected works is now in the process of publication. It includes even the original version of the *1812 Overture* containing the tune of the "Russian Czarist Hymn." In actual performance, this *Overture* is given in a revised version, replacing the objectionable tune by the contrapuntally suitable final chorus from Glinka's opera *A Life for the Czar*, which in turn has been retitled *Ivan Susanin*.

No self-respecting musicologist subscribed to the once current notion that Tchaikovsky ended his life by suicide. I was therefore surprised to hear in Russia an elaborate story supporting the suicide version. According to it, Tchaikovsky became homosexually embroiled with a Grand Duke. The scandal reached the Court, and an order for Tchaikovsky's arrest was issued. It is claimed that the original order is still preserved in the Soviet State Archives, bearing the personal endorsement of Czar Alexander III: "Be it thus!" Tchaikovsky's brother and biographer, Modest, was warned of the imminent threat of arrest by the composer Alexander Taneyev (uncle of the more famous Sergei Taneyev) who was a member of the Ministry of the Court, and summoned a family council and a few close friends, all homosexuals, as was Modest himself, to decide what to do. Modest declared that the only way to prevent the ultimate disgrace was for Tchaikovsky to kill himself. He drank poison, and the symptoms were disguised as a cholera infection, the disease of which Tchaikovsky died in actual fact. In support of this theory, it is mentioned that Tchaikovsky's body was laid in an open coffin, while cholera victims were invariably buried in sealed zinc caskets, and that his friends were allowed to kiss him in death.

A pendant to the story of Tchaikovsky's suicide is the tale I heard in Moscow that Nicholas Rubinstein, Director of the Moscow Conservatory and Tchaikovsky's friend, died as a result of a severe beating administered to him by a Grand Duke in Paris for having seduced his daughter. Tchaikovsky knew about it, and the fear of being similarly assaulted led to his acceptance of the plan to commit suicide by cholera. Another strange thing about Nicholas Rubinstein was that when his body was exhumed for reinterment it was found in a state of complete preservation, without a taint of corruption, but it dissolved into dust when it was touched. This has to be accepted as a fact, for I heard this account from witnesses who had actually viewed the body, and the incorruptibility of his remains was explained by the extraordinary dryness of the soil of Rubinstein's burying place.

The willingness on the part of some Soviet scholars to accept melodramatic accounts of historic events, in musical biography and in other fields, occasionally reaches mystical extremes. Thus the Soviet musicologist Igor Belza revived the long discarded legend that Mozart was poisoned by Salieri, basing his theory on a hypothetical document supposedly sequestered by the Archbishop of Vienna, which no one has ever seen. Perhaps Belza's motivation in reviving the legend was due to his desire to provide documentary background to Pushkin's drama *Mozart and Salieri*, which of course remains a Russian classic regardless of its historical untruth.

In a society in which atheism is the official religion and the perishability of all flesh is a dogma, it is amazing to find a constant accent on spiritual values in the arts. Paradoxically, spirituality is combined with the tenet of Socialist Realism, which represents the final stage of dialectical synthesis. Western modernism is attacked in the Soviet press not because of its innovations, but because of its materialism and lack of exaltation, and its failure to give expression to the national characteristics of the people. The superiority of Socialist Realism to Western modernism is revealingly explained in *The Brief Musical Dictionary*, published in 1959: "Socialist Realism demands from the artist a true, historically concrete, representation of reality in its revolutionary development, serving the task of Communist education of the masses. It opens wide opportunities for the revelation of individual qualities and presupposes a wealth and variety of artistic means and styles, a broad creative initiative in the struggle for Communist ideology, party loyalty and the national essence of all art. Socialist Realism demands irreconcilable struggle against antinational modernistic trends which reflect the decline and decay of contemporary bourgeois art."

The Soviet cosmonauts officially reported to Khrushchev that they encountered no angels in the skies, but "my angel" still remains the highest term of endearment among Soviet lovers. The Russian words for milady, master, etc., have been successfully removed, but expressions such as "for God's sake" or "I swear by God" remain permanently in Soviet speech. The Russian word "spasibo"—"thank you"—is etymologically derived from "Save, Oh God." Of course, here God is a mere expletive. But on some other occasions, God seemed to be elevated to an active deity. Before my final departure from Moscow, the girl secretary of the Foreign Commission of the Union of Soviet Composers wished me Godspeed, and I could not refrain from remarking that I thought God had been abolished. She replied, with wry humor, that it was not necessarily so. Then the entire company that came to see me off resorted to the ancient Russian ritual of sitting down for a minute before starting for the airport.

The belief in supra-human possibilities and attainments has, of course, nothing in common with religious mysticism, so popular in pre-Revolutionary Russia, but its overtones are somehow brought into Soviet science. Reaching for the moon becomes a part of the Seven Year Plan rather than a sentimental dream. In this connection it is interesting to quote from a letter from Leo Theremin, inventor of the Thereminovox, the musical instrument familiar from its employment on the sound track of science fiction movies: "There is every reason to believe that in the near future the length of human life may be increased at will. Then I will be able to devote more time to the solution of purely musical problems." The letter, dated Moscow, December 28, 1962, is remarkable in its positive assertiveness, particularly so since it is addressed to a colleague abroad. Theremin is a scientist, an electrical engineer by profession, and is not generally given to frivolous pronouncements. Who knows? His letter may portend a spectacular breakthrough in Soviet biology.

Incidentally, Theremin was widely reported to be dead. There were rumors that he was shot upon his return to the Soviet Union from America in 1938. Until recently, his name was ominously absent from Soviet publications dealing with electronic musical instruments, a field in which he was a pioneer. I am happy to inform his numerous American friends that he is very much alive in Moscow. I have his personal address.

In Russia, I enjoyed free and relaxed intellectual association with many people of many different professions, was invited to their homes, had meals with them, and watched Soviet television with them. Political subjects were avoided, not because there was any danger to my hosts in political discussion, but simply because such exchanges of widely divergent views would have led to mutual embarrassment without any gain on either side.

The nearest I came to a polemical exchange was in connection with a story published in *Pravda* at the time of Edward Kennedy's election to the Senate in November 1962. After passing a few contemptuous remarks about young Kennedy's lack of integrity, the author of the article appended an erudite-sounding footnote: "Edward Kennedy is familiarly known as Ted, an abbreviation of the American slang expression Teddy-boy, which means a beatnik." Somehow this particular brand of massive misinformation irritated me, and I mentioned it to a musical friend, himself a contributor to *Pravda*. He agreed with me that such reporting is "inadmissible" (a favorite word in Russian polemical journalism), and suggested that I write a letter to the editor about it. But I decided to refrain from tangling with *Pravda*.

Not all Soviet misinformation about America is malicious. Most of it is due to simple ignorance. For instance, several of my Soviet colleagues imagined that *West Side Story* had the Pacific Coast for its locale, interpreting West Side as the left side of the map of America.

Massive misinformation about America in the Soviet Union is matched by conspicuous misinformation about the Soviet Union in the American news media. When cosmonaut Titov orbited his way around the earth, screaming headlines in American newspapers proclaimed: I AM EAGLE CRIES SOVIET COSMONAUT. There was editorial comment drawing pregnant parallels between Titov's self-intoxication in his celestial pride as a soaring eagle and the American astronauts' humble invocation of God's help in their courageous adventures. But Titov's Eagle was simply the code call of his spaceship. All Russian spaceships are named after birds, and the Russian word for Eagle, "Oryol", has the liquid consonants *r* and *l* which are always favored in space communication for clarity.

What fantastic notions regarding the United States are entertained by some sincere and intelligent people in the Soviet Union was illustrated to me on the occasion of my lecture at the Kiev Conservatory. During the discussion period, one of its professors showed to me his piano manual for beginners. "I would be glad to present a copy to you," he said, "but there are in my book several piano arrangements of revolutionary songs, and I fear that it might get you in trouble when they search your luggage in America." At first, I thought he was joking, but he added: "They don't allow revolutionary songs in America, do they?"

My guide sheet from the State Department under the program of Cultural Exchange does not require militant flag waving, but this time I saw red, or rather red, white and blue. Almost uncontrollably I launched into an impassioned oration. "America is a free country!" I exclaimed. "No one has a right to confiscate anything I choose to bring along with me. As for the idea that an American customs officer would search the music in my baggage for revolutionary subject matter, it is absurd beyond imagination!"

The poor professor was bewildered by my outburst. He was solely motivated by my safety, he protested. "You are a valuable person," he said, "and I did not want you to lose your position in America on account of my book. But if you feel there is no risk, please, accept it from me." And he inscribed the volume to me. I got it through the American customs without being arrested or jailed.

Not only specialists, but all Russians seem to be electrically charged with a collective desire for limitless achievement. There is an atmosphere of cultural explosion which is unlike anything in any other country on earth. Sociologists will say that this cultural explosion is an optical illusion due to the former backwardness of Russian standards, so that the rate of advance appears greater than in the nations of older civilizations. But this view fails to take into account the flame of intellectual curiosity that has been lighted simultaneously in the minds of the Soviet people. It does not explain the universal respect that Russians, both educated and uneducated, have for culture, knowledge and ability. Some years ago a series of articles was published in the American press dealing with the high standards of Soviet schools, the long hours, the rigid examinations, the high demands of scholarship. The purpose of these articles was to awaken America to the deficiencies of its own educational system. I had to smile when I read the schedule of Russian classes and subjects. The hours and the courses were identical with those of pre-Revolutionary Russia at the time when I went to High School in St. Petersburg. To be sure, there were changes in subjects. Instead of daily courses in Divine Law there are now courses in Marxism and Communism, English has supplanted Latin. But mathematics, physics, biology, geology, mineralogy, astronomy, history, literature—all these courses are similar to the ones I had to take. But education in old Russia was mainly for the intelligentsia. Now it has spilled over. Education became an envied status symbol. It does not end with school, but continues into adult life.

Let me give an illustration of this educational spilling over into the masses. I took a taxicab to an address on Alexei Tolstoy Street in Moscow, and the driver remarked that the street was named after the Soviet writer Alexei Tolstoy, not after the great Leo. This distinction, incidentally, escaped the notice of a Reuters dispatch widely published in the American press in October 1963, which stated that five streets in Moscow were named for Leo Tolstoy. For the sake of the record, it ought to be mentioned that there was another Alexei Tolstoy, a 19th-century poet and dramatist.

My interest encouraged the driver to give me a well-balanced lecture on other literary streets of Moscow. He freely cited such relatively obscure names as Herzen and Ogarev. We passed by an ancient church in the old part of Moscow, and he observed: "Pushkin was married in this church." He expanded his remarks into general Pushkiniana, adding that it was on account of his wife that he fought his fatal duel. What was amazing to me was the didactic quality of his exposition, a characteristic that I found among many Russians of different social groups. I asked him how he happened to know so much about literature. He replied, with a certain show of pride, that after all he was not uneducated.

After a pleasant afternoon at the house of the celebrated composer Aram Khatchaturian and his wife Nina Makarova, also a composer, I went to the post office to mail to myself in Boston the orchestral score of Khatchaturian's ballet *Spartacus* which he gave me for a present. I used to send most of the music I received in Russia this way, since it was unthinkable to carry it back with me on the plane, the quantity was so enormous.

Soviet post offices have an admirable service: for 15 kopecks the postal clerk will wrap up your package, address it, weigh it, put pretty postage stamps on it and mail it for you. The clerk, a youngish girl, cast an appreciative glance at the score and asked: "Do you think that *Spartacus* is really superior to *Gayane*?" I was quite impressed by this exhibition of specialized knowledge at the post office, and ventured some appropriate remark to the effect that *Gayane*, with its famous Sabre Dance, was more popular than Khatchaturian's later *Spartacus*, but that musically the latter was perhaps the more significant.

At that point, a young man stepped up to the clerk's window, and I heard him whisper: "Es-Shay-Ah?" "Yes," was the reply. "Boston!" The vocables Es-Shay-Ah stood for the U.S.A. The young man carried an issue of the Russian language magazine *Amerika* published by the U.S. State Department in Moscow, with Jacqueline Kennedy's picture on the cover. Not realizing that I could speak Russian, he began to compose a laborious English sentence. I interrupted him to save him the trouble. He fired a number of questions at me. What did I think of modern art? Why did Marilyn Monroe kill herself? Was she really deprived of means of existence because of her progressive views? And what about that British movie star who committed suicide shortly afterwards? Was it true that she was ostracized by the British film colony because she bore an illegitimate child whose father was colored? These items were published under the rubric "Behind the Iron Curtain" in *Pravda* and other Soviet newspapers, retailing the dismal side of life in the capitalist camp.

I answered these queries as informatively and as concisely as I possibly could. Then he asked me if I had seen any Brigitte Bardot films. I replied that I had seen them all. He became positively excited. Did I, specifically, see *La Verité*? Yes, I did, twice. He became positively maudlin. He groaned. He said the film was shown during the French Film Festival but invitation cards sold illegally, for as much as 50 rubles apiece. "Why was it not allowed to be shown?" he asked. "Perhaps such a picture would present no interest to the Soviet public." "O, no!" he moaned, "the hall would have been filled to capacity for months and months!" I then ventured the opinion that the picture must have been unacceptable on moral grounds, since Brigitte appears in it in various states of nudity. He observed that there is nothing wrong in nudity if the actress is pretty, and wasn't Brigitte attractive? At that juncture, I resorted to inarticulate mumbling. He took a small book out of his overcoat pocket. It was a volume of Yevtushenko's poems. "This is difficult to get." he said. "Would you accept it as a souvenir?" But I felt it was not fair to accept a gift so difficult to duplicate.

Poetry is a best-selling commodity in the Soviet Union. Incidentally, *best-sellair* is a Russian neologism in good standing. When I stepped into a Moscow bookstore and scanned the exhibits of new books, a salesman declared as if anticipating my request: "Poetry *nyet!*" I knew that it was practically impossible to get a ticket at one of Yevtushenko's poetry readings, but what surprised me was the tremendous sales of all kinds of poetry, even 19th-century poetry. This was a new development, apparently peculiar only to Soviet Russia. As a boy, I recall Mayakovsky's readings of Futurist poetry in St. Petersburg, but there were no crowds eager to attend. Nor were there crowds for the erotic poet Balmont, or the peasant poet Yessenin. Why did poetry come to such unique distinction in a land of dialectical materialism? The facile answer is that Yevtushenko provides an emotional outlet to a generation hungry for self-expression, and that his poetry is covertly political in its overtones. But this theory is obviously contrived. The young men and women who watch him perform are his fans, *Bolelshchiki*, as the new Soviet word etymologically derived from the idiom "to be sick over" has it. Their sympathetic response comes fundamentally from the same reaction that actors and singers have received from time immemorial.

Intellectual fermentation that gives rise to the popularity of poetry in Russia is extended also to the fields of music and even chess. Thousands of people gather in front of a hall where a chess tournament is in progress, watching the games on large chessboards placed on the walls. The names of grandmasters of chess are known virtually to everyone in Russia.

After a Moscow concert I went to a restaurant with a company of musicians and composers. The restaurant orchestra played Russian ballads and American jazz. Suddenly, the master of ceremonies approached our table and asked if the composer Yuri Sviridov was one of the guests. Indeed he was, but he did not want to make his presence known, and twitched his eyes to give us all a signal to that effect. "I love Sviridov's music," the man said, "and I want to shake his hand." But Sviridov's anonymity was preserved. I was very much impressed by this manifestation. Sviridov is the composer of symphonic and vocal works of large dimensions, hardly the type who would attract a large following. Shostakovich, who is the most popular Soviet composer today, would not be able to escape notice in a public place because his photographs are so well known. But Shostakovich is extremely shy by nature and avoids large gatherings where he might become the target of attention.

Affectionate popularity of artists and musicians is not confined to Soviet figures. Van Cliburn who won the Russian hearts as well as the first prize at the Tchaikovsky Competition of 1958 arouses sentimental adulation among Russian females of all ages. The degree of Van Cliburn's popularity can be judged by the fact that candy stores make a brisk sale of chocolate boxes in the shape of a grand piano with Van Cliburn's picture on top. It so happens that his first name is easily Russianized as Vania, and it is by this name that he is usually acclaimed.

To poetry, chess and music, must be added the great art of Russian puppetry, a mechanical offspring of the ballet. But where the ballet in Russia continues to develop along the classical lines, Russian puppeteers develop satire.

On the night of November 7, 1962, after the last procession passed through Red Square to celebrate the 46th Anniversary of the Soviet Revolution, I went to see the famous State Central Puppet Theater directed by Sergei Obraztsov, which made such a sensational success in New York in September 1963. (For some reason the name of the director was misspelled in all American advertisements and programs, leaving out the essential letter "z" in his name.) It was a variety program under the title "An Unusual Concert." With nostalgia, I recognized the name of the author of the script, Alexei Bondi, who was my classmate and close friend in High School 4 in St. Petersburg, who died some years ago. He was also a contributor to my home journal, *The News of the House of Slonimsky*, and it seemed that I could recognize his peculiar type of wit even if his name were not given in the program.

Obraztsov's puppets were more alive than some actors. Their limbs articulated acrobatically, the puppet cellist moved his bow in perfect synchronization with the sounds produced by a human cellist in the orchestra pit. The puppet conductor gave cues with professional efficiency. Among the characters there was an American movie star, a French couple dancing a tango, and, inevitably, a reader of poetry named Jaundice. The surnames of the characters were selected with pointed appropriateness: Conductor Tougher, pianist Patient, coloratura soprano Veronica Disjointed. Remarkably, the real names of the puppeteers had a similar quality of morality plays, beginning with the director himself whose name Obraztsov means Exemplary. The name of the choreographer was Samodur, which means Self-Willed Fool.

Emerging from the theater, I made my way through the milling crowds to Mayakovsky Square. The busses and the Metro did not run on this great Soviet holiday, and it was impossible to find a taxicab. My attention was attracted by a group of people gathered around a militiaman who was engaged in conversation, gesticulating seemingly in sign language, with a dark-skinned young man. Somebody asked me: "Do you speak English?" I approached the dark-skinned man and asked him in English what the trouble was. He was overjoyed at this intercession, and explained to me that he was a member of the parliament of Ceylon, a guest of the

Soviet Government, and had just attended a reception given by Khrushchev in the Kremlin. Somehow he had lost his interpreter and did not know how to get back to the Budapest Hotel where he was staying. But where was the Budapest Hotel? The militiaman named the street, but some one remarked that it was the Bucharest Hotel, not the Budapest, that was situated at that address. Maybe, the Budapest Hotel was renamed Bucharest, or vice versa, the militiaman observed. In this confusion I decided to take charge of the situation. I led the young Ceylonese (he turned out to be the youngest member of the parliament at the age of thirty-two) to a telephone booth in order to make a call to his hotel. But I did not know how to operate the instrument. In dim light I read the instructions: Drop a 2-kopeck coin into the slot, then dial the number. But there was no telephone directory in the booth, and my friend from Ceylon did not know his phone number. Besides, I did not have the right coin, and neither did he.

On this chilly evening, the only refreshment stand on Mayakovsky Square retailed ice cream, and it was presided over by a formidable looking woman. I asked her if she could give me some change to make a phone call, but she said *nyet*, she had none. I offered to buy a two-kopeck coin for ten or fifteen kopecks but she did not deign to respond to such an insulting proposition. I was stalemated. Fortunately, a kind-hearted Soviet citizen proffered the requisite coin, and I accepted his donation with thanks. I called Information, but I must have pushed the wrong button, for the coin sank into the innards of the telephone with a sickening clink. I got the number of the Budapest Hotel, but I realized that I had to have another two-kopeck coin for the call itself. A group of well-wishers remained with me, and the wife of the original donor produced another coin.

Finally I reached the hotel. A woman's voice answered identifying herself: "Commutator." The word was new to me, but apparently it meant switch operator. Excitedly, I explained to her that a guest of the Soviet Union personally invited by Premier Khrushchev was lost and needed immediate assistance. But the commutator cut me short, and said I would have to call the manager. Seconds clicked ominously somewhere on the line, and I had a sinking feeling that we would be disconnected any moment. But the manager appeared, and I repeated my story in an even more melodramatic version. He seemed unmoved. It was not his duty to attend to lost tenants, he explained, but he would try to locate the inter-

preter. At last, the interpreter got on the wire, and said he would immediately drive to Mayakovsky Square and pick up his lost charge.

Half an hour elapsed, but there was no sign of him. In the meantime,
the Ceylonese M.P. was visibly freezing. He wore a light overcoat more
suitable for a rainy day on the Equator than for Moscow in November. I
suggested that we have a glass of hot tea. But where? The only place to
eat was a large restaurant, but a printed sign in the window warned: NO
ROOM. We returned to our booth. We exchanged our addresses and he
said that should I come to Ceylon, he would introduce me to the
Parliament. But what happened to the interpreter? I had to make another
phone call. The ice cream woman finally relented and sold me a two-
kopeck coin for twenty kopecks. Once more I got through to the
Budapest Hotel, and the manager told me that the interpreter did not
have a car and had left on foot. I had hardly finished the call when a young
man, running and panting, reached the booth and took the M.P. by the
hand. He spoke fairly good English for an average interpreter. I was about
to start on my three-kilometer trek to my hotel, when a miracle happened. A taxicab materialized out of nowhere, and the driver took us on.
They insisted on taking me home first, in appreciation of my help, and
soon I was in the warm comfort of my hotel room.

The most striking phenomenon that I encountered in the Soviet
Union was what I would like to call Articulate Collectivity of the Soviet
Man. Individual characteristics are as varied in the Soviet population as in
any country in the world. But there seems to be present an almost mystical feeling of being part of a universal community. A corollary to this is a
didactic and forensic eloquence of Soviet men, women and children. I
attended many political and professional meetings in the Soviet Union,
including the grandiose session of the Communist Party leaders in the
new, architecturally modernistic and acoustically perfect Hall of
Congresses in the Kremlin. I could not help being impressed by the
almost histrionic ability of Soviet men, women and even children to
express their views in an articulate prose, in impeccable syntax. A cosmonaut reporting to Khrushchev speaks out as though he was trained by
Stanislavsky. A small girl offering a bouquet to a hero of the Soviet Union
delivers her piece as though she is a prodigy movie star. Soviet composers
speak with an air of a professional orator, and so do painters, architects,
scientists. Most of them can write as well as they can speak. Perhaps training in dialectics has something to do with this easy formulation and deliv-

ery of ideas. Perhaps a sense of professional responsibility has been extended to comprise the entire nation, so that each citizen regards himself as a representative not only of his own individuality but of the entire community when he rises to speak. And finally, this universal participation in common endeavor makes a rebellion against the regime unthinkable in the Soviet Union. Passive resistance, however, is beginning to be felt. When, in December 1962, Khrushchev delivered his thunderbolt against the expressionist art exhibited at the ancient Manege building (where Czarist horses were formerly bred), the public did not recoil in horror from the accursed place as it would under Stalin's "cult of personality" but queued up in hundreds the next day to see the forbidden fruit.

Still, despite all its power, the Soviet government resorts to moralistic persuasion while abstaining from punishment. Government agencies constantly "put to shame" their delinquent citizens and educate them to be honest, polite and cooperative.

It was different in my remote youth. At that time there was daring and challenge in throwing mental pebbles at the 300-year-old dynasty. As a boy of fourteen I edited a handwritten periodical named *Illegalities* whose purpose was to defy parental and pedagogical authorities, and, by extension, any government at all. Now that this rebellion has consummated in the formation of a government a thousand times as powerful as the old regime, direct rebellion is out of the question.

But if the Soviet Government is so powerful, why is it necessary to play parent and teacher to the people, to argue and to persuade, to cajole and to remonstrate on the pages of *Pravda*, in the public posters, on the radio, even on the movie screen?

This moralistic pressure, without an explicit threat of punishment, had some morbid fascination in it. What chance has it to succeed? Still, it would not have been practiced if it had been totally ineffective.

The method of "putting to shame" apparently works in collecting fares on trolley busses. There is no conductor, and passengers not having the right change are expected to pool their resources with others and drop the coins in a tiller. When a bus is crowded, money has to be passed from passenger to passenger, and the change returned by the same system of relays. Surely there was every chance to be a "rabbit," an old slang expression for stowaways. But the punishment is so painful that few attempt to cheat. Such rabbits are photographed, and their pictures, together with their names and occupations are exhibited in the vehicles of communal transport in which they violated their trust, with an appropriate description of their misdeeds. They are "nailed to the pillar of shame." Other passengers are encouraged to report. In Soviet society squealers are not despised if they squeal in a righteous cause. Rabbits beware!

Persuasion plays an important role in practical journalism. Editorial exhortations, with captions employing the curious form of imperative infinitive, with an exclamation point at the end, are made in a variety of cases. I read in a Soviet paper an earnest injunction to chess grandmasters to stop the practice of playing for a draw and to inject a fighting spirit into their games. Appeals to musicians to write great symphonies and to writers to publish great novels are frequent.

In a movie theater I saw an interesting string of short vignettes denouncing some egregious malefactors by name. The most striking one, enacted with consummate skill, dealt with a case of cheating in alimony payments. It opened in the manner of a thriller. A man enters a photographer's studio and asks if his coffin is ready. Yes, it is, and the rent is reasonable. The visitor lies down in the coffin, crosses his hands on his chest, and the photographer takes a picture. The next scene is in the room of his estranged wife. The postman brings a letter. She opens it. It contains a photograph of her husband in death. She gasps, and reads the letter written purportedly by a friend, notifying her of the death of her husband and offering condolences. The woman sinks into a chair in utter desolation. How will she meet her everyday expenses now that her alimony will cease? The scene changes, showing the blackguard carousing with a woman accompanied by the treacherous photographer. By declaring himself dead he got rid of the duty to pay alimony. BUT THIS IS NOT THE END, shouts the voice from the screen. The perpetrator of this heartless fraud is tracked down, arrested, and sentenced to a term in a prison camp, his earnings are turned over to his estranged wife until her alimony payments are taken care of. Then the picture of the real life defaulter is shown on the screen, his name and his age (twenty-nine) are given, and a voice of restrained indignation warns other delinquent husbands of the fate that awaits such moral monsters.

The next vignette dealt with the manager of an automobile distributing agency who took bribes from customers to give them priority. He was caught easily when he suggested an underhand deal to an honest citizen.

The last vignette was more light-hearted, in the form of an animated cartoon, showing a flighty young female lounging on a modernistically shaped sofa, with abstract expressionist paintings on the wall, and with a copy of *Vogue* thrown carelessly on the table, and a jar of Parisian perfume before a mirror. She titivates herself busily, while a rhymed doggerel is run on the screen shaming girls who "catch foreign tourists at airports and railroad stations" and demean themselves by accepting worthless knick-knacks and fashion magazines from strangers.

The pride of being a Soviet citizen is reflected in the flaunting of honorary titles that to a westerner appear embarrassing. A woman farmer writes a letter to the editor of *Pravda* signing it Heroine of Agricultural Labor. A cosmonaut signs his name appending his legitimate title, that of a Hero of the Soviet Union.

When I took the famous Red Arrow train from Moscow to Leningrad, the announcer on the public address system with loudspeakers in every compartment, recited metrically in resonant tones: "We are now coming into Leningrad, City Hero, Bearer of the Order of Lenin." Cities, like individuals, receive their official honors.

In view of the spectacular Soviet achievements, how can one explain the constant breakdowns in the manufacture of consumers' goods? The pages of *Pravda* and the cartoons of *Krokodil* denounce inefficiency, incompetence and greed of Soviet industrial managers in devastating terms. An uninformed visitor to Russia would not see the Sputniks but will observe the shabby condition of housing, the lack of expressways, the scarcity of privately owned cars. But there are surprises in daily innovations. You can make a televised phone call, from a television booth in the post office in one city to a television booth in another. The glories of the Moscow Metro are well known. When I was a boy in St. Petersburg, one of my regrets was that no subway could be built there on account of the swampy terrain. Now, returning to the city of my birth, I took a pleasure ride in the new Leningrad Metro. The problem of subterranean waters was solved by digging deeper and deeper until a layer of solid rock was reached. The escalators in the Leningrad subway are probably the longest and deepest in the world. I timed the descent at one Leningrad Metro station at four minutes moving at the regular speed.

Many simple things that would make a Soviet man or woman happy are non-existent in the Soviet Union. Ballpoint pens are the most wonderful gifts that can be recommended for tourists to take to Russia. As far as I could judge from my experience and that of others, the Soviet customs do not object to the importation of such gifts as long as there is no suspicion that they are for barter or sale. Chewing gum is popular with adolescents, but its appeal seems to be diminishing among Soviet youth. Once in a museum I was approached by a boy about seventeen years of age who asked me in English whether I was a foreigner. I replied in Russian that I was. He asked me, again in English, whether I had any ball-point fountain pens to sell, or to exchange. I said no, and did not pursue the conversation so as not to get the boy into any kind of trouble.

Russian hospitality is proverbial. Now, fortunately, there is enough food to entertain guests to a Russian heart's content. The schedule of eating has changed. The Russians now have a midday meal served as late as 3 o'clock, and a late supper at 9 or at 10. There is somehow always enough food to take care of an unexpected guest. I will never forget an unexpected snack in Aram Khatchaturian's apartment in Moscow. I bumped into him on the street near the Union of Soviet Composers, and he suggested that I drop in for a few minutes. Typically, these few minutes expanded into nearly three hours. First we talked about music. Then his wife, Nina Makarova, herself a composer, came in. She remembered that I was the first to put her name in an American music dictionary. We chatted some more, and I was invited to partake of tea. Khatchaturian apologized that there was nothing to eat in the house. We sat down at the table; there was caviar, cold cuts and hors d'oeuvres. Then, as if by magic, a tureen of delicious hot soup was brought in. It was followed by a plate of Volga sturgeon, and fried chicken. To round off the meal, there was mousse, some kind of Russian soufflé, and, finally, tea. For an empty kitchen, this was a highly creditable showing. Khatchaturian himself was amused, and told a story about a hostess who left a note for a house guest: "If you can't find anything to eat, take a leg of ham from the icebox and serve it with purée."

The most artistic consumers of food in the world are found in Tbilisi, in Soviet Georgia, where I had the greatest gastronomic feast of my life, at the home of Alexei Machavariani, President of the Georgian Composers' Union in Tbilisi. Georgian shashlik is known all over the world, but in order to appreciate its infinite potentialities, one must eat it in Tbilisi. Georgians are also wine enthusiasts. Since I was a guest of honor at Machavariani's table, I was toasted copiously. Among those present was the Georgian composer Andrei Balanchivadze, brother of the choreographer George Balanchine (who cut off the Georgian ending of his name to make it easier for his western followers to pronounce).

Balanchine had been to Tbilisi just before my arrival there, and the two brothers got along together famously. Balanchivadze told me that Balanchine intended to send him an American car, but the idea had to be dropped. The customs duty would have been three times the cost of the car, and besides it would have been impossible to obtain spare parts in case of disrepair. One of my newly acquired Georgian friends, the composer David Toradze, turned out to be the best jazz pianist east of the Elbe River. He picked up his jazz technique from the shortwave broadcast of the Voice of America. I told him that he could make a fortune playing jazz piano in nightclubs in New York. Toradze is married to Georgia's beauteous movie actress Lian Asatiani.

In Georgia, when the master of the house offers food or wine, you cannot refuse. If you hesitate, he says solemnly "I am Tomada," the Georgian word for boss. (The American word boss is common in Soviet usage, too, but it is applied deprecatorily only to American monopolists and imperialists.) This declaration of absolute power applies to speeches as well. After the Tomada has had his say, you can take over by saying "Allah verdyi!" which means "Allah be with you," and make your own speech.

The Tomada ritual made me miss the train for my next point of destination, Erevan in Armenia. Balanchivadze invited me and a group of friends to a restaurant outside Tbilisi, and there we ate and drank copiously. The train time was approaching, but Balanchivadze uttered the magic word Tomada, and I had to drink some more. When we finally got off, there was unexpected traffic congestion, and we reached the railroad station as the train was pulling out. My greatest regret in not getting to Erevan in time was that I missed a performance of Khatchaturian's ballet *Spartacus* which was put on expressly for me by the State Opera House of the Armenian Socialist Soviet Republic.

The weird sensation of being an Outside-Insider continued to haunt me. In my Russian childhood, domestic servants were practically slaves, and their time was available to the household day or night. The average wages paid to a maid, who was also cook and nurse, were three rubles a month. All the servants lived on the premises. There was a class distinction between "booted" servants who wore shoes and "unbooted" ones who ran around the house barefoot.

These feudal customs are naturally abolished in Soviet society. All servants are booted now. In addressing their employers, the Soviet "domestic workers," as they are now called, use the polite form of first names and patronymics rather than the Russian equivalents of Milord and Milady; the employers use a similar form. Like their feudal predecessors, Soviet domestic workers are universally gifted. They sweep the floors and cook meals; they launder and they sew missing buttons on shirts and jackets. Their wages average 75 rubles a month, about twenty-five times as much in purchasing power as their pre-Revolutionary counterparts. They are infinitely more knowledgeable and take great interest in public affairs.

My observation was that the word Tovarishch (such as in Khrushchev) was not universally used in the Soviet Union. A restaurant waiter was a tovarishch, and a taxi driver might be. I was addressed as a comrade only when someone did not realize I was not a Soviet citizen. Otherwise I was a gospodin. But customarily, a young man was addressed as young man, and a young woman by the poetic word which had supplanted the expression "young lady."

Respectful treatment of servants in public places is demanded of all. The Soviet composer Mosolov was once kicked out of the Union of Soviet Composers for conducting himself "in the glorious old Russian style," abusing a waiter in the restaurant of the Press Building in Moscow.

Barbers are called "Masters." It seems that Russians have their hair cut more often than citizens of other countries, for there is always a waiting line in Soviet barber shops. Despairing of ever getting my hair cut. I asked the receptionist at the barber shop in the Sovietskaya Hotel in Moscow, where I was staying, whether there was any time of day when I could get service without waiting. "But aren't you an Intourist?" she asked. Yes, I replied, but what difference does it make? "Intourists don't have to wait their turn," she explained, and led me to a barber's chair. I cast a furtive glance at the people waiting in the anteroom, but they looked at me without anger, and their lips formed no muttering imprecations.

I carried with me to the barbershop a copy of *Time* Magazine which I got from the American Embassy. I folded it so as to conceal a menacing-looking picture of Khrushchev on the cover. Two middle pages with colored advertisements of 1963 automobiles became detached and fell on the floor. The master next to my chair picked it up and asked me: "Amerikanskaya machine?" Yes, I said, and handed the pages over to him. He carefully propped the advertisement against the mirror. I was having my hair cut by a woman, and she seemed entranced by a cigarette ad GIVE A MAN A CAMEL. I tore out the page carrying the ad. She smiled: "For me?" Then she put it up on her barber's stand.

I paid 35 kopecks for my haircut. I made a carefully worded inquiry as to the acceptability of a tip, and was told that tips were not allowed. But I managed to slip a tip to the manicurist in Armenia who charged me only 20 kopecks for the service.

At the official rate of exchange, the new ruble revalued some years ago by slashing off a cipher from the old ruble, places it above the American dollar. In this respect at least, Lenin's earnest admonition to the Soviet people to overtake and surpass America has actually come to pass. Is this rate realistic? Yes and no. In terms of manufactured goods, particularly clothing, the prices are disproportionately high. But hotel rooms are ridiculously cheap. I had to pay for my hotel room only once, when my plane was grounded by fog in Kiev. For 6 rubles I got a suite of rooms in a remodeled old mansion, comprising a bedroom with a four-posted bed under a canopy, a bathroom with a marble tub the likes of which one could find only in Ancient Rome, and a drawing-room complete with chandelier, vintage upright piano and a 19th-century grandfather clock.

A box seat at the Bolshoi Theater, which I had at a gala performance of Prokofiev's opera *War and Peace*, was priced at 3 rubles and 20 kopecks. (A ruble contains 100 kopecks.) A good seat for a symphony concert may be had for a ruble; a movie ticket costs 25 kopecks. A copy of *Pravda* sells for 3 kopecks. Books are very cheap, but candy is expensive. I paid 12 kopecks for a piece of caramel candy, twice the price of Khrushchev's 64-page octavo pamphlet, *High Idea Content and Artistic Mastery is a Great Force of Soviet Literature and Art.*

The winter of my Russian travels was abnormally mild. The receptionist at the Sovietskaya Hotel observed superstitiously that those atomic tests had done something terrible to Russian winters—not a sign of snow, and it was already December. But snow did fall in beautiful soft layers a few days before my final departure from Moscow, and Moscow looked like a picture on an old Christmas postcard. I had to get up very early; the radio went on at 6 o'clock in the morning—there are no broadcasts after midnight. For the last time I heard the glockenspiel play the tune of Shostakovich's song "Fatherland Knows," which always preceded the early morning news broadcast. It was almost with nostalgia that I listened to the didactic persuasive voices of a man and a woman speaking in short relays and reporting the events of the day before, the failures of insidious imperialists' adventures in southeast Asia, the growing unemployment in the United States, persecution of progressive elements in England and

France, the victories of Soviet athletic teams in western Europe, criminal preparations for nuclear tests in the Pacific . . .

But my thoughts were with the real marvels of new Russian culture and with the wonderful people who worked for its triumphs with such fantastic devotion. In one of his novels, Turgenev describes a visit to an industrial exhibition in London, and through the mouth of his hero, a Russian with a Western outlook, points out, with an anti-patriotic sneer, that every nation is represented at this exhibit. Even Patagonia contributed something, but not Russia, which is so backward that its people cannot invent even a screwdriver. Turgenev is not a very popular author in the Soviet Union, perhaps on account of his attitude of westernized disdain, but it would be interesting to speculate what Turgenev would have said had he known that in a hundred years Russia would travel from inner darkness into outer space.

INDEX

Abraham, Gerald, 19
adaptationism, 179–80
Alesksey, Tsar, 6–7
Alexandroff, Anatol, 147
Alexandrov, Alexander: "Gimn Partii
    Bolshevikov" (Hymn of the
    Bolshevik Party), 19, 165
Altschuler, Modest, 50
Alyabyev, Alexander, 8
Amirov, Fikret, 196–97
Andreyev, V., 5
Araja, Francesco, 8
Arensky, Anton, 12, 45, 55
Armenian Radio, 223–24
Asafiev, Boris, 18, 58, 147
Asatiani, Lian, 239
Association of Contemporary Music in
    Leningrad, 16
Association of Proletarian Musicians,
    182
Auric, Georges, 128

Bair, 145
Bakunin, Mikhail, 187
Balakirev, Mili, 41, 166, 169, 195;
    Islamey, 9; The Mighty Five and, 9,
    25–26, 35; Rimsky-Korsakov and,
    38; Russian folk songs and, 4, 24;
    "Vision," 28
Balanchine, George, 238–39
Balanchivadze, Andrei, 238–39
Balasanian: *The Song of Wrath,* 163
Ballet Russe (*see also* Diaghilev), 13,

16, 63; Russian composers and,
    13–14
Balmont, 231
Barber, Samuel, 206, 207, 209
Bartók, Bela, 129, 211
Beethoven, Ludwig van, 4, 98, 129,
    150, 154, 198; *Eroica,* 16, 98;
    Razumovsky Quartets, 23
Belaieff, Mitrofan (Belaiev), 42, 49–50,
    55
Belyi, Victor: *The Red Square, Nov. 7,
    1941,* 147
Belza, Igor, 225
Benois, Albert, 63
Benois, Alexandre, 63
Berezovsky, Maxim, 7
Berg, Alban, 183, 192, 210; *Wozzeck,*
    128
Berlioz, Hector, 29
Bezimensky, 94–95
Blanter, Matuei: "Katyusha"
    (Katherine), 19, 164
Blazkov, Igor, *114a,* 216–18
Bolshoi Theater, 218
Bondi, Alexei, 232
Borodin, Alexander, 19, 140, 166, 169;
    "Conceit," 28; The Mighty Five and,
    9, 25–26, 35; prime number signa-
    tures and, 22; *Prince Igor,* 10;
    Second Symphony, 10; *In the
    Steppes of Central Asia,* 10; "The
    Sea," 28
Bortniansky, Dmitri, 7

Boston Symphony Orchestra, 52
Brusilovsky, Eugeni: *Kijz-Zhybek,* 162
Busoni, Ferruccio: *Doktor Faust,* 128

Carter, Elliott: Second Sting Quartet, 207
Casella, Alfredo, 128, 129
Catherine the Great, 8
Cavos, Catterino, 63
Cephalus and Procris, 8
Chaliapin, Feodor, 27
Cherepnin, Nicolas, 80 (*see also* Tcherepnin)
Children's Theater in Moscow, 82, 143, 157
Chisko, Oles (*see* Tchisko)
Chopin, Frédéric: *Nocturne,* 74; *Valse brillante,* 74
chromatic tones, 186
Chronicle of Prince Igor, 5
Cimarosa, Domenico, 8
Cliburn, Van, 231
Collet, Henri, 128
color associations in music, 13, 37–38
Communist Party: Central Committee of, 169, 171, 174, 176
Conservatory of Tiflis, 65–66
Coolidge, Elizabeth Sprague, 77
Copland, Aaron, 207
Cowell, Henry, 129, 209
Cui, César, 9, 25, 26, 29, 35, 42
Czar Alexander III, 224
Czech composers, 25

Dankevich, Konstantin, 196, 218
Dargomyzhsky, Alexander, 27, 29; *Kamennyi Gost,* 9; *Kazatchok,* 25; *Russalka,* 9
Debussy, Claude, 38, 73, 208; *La Mer,* 28
Denza, Luigi: "Funiculi Funicula," 23
Deshevov, Vladimir: *Ice and Steel,* 15; *The Rails,* 16, 150
Diaghilev, Sergei, 157; Ballet Russe in Paris and, 13, 74 (*see also* Ballet Russe); Russian composers and, 13–14, 79–80

Dolzhansky, A.: *Brief Music Dictionary,* 215
Druskin, Mikhail, 184–85
Dukelsky, Vladimir, 14
Dunaevsky, Ivan, 136, 148, 173
Dunayevsky, Isaac, 19; *Song About Love,* 153
Durey, Louis, 128
Dushkin, Samuel, 78
Dzerzhinsky, Ivan, 15, 136, 145–46, 163; *Blood of the People,* 145; *Podniataya Tselina (Ploughed-up Fallowland),* 15, 145, 159, 161; *Tikhyl Don (Quiet Flows the Don),* 15, 133, 140, 145, 161

Edition Russe de Musique, 51
Eisler, Hanns, 173, 184, 193
Elson, Louis, 38
Engel, Julius, 55
Essipova, Anna, 80

Falla, Manuel de, 38
Feinburg, Samuel, 147
Findeisen, Nicolas, 7
folklore: Jewish, 18, 147; Russian. *See* Russian folklore
Fomin, Evstigney: *Amerikantsy,* 8
formalism, 169, 177, 215; critique of, 169–74; definition of, 215
Franck, César, 56
Frolov: *Enke Bular Bator,* 163

Gadzhibekov, Uzeir: *Ker-Ogly,* 136
Galuppi, Baldassare, 8
Georgian Composers' Union, 207, 212
Gershkovich, F., 185–87
Gershwin, George, 197, 209
Gide, André, 78
Gladkovsky and Prussak: *Za Krasnyi Petrograd,* 15
Glazunov, Alexander, 12, 50, 55, 65; compositions of, 42; *From the Middle Ages,* 42; Liszt and, 43; modernism and, 44; national music and, 41; oriental music and, 43; reception

of, 42; Rimsky-Korsakov and, 41; St. Petersburg Conservatory and, 43
Glebov, Igor, 18, 147
Glière, Reinhold, 12, 18, 79, 144; *Cossacks of Zaporozh*, 46; *Fantasy for the Festival of the Comintern*, 45; harmony of, 46; *Hitler's End Will Come*, 138, 144; Kiev Conservatory and, 46; *March of the Red Army*, 45; Moscow Conservatory and, 46; *Red Poppy*, 23, 46–47, 136, 159; Russian folk music and, 47; Scriabin and, 46; *Shakh-Senem*, 45, 162; Soviet music and, 45; Third Symphony, 46
Glinka, Michael, 8, 22, 63, 76, 166, 215; *Ivan Susanin (A Life for the Tsar)*, 8, 26–27, 57, 63, 135, 166, 224; *Kamarinskaya*, 9, 25; *Ruslan and Ludmila*, 8, 26
Gnessin, Mikhail (Michael), 18, 144, 147; *Symphonic Monument*, 195
Goedicke, Alexander, 144
Gogol, Nicolai, 17, 29, 85, 145, 156
Goldenweiser, Alexander, 139
Gorky, Maxim, 50
Gounod, Charles: *Faust*, 160
Grabovsky, Leonid, *114a*, 217
Grazia, Sebastian de, 120
Grein, Gregory, 18
Gretchaninov, Alexander (Gretchaninoff), 8, 12, 13, 29–30
Gruber: *History of Music Culture*, 142
Gulak-Artemovsky, Semyon Stepanovitch, 211

Hanslick, Eduard, 38
Harishkin, Simeon, 6
Harris, Roy, 122, 207, 209
Hindemith, Paul, 172
Hippius, Zinaida, 58
Honegger, Arthur, 128, 129, 211; *Pacific 231*, 16

Ilya Murometz, 46
Interpunctus, theory of, 68–69, 70

Ippolitov-Ivanov, Mikhail, 12, 45
Italian music: influence on Russia by, 8
Ivan the Terrible, 7
Ives, Charles, 209; *Three Places in New England*, 207

Jatchaturyan (*see* Khatchaturian)
jazz, 197; American, 152–53, 173; popularity of, 174; Soviet, 18, 110, 153, 173–74
Jrennikov, Tijon (*see* Khrennikov)
Jurgenson, 51

Kabalevsky, Dmitri, 18, *114a*, 161, 177–78, 196, 198; *At the Approaches to Moscow*, 146; *Sonatina for Piano*, 159
Kalafati, Vasili, 72
Kalinnikov, Vassily: First Symphony, 12
Kastalsky, Alexander, 24
Keldysh, Yuri, 205
Ketelbey, Albert: *In a Persian Market*, 154
Khatchaturian, Aram, 18, 144, 146, 161–62, 163, 171, 200–203, 229, 238; formalism and, 169; *Gayane*, 168, 202, 229; *Heroic Moscow*, 146; "On Creative Boldness and Inspiration," 176–82; *Poem about Stalin*, 146, 167; *Rhapsody-Concerto (Rhapsody)*, 199; *Spartacus*, 201–202, 229, 239; *Symphonie-Poème*, 170–71
Khomiakov, 28
Khrennikov, Tikhon (Kehrennikov, Tikkon) (Khrennikoff, Tikhon), *114b*, 114e, 146, 161, 170, 172, 175, 196–97, 213; *The Blood of the People*, 168; *Brothers*, 15; *During the Storm*, 140, 146, 213
Khrushchev, Nikita: critique of modern music by, 183, 184, 187, 208–209, 235; musical tastes of, 215, 241
Kiev Conservatory, 218, 227
Kind, Johann Friedrich, 63
Knipper, Leo (Lev), 18, 139–40,

146–47, 161; Fourth Symphony,
164; "Polyushko Pole"
(Meadowland), 19, 163, 164;
Severnyl Veter (North Wind), 15
Koussevitzky, Serge, 49, 51–52
Koval, Marian, 139, 175; *Emelian
Pugatchov,* 101, 139, 144, 147, 167
Kozlovsky: *Ulugbek,* 163
Krashnukha, G., 154
Krein, Alexander, 18, 144, 147; *Ode to
Lenin,* 147, 167
Krein, Gregory, 147
Krein, Julian, 18, 147, 194
Krenek, Ernst, 128, 211
Krylov, Pavel, 177
Kryzhanovsky, Ivan, 58

Lee Fisien Ming, 69
Lenin, V. I., 167, 171
Leningrad: Association of
Contemporary Music, 150, 174;
Conservatory, 129, 133, 193, 195;
Philharmonic Orchestra, 115, 142
Les Sylphides, 74
Leskov, 88
Lesur, Daniel, *114b*
Liadov, Anatole, 4, 12, 55, 58, 80;
Russian folk songs and, 24
Liatoshinsky, Boris, 147; *Shchors,* 15,
162
Litinsky, Genrik, 195; Sonata for Viola,
194; Sonata for Violin Alone, 194
Lockwood, Normand, 36
Lourie, Arthur, 127–28
Lvov, Alexei, 7
Lvov, G., 170–71
Lvov, Nicolas, 4, 23

Machavariani, Eugene, *114a,* 238
Makarova, Nina, 18, 147, 162, 200, 229,
238; *Zaya,* 202
Malko, Nicolas, 92
Manfredini, Vincenzo, 8
Markevitch, Igor, 14
Marshak, 122
Martynov, Ivan, 205

Marxism: artistic, 129
Medtner, Nicolas, 12
Meitus, Julius: *Dnieprostroy,* 150
Melgunov, 21, 24
Meyerbeer, Giacomo: *The Hugenots
(The Decembrists),* 15, 135, 160
Miaskovsky, Nicolas: absolute music
and, 58; "Autobiographical Notes,"
58–59, 159–60; compositions of, 58;
Eighteenth Symphony, 60; Fifteenth
Symphony, 60; folk motives and, 60;
formalism and, 169, 171;
Fourteenth Symphony, 60; Glière
and, 58; Hippius and, 58; "Lenin
Song," 59; Nineteenth Symphony,
60–61; Rimsky-Korsakov and,
57–58; romanticism of, 58; second
symphonic period of, 59;
Shostakovich and, 131; Sixth
Symphony, 58–59, 133; St.
Petersburg Conservatory and, 58;
symphonies of, 18, 213; third symphonic period of, 59; Thirteenth
Symphony, 59; Twelfth Symphony
(*Collective Farm Symphony*), 59,
133, 140; Twentieth Symphony, 60;
Twenty-first Symphony, 60–61, 143;
Twenty-second Symphony, 61–62,
143; Twenty-third Symphony, 61–62,
143; "Wings of the Soviets," 59
Mighty Five, The (*see also* Balakirev),
9, 10, 26, 35; influence of, 12, 73
Milhaud, Darius, 129, 211; *Les mal-
heurs d'Orphée,* 128
modernism: denunciation of, 168–74,
183, 225; Soviet, 156
Mogutchaya Kutchka (*see* Mighty Five)
Mokreyeva, Galina, 216–17
Mokroussov, Boris: *Anti-Fascist
Symphony,* 138–39, 144
Montagu-Nathan, M., 19
Morozova, Margarita, 50
Moscow: Conservatory, 11, 46, 139,
224; Festival of Music, 139, 141,
143; School, 12
Mossolov, Alexander, 191, 195, 239;

Iron Foundry, 95, 144; *Zavod*, 16, 150
Moussorgsky (Mussorgsky), Modest, 27, 35, 195; *Boris Godunov*, 10, 110; influence of, 140; *Khovanshchina*, 10; *Marriage*, 10; The Mighty Five and, 9, 25; national folklore and, 10; *Pictures at an Exhibition*, 10, 195; prime number signatures and, 22; RAPM and, 129, 154; *Rayok*, 29; *The Songs of Death*, 29
Mozart, W.A., 225
Mravinsky, Eugene, 121
Muradelli, Vano, 18, 138, 147, 171; *Great Friendship*, 169–70
Mystic Chord, 13

Nabokov, Nicolas, 14, 114d
national traditionalism, 215
Nationalist School of St. Petersburg, 12, 195
naturalism, 155
Nekrasov, Nikolai, 29
neo-classicism, 175
Nestiev, I., 173
Nestor, 6
New Economic Policy (NEP), 128, 134, 153
Nicolayevna, Nadezhda (Purgold), 34
Nikolaev, Leonid, 91, 122
Nono, Luigi, 184

Obraztsov, Sergei, 232
Ogolevetz, Alexi, 174
Oistrakh, David, 215
Orlov, G: *Musikalnaya Literatura*, 20
Ostretsov, 89, 97
Ouchkoff, Natalie, 51

Paisiello, Giovanni, 4, 8, 23
Paliashvili, Zakhari: *Abessalom and Eteri*, 163
Palmer, Robert, 36
Paltchikov, N., 4, 21, 23, 24
Paris Commune, 160
Pashkevitch, Vassily: *Tsarevitch Fevey*, 8

Patti, Adelina, 29
Pavlova, Anna, 66
Pervi Simfonitcheski Ansamble (First Symphonic Ensemble) *(Persimfans)*, 15, 129, 151
Peter the Great, 7
Petrograd Conservatory (*see* St. Petersburg Conservatory)
Petrov, 60
Petrushka, 63
Petyrek, Felix, 36
Pijper, Willem, 36, 68
Polovinkin, Leonid, 147
Popov, Gabriel (Gavril), 147, 161, 169, 171; *Expressions*, 173
Popov, George, 128
Poulenc, Francis, 128
Pratch, Ivan, 4, 23, 24
Principles of Proletarian Music, 16
Production Collective of Composers (PROCOLL), 152
progressivism, 215
Prokofiev, Sergey, *114d*, 180, 192, 219; *1941*, 168; *Alexander Nevsky*, 17, 82, 101, 139, 143, 166, 180; *Ballad of an Unknown Boy*, 17, 143; ballets by, 81; *Classical Symphony*, 81; *Desert Island*, 80; Diaghilev and, 79–80; displaced tonality of, 157; *Feast During the Plague*, 80; film music of, 81, 139; formalism and, 169; *The Giant*, 80; Glazunov and, 44; Glière and, 80; *Le Pas d'Acier*, 16, 79–80; *Lieutenant Kizhe*, 82; *Love for Three Oranges*, 128; *March for Band*, Opus 99, 157–58; *Ode on the End of the War*, 168; *Overture on Russian Themes*, 82, 133; *Partisans of the Ukraine*, 143; *Peter and the Wolf*, 82, 143, 157–58; piano concertos by, 82; *The Prodigal Son*, 81; Scythian Suite, 80–81; *Seven, They Are Seven*, 81; socialist realism and, 79; Soviet music and, 14, 79, 133, 156–57, 163, 167; *The Tale of a Real Man*, 171–72; *War and Peace*, 17, 143, 211, 241

Prokofieva, Lina, *114b*, 219
Protiv Nepmanskoy Musiky, 153
Puccini, Giacomo: *Tosca*, 15, 160
Pushkin, Alexander, 9, 11, 36, 76, 80, 100, 225

Rachmaninoff, Sergey (Rachmaninov), 19, 29, 51, 166; second Piano Concerto, 12
RAPM. *See* Russian Association of Proletarian Musicians
Ravel, Maurice, 10; *L'Enfant et les Sortileges*, 128
Rebikov, Vladimir, 13
revolutionary songs, 5, 127
Riemann, Hugo, 67
Rimsky-Korsakov, Andrey, 194–95
Rimsky-Korsakov, George, 129, 152
Rimsky-Korsakov, Nicholas: *Capriccio Espagnol*, 38; *Chronicles of My Musical Life*, 19, 33; color associations and, 37–38; compositions of, 36–38; eight-note scale of, 68; folk songs and, 4, 22; *The Golden Cockerel (Le Coq d'Or)*, 36–37, 67; influence of, 30, 39–40, 80; *Kaschey the Immortal*, 37; The Mighty Five and, 25–26; *Mlada*, 36; nationalism and, 35; *Neapolitan Song*, 23; oriental themes in, 38; reception of, 33; rhythm and, 37; *Russian Easter Overture*, 38; Russian folk songs and, 24, 29; *Sadko*, 5, 9, 37, 39; *Scheherazade*, 10, 33, 36, 38, 40; *Serbian Fantasy*, 25; *Skazanye o Nevidimom Grado Kitezhe (The Invisible City of Kitezh)*, 10, 104; *Snegurotchka (Snow Maiden)*, 9, 38; St. Petersburg Conservatory and, 35; Stravinsky and, 13; tone-painting and, 68; *Tsar Saltan*, 10; *Tsarskaya Nevesta*, 10; *Zolotoy Petushck*, 10
Rogowski, Ludomir, 36
Roslavets, Nicholas (Roslavetz), 128, 156
Rubinstein, Anton, 19, 35; *Demon*, 11

Rubinstein, Madame Ida, 78
Rubinstein, Nicholas, 11, 224–25
Russia: Christianization of, 7; European, 3; art songs, 8; ballet, 8, 232; *byliny*, 10; city songs, 23; gypsy songs of, 23; language, 222–23, 226; minstrels, 6; national culture, 13; nationalism, 8, 10–12, 26–27, 158; orientalism, 26, 36, 39–40, 163; popular songs, 163; puppetry, 6, 232; romanticism, 13, 29–30; system of notation, 7; tone-painting, 28
Russian Association of Proletarian Musicians, The (RAPM), 16, 129–32, 166, 191; dissolution of, 134, 192; ideology of, 152, 154; *Nevinnaya Propaganda Imperialisma*, 154; *Za Proletarskuyu Musiku*, 152–53
Russian church music, 8, 19; notation and, 19
Russian Civil War songs: "Yablotchko" (Little Apple), 23, 47
Russian folk music, 3, 160; Caucasian, 167; characteristics of, 4, 21; classification of, 21; collections of, 4, 22, 24; development of, 7; folklore and, 5; influence of, 11, 131, 158, 162; peasant songs, 24; polytonality of, 4, 21, 24; recording of, 4, 24; rhythms in, 22; Soviet music and, 19, 164, 195
Russian folklore, 9, 163, 177; colorism and, 13; influence of, 10
Russian music, 3; academism of, 161; after 1917 (*see* Soviet music); choral, 7; classical, 165, 170, 173, 179; diatonic language of, 159; evolution of, 8, 11, 19; impact of, 30; influence of folklore on, 9, 11; modernism and, 161, 166; national, 13, 25, 26–27, 127; of national minorities, 127, 134, 163; nationalism of, 9, 10–11, 165–67; nineteenth-century, 19, 131, 168, 172; old, 19, 22; polytonality and, 7, 93, 129; popular, 163; RAPM

and, 16; religious, 3, 7, 19; rhythm in, 22, 24; secular, 8; Soviet music and, 127, 156, 162–64, 170, 191–92; Wagner's influence on, 27

Russian Musical Gazette, The, 55

Russian musical instruments, 5–7, 163; old, 19

Russian National School, 8, 29, 154, 169

Russian opera (*see also* Soviet opera), 8, 10–11; development of, 15

Sabaneyev, Leonid, 19

Salieri, Antonio, 225

Saminsky, Lazare, 58

Samosud, Samuel, 88–89, 103

Sarti, Giuseppe, 8

Satie, Erik, 128

Schillinger, Josef, 128, 174

Schneerson, Gregory, 142, 209; American music and, 153, 174; Eisler and, 173; Miaskovsky and, 60–61; *Music Living and Dead,* 210; Shostakovitch and, 97

Schöenberg, Arnold, 131; dodeca-phonic music and, 197; film music, 186; influence of, 67, 173, 192, 210; method of composition, 183–87; Soviet criticism of, 172, 183–87, 208; twelve-tone system, 128

Schuller, Gunther: *Jazz Abstractions,* 207

Schuman, William: Third String Quartet, 207

Scriabin, Alexandre, 19, 71, 156; Belaieff and, 49–50, 55; *clavier à lumières* and, 13, 49; *Divine Poem (Poème divin),* 13, 49, 50, 54; Koussevitzky and, 49, 51–52; Morozova and, 50–51; *Mystery,* 13; Mystic Chord and, 13, 48, 53; mysti-cism of, 51; Ouchkoff and, 51; phi-losophy of, 48; *Poem of Ecstasy (Poème de l'extase),* 13, 49, 51, 54; *Poem of Fire (Le poème du feu),* 13, 48, 54; *Prometheus (Promethée),* 13,

48–49, 54; reception of, 51, 55–56; Second Symphony, 54–56; United States and, 50; Wagner and, 48

Scriabin, Julian, 52–53

Scriabin, Tatiana, 53

Serov, Alexander, 11, 21; *Vrazhya Sila,* 10–11

Sessions, Roger, 186

Shaporin, Yuri (Youri), 138, 139, 169, 194; *The Decembrists,* 136–37, 193, 218; *Na Pole Kulikovom (On the Kulikov Field),* 17, 101, 139, 144, 166; *Skazanye o Bitve za Russkuyu Zemlyu* (Chronicle of a Battle for Russian Land), 18, 168

Shebalin, Vissarion, 18, 147, 161, 169, 171

Shekhter, Boris, 147; *Yusup and Akhmet,* 162

Shirinsky, Vassili, 147

Sholokhov (Sholohoff), 136, 145; *Soil Upturned,* 136, 140; *Tikhyl Don* (Quiet Flows the Don), 15, 133, 136, 140

Shostakovitch, Dmitri, 16–17, *114e,* 134, 167, 168, 177, 192, 196–98, 208, 231; absolute music and, 145; American music and, 122; *The Bolt,* 88; *Boris Godunov* and, 110–11; 'Cello Sonata, 117; chamber music of, 109; Eighth String Quartet, 212, 214; Eighth Symphony, 17, 120–21; Fifth Symphony, 17, 97–99, 121, 141, 145, 155; film music and, 110, 122, 171; First Symphony, 91–93, 95–96, 99, 116, 141, 145; Five Fragments for Orchestra, 119; folkore and, 100, 122, 145; *Forest Cantata,* 171; Fourteenth Symphony, 184; Fourth Symphony, 97, 119, 132, 175, 193; *The Golden Age,* 17, 86–88, 156; jazz and, 110; *Lady Macbeth of the District of Mtsensk (Katerina Izmailova),* 16, 88–91, 116–17, 131–32, 136, 140–41, 145, 155, 158, 191; *The*

*Limpid Stream (The Lucid Stream)
(The Sparkling Brook)*, 90, 117, 132,
141, 145, 155; list of works by,
111–14; *May First* (Third
Symphony), 17; musical satire of,
88–89, 117, 156; *The Nose*, 17, 71,
85, 131, 145, 156, 192; Piano
Concerto, 110, 193; Piano Quintet,
17, 107–108, 119, 145; Piano
Sonata, op. 64, 121–23; polyrhythmy
of, 93; polytonality of, 93; reception
of, 85–86, 88–91, 100, 103, 105, 108,
115–16, 119, 120–22, 131–32, 134,
141, 155, 161, 169; Second
Symphony (October Symphony), 17,
93–95, 98, 141, 150; Seventh
Symphony (Leningrad Symphony)
(War Symphony), 17, 84, 101–107,
115–19, 120–21, 123, 141, 142–43,
145, 155, 167; Sixth Symphony, 10,
100–101, 108, 141, 155; Sonata for
'Cello and Piano, 108; "Song of the
United Nations," 122; Soviet music
and, 155–56, 161, 170, 175, 180,
182; String Quartet, 108–109, 184;
Svetly Rutchey, 16; Tass Windows
and, 111, 119; Tchaikovsky and, 86;
"The Golden Key," 123; Third
Symphony (May First Symphony),
95–96, 141; wartime and, 138
Slonimsky, Alexander, 206, 213
Slonimsky, Electra, *114c*
Slonimsky, Mikhail, 205
Slonimsky, Sergei, *114c*, 184
Socialist Realism in music, 14, 47, 79,
154, 160, 183, 225
Society of Quarter-Tone Music, 152
Sokalsky, Pyotr, 3, 21–22
Solertinsky, Ivan, 85–86, 91, 183
Soviet composers: attack on Soviet
Union and, 138–39, 144, 168; musi-
cal styles of, 158–59, 161, 168;
nationalism and, 17; older genera-
tion of, 18; operas by (*see* Soviet
opera); Spanish Civil War and,
138–39; triadic parallelism and, 158,

161; war and, 138–43, 168; Western
music and, 158
Soviet music, 14, 19, 45, 183, 191, 209;
American music and, 196–97, 207;
characteristics of, 156–57; classicism
and, 175; development of, 14,
127–34, 149–75, 176–77, 214; early,
128, 162; esthetics, 14; in films, 146;
first period of, 128, 134, 149, 150;
folklore and folk music influence on,
145, 162, 169–70; formalism and,
169–71; formative factors in, 157;
ideology of, 16, 129–30, 165–74,
178; influence of western music on,
128–31, 153, 183; mass songs, 19,
165; modernism and, 93, 168,
170–75, 183, 225; national anthem,
165; opera (see Soviet opera); polytonality and, 129, 162, 169; popular,
164; pre-modern trend in, 152;
Prokofiev and, 157; proletarianism
and, 162; Russian music and,
191–92, 195; second period of, 130,
134, 149; Socialist Realism and, 79,
134, 150, 154, 160, 167, 170, 183;
third period of, 131–33, 134, 149;
threnody, 127; tonality and, 162, 169
*Soviet Music. See Sovietskaya Musyka
(Sovetskaia Muzyka)*
Soviet opera (*see also* Russian opera),
135–37, 178; caricature in, 136;
national minorities and, 136;
Socialist Realism in, 161; subjects
of, 140, 146, 160
*Sovietskaya Musyka (Sovetskaia
Muzyka)*, 134, 191, 211;
Khachaturian and, 176–78;
Miaskovsky and, 58, 133, 140, 159;
music critiques in, 139, 171–74;
Soviet music and, 20
St. Petersburg Academy of Science,
24
St. Petersburg Conservatory, 11, 12, 35,
58
Stalin, Josef, 145, 172; cult of personal-
ity of, 235; death of, 177; Socialist

Realism and, 16, 127, 133, 150, 171;
Soviet music composed about, 167
Stallin, Jacob von, 6
Stanislavsky, Konstantin, 27
Starokadomsky, Mikhail, 18, 147, 161
Stasov, Vladimir, 9, 25, 26, 35, 42
State Central Puppet Theater, 232
State Little Opera Theater, 85
State Music Publishing House, 20, 214
Steinberg, Maximilian, 18, 73–74, 91,
147; *Turk-Sib,* 144, 159, 195
Stokowski, Leopold, 116, 193; *Music
for All of Us,* 211
Strauss, Richard, 208; *Aus Italien,* 23
Stravinsky, Igor, v, xi, 128, 131, 210;
American tours of, 77; *Berceuses du
Chat,* 75; Capriccio for piano and
orchestra, 77; *Card Party,* 78;
change of styles and, 75–77; *Chant
funèbre, op.* 5, 74; Concerto for 16
instruments *(Dumbarton Oaks),* 78;
Concerto for 2 pianos, 78; Concerto
for piano and orchestra of wind
instruments, 77; Diaghilev and, 74,
76; *Duo Concertant,* 78; Elizabeth
Sprague Coolidge and, 77; Fantastic
Scherzo, op. 3, 73, 74; *The Firebird,*
13, 74, 76, 217; *Fireworks,* 74; First
Symphony, 73; influence of, 73; *Le
Baiser de la Fée,* 77; *Le Faune at la
bergère,* 73; *Le Rossignol,* 74; *Le
Sacre du Printemps,* 14, 75, 76; *Les
Noces,* 75; *l'Histoire du Soldat,* 76,
77; *Mavra,* 76, 128; modern music
and, 74; The Octet for wind instruments, 76–77; *Oedipus-Rex,* 77, 78;
Pergolesi and, 76, 77; *Perséphone,*
78; Petrouchka chord and, 75, 76;
Petrushka (Petrouchka), 13, 23, 63,
74; polytonality and, 75; *Pribaoutki,*
75; *Pulcinella,* 76, 77; *Ragtime,* 76;
Renard, 75; Rimsky-Korsakov and,
73, 74; Russian folk songs and, 22,
75; Russian national music and, 13;
Russian Revolution and, 75; Scriabin
and, 52; *Symphony of Psalms,*

77–78, 116, 192; Tchaikovsky and,
76; Tcherepnin and, 67; Volga
Boatmen's Song and, 75
Stravinsky, Sviatoslav, 78
Sumarokov, 8
Susanin, Ivan, 63 (*see also* Glinka,
Michael)
Sviridov, Yuri, 231; *Pathetic Oratorio,*
212
Szabo, F., 5

Tailleferre, Germaine, 128
Taneyev, Alexander, 224
Taneyev, Sergey (Taneiev) (Taneev), 12,
45, 55, 58, 224
Tasin, Dima, 139, 144
Tchaikovsky, Hippolytus, 64
Tchaikovsky, Peter (Chaikovsky), xi, 9,
19, 76, 150, 224–25; *1812 Overture,*
166, 224; *Eugene Onegin,* 11, 136;
influence of, 12, 13, 35, 168; nationalism of, 11, 27–28; *The Nutcracker,*
11; *Pathétique,* 11, 166; *Pique-
Dame,* 11, 191, 193; popularity of,
136; Quartet, op. 11, 23; Russian
church music and, 8; Russian folk
songs and, 4, 11, 24, 100; Russian
romanticism and, 29–30; *Sleeping
Beauty,* 11; *Swan Lake,* 11; sym-
phonic poems of, 11
Tchemberdzhi: *Karlugas,* 162–63
Tcherepnin, Alexander, 72
Tcherepnin, Ivan, 71–72
Tcherepnin, Nicolas, 12, 29; American
period of, 71; Conservatory of Tiflis
and, 65–66; electronic music and,
71, 72; folk music and, 69; Fourth
Symphony, 65; *Ivan the Terrible,* 64;
Le Pavillon d'Armide, 63; nine-note
scale and (Tcherepnin Scale), 67–68;
Pièces sans titres, op. 7, 64; Second
Piano Sonata, 71–72; Second
Symphony, 71; *Story of Ivan the
Fool,* 71; Stravinsky and, 67;
Symphonic Prayer, 71; Symphony in
E, Op. 42, 69, 71; theory of

Interpunctus and, 68–69, 70; thir-
teenth piano sonata, 65; Trio, Op.
34, 71
Tcherepnin, Serge, 71–72
Tchishko (Chisko), Oles: *Battleship
Potemkin*, 15, 136, 160
Theremin, Leon: *Emiriton*, 15;
Persymfans, 129, 151; the
Thereminovox and, 15, 151, 226
Thomson, Virgil, 207
Titov, Nicolas, 8
Tolstoy, Alexei: Shostakovitch and,
103, 105. 115, 155; Soviet music
criticism of, 97; writing of, 123, 137,
141, 229
Tolstoy, Leo, 17
tonality, 186, 201
tone clusters, 129
Toradze, David, 239
Toscanini, Arturo, 107, 116, 119
Traetta, Tommaso, 8
Tritone, 152
Trutovsky, Vasily, 4, 22–23, 24
Tsarist National Anthem, 7
Turgeniev, Ivan, 26, 242
twelve-tone system, 184, 192, 201, 208,
210

Union of Composers of the Soviet
Union, 204–206, 212–15; charter of,
214–15; criticism of, 170–71,
177–78; directives of, 162, 170–71;
February 1948 resolution, 170, 172,
176, 181; leading members of, 175;
*The Paths of Evolution of Soviet
Music*, 172; Russian folklore and,
162

Union of Composers of Ukraine, 218

Varese, Edgar: *Ionization*, 193
Varlamov, Alexander, 8; "Red Sarafan,"
23
Varzar, Nina, 91
Vasnetzov, 139, 144
Vassilenko, Sergey, 12, 18, 79, 144, 159;
Red Army Rhapsody, 159
Veprik, Alexander, 18
Verdi, Giuseppi, 136
Verstovsky, Alexey: *Askoldova Mogila*, 8
Vienna School: New, 185; Second, 184
Volga Boatmen's Song, 3, 75
Von Meck, Madame, xi, 28, 38

Wagner, Richard, 27; *Parsifal*, 10
War Communism, 127–28
Webern, Anton von, 128, 183, 184–85,
210; *Der Freischutz*, 63
Weissberg, Julia: *Negro Lullaby*, 195
whole-tone scale, 13
Wieniawski: *Souvenir de Moscow*, 23
Worker and the Theatre, The, 90–91

Yarustovsky, Boris, 196–97
Yessenin, Sergei, 231
Yevtushenko, Yevgeny, 230

Zakharov, Vladimir: *Provozhanye*
(Farewell), 19; "Taking Her Home,"
164–65
Zamiatin, Evgeny: *The Flea*, 194
Zaslavsky, David, 172
Zhdanov, Andrei, 172–73, 176–77, 179,
182
Zhelobinsky, Valery, 18, 147